Stories from My Life

Studies in Austrian Literature, Culture, and Thought

Translation Series

Oskar Kokoschka

Stories from My Life

Translated by
Michael Mitchell,
Eithne Wilkins and Ernst Kaiser

ARIADNE PRESS
Riverside, California

Ariadne Press would like to express its appreciation to the Austrian Cultural Institute, New York and the Bundeskanzleramt – Sektion Kunst, Vienna for their assistance in publishing this book.

Translated from the German
Das schriftliche Werk, Hans Christians Verlag
A Sea Ringed with Visions
Thames and Hudson, 1962, London

World Rights © Thomas Sessler Verlag, Wien

Library of Congress Cataloging-in-Publication Data

Kokoschka, Oskar, 1886-1980
    Stories from my life / Oskar Kokoschka : translated by Michael Mitchell,
Eithne Wilkins and Ernst Kaiser.
            p.   cm. -- (Studies in Austrian literature, culture, and thought.
    Translation series)
    Originally published in German in 1974 as v. 2 of the author's Das schriftliche
Werk under the title: Erzählungen.
    ISBN 1-57241-062-0
    I. Title. II. Series.
PT2621.0664E79   1998
760'092--dc21

                                                        98-20564
                                                        CIP

Cover:
Art Director, Designer: George McGinnis
Drawing: Oskar Kokoschka

I told these stories to Olda,
later wrote them down, and dictated them to her.
This volume, therefore, belongs to Olda. O.K.

CONTENTS

Preface

In this book I am going to tell not my life history, but a random selection of stories from my life, in no particular order, just as they occur to me.

While academic history, starting out from the taste, ethics and philosophy of the age, seeks to establish objective truth, the credibility of a view of the world which is based on personal experience comes from its internal cohesion.

Dogmatism, excommunications, bodies burned at the stake provide the picturesque lighting along the road indicated by the theoretical truth for which the spirit informing history is not mankind, but a disembodied specter.

It is our capacity for experience which lifts humanity out of the transitory stream of ahistorical existence, and the truth which appears in experience is one we can vouch for personally. The self speaks directly, telling what has happened and what is happening; the unconscious or suppressed beings, the mute masks, the masses for whom speech is, or has become alien achieve full humanity.

Objective, so-called 'higher' truth can confuse our perception of what human life is, sometimes even openly contradict it. That personal truth which we call experience is an act of parturition. To profess this inner experience is a social function.

Experience is the birth of reason. It is in this act, without which the world would remain chaos, that we liberate ourselves, overcoming our alienation, the depths that separate our selves from our neighbor, animating the inanimate, turning inert matter into material cause. Our mother tongue, which whispers the names of all things and with which the history of every human being truly begins, is reason.

'The common herd follow the executioner' — a philosophy of history can, if it so desires, base its justification on that. It sees the workings of some assumed 'higher' fate as a better truth than that of our experience.

So-called 'higher' truth, derived from the old demiurge, opposes earthly reality with abstractions hostile to it. Our reason, however, cannot constantly abandon the human perspective, since an overemphasis on divine matters suppresses creative power within the human sphere.

Right down to the Middle Ages the Latin word generally used for the rural population, which had not converted to the new god as quickly as city folk, was 'heathens' — *pagani*. Even today, we call that unbroken chain of human beings who, thanks to a special sharpness of their senses, experience nature directly, geniuses, after those forgotten heathen spirits that once informed fields and meadows, woods and rocks.

The genius professes himself teacher of an undying art which has the task of preserving for earthly life that measure of reason without which humanity would have no history.

The root cause of every crisis which brings down catastrophe on mankind is a superstition, since the uneducated masses cannot forgive the passion for creative reason which they do not share.

The magic of art is the only magic that is not based on superstition. Has today's society turned its face away from living art because it cannot bear to look truth in the face? Today there is the 'higher' truth, to which people pay no more than lip-service, and a deeper truth, on which no one has the courage to base his life. The flood of art-books has resulted in a legend according to which geniuses live in ivory towers, in garrets, where they wrestle with the unknown god. The academic view of history takes a psychological interest in the artist, whose urge to communicate scholars equate with the delusion of messianic status. The first principle of the history of art is that the artist must be dead; that is what academic historians call 'maintaining the necessary historical distance.'

Current attitudes and practices, the taste, ethics and philosophy of the age, do not suggest our human existence is guided by reason. Therefore the artist must reject the unsocial 'higher' truth, in which the combination of reality and ideology can only be achieved at the cost of reason, and open himself with the utmost honesty to a profounder truth.

One evening in the spring of 1909 in Vienna (I will describe it in fuller detail later on), I was going home with a friend from the premiere of my first play, *Murderer, Hope of Women*, which had been performed in the open-air theater of the *Kunstschau* exhibition.

Why in those days educated people in particular tried to by-pass truth with their eyes closed is no longer a mystery to me today. Since I have matured, I can see that that is precisely what their 'higher' fate consists of. But at the time the fact that both the pictures I painted of those people and my plays aroused such an acrimonious fury of opposition had a different significance for me. I was still a stranger in the world of the grown-ups who alone had the right to pass historical judgment on people. A few years later, during the World War, it became apparent how little concern they had for human lives.

The basic idea of my first play is that man is mortal and woman immortal, and that in modern life it is only the murderer who wants to reverse this basic fact. With this I had offended against the empty-headedness of our male society, immediately being seen as an affront to all right-thinking people.

That night I was standing in St. Stephen's Square in a state of intense excitement, animatedly discussing the events of the evening with the friend who had played the male lead in the play. Gatecrashers, Bosnian soldiers from the barracks opposite, had joined in the rumpus kicked up by the paying audience, so that the literary dispute would have degenerated into bloody warfare had not Adolf Loos and a small band of his faithful followers intervened and saved me from being beaten to death.

It was midnight. Since childhood the full moon has always upset my nerves; at home they had to take special precautions to stop me from climbing out of the window in my sleep.

There is a picture I painted of my friend which is now in the museum in Brussels. I called it 'Actor in a Trance,' and if you look at the staring blue eyes of the figure you will perhaps understand what was behind the experience I am about to relate and which I cannot adequately describe in words. I saw his eyes open wide and, bewildered by the sudden, silent look of horror on my companion's face, I looked around. Over the whole square the bumps of the cobbles, each framed in shadow, reflected the moonlight, like the glistening scales of fish seen through the meshes of the net; only my own shadow had separated from my feet, as if the ground beneath me had started to move and my shadow with it.

A moment of suspended consciousness. The only reason I can give is the agitation I have just described, the abnormal state of a young man suddenly, and for the first time, dragged into the screaming, raging maelstrom of a public brawl. The whole thing probably only lasted for fractions of a second: I appear to rise up into the air, vainly try to get my feet back on the ground, and am forced to move my whole body, finding myself eventually in a horizontal position with my left side pointing slightly toward the ground. In water, or some other element heavier than air, there would have been nothing unnatural about it.

I did suffer from a similar delusion many years later, during World War I, after my sense of balance had been disrupted by a head wound which destroyed the labyrinth of the left inner ear, the organ controlling it. However, that abnormal reflex was still many years away, and, anyway, it had a perfectly natural explanation and corrected itself with time and experience.

What is the significance of the fact that, in the case just described, the effect appeared before the cause, casting doubt on a universally accepted law of reasoning? Are there not many people who at some time in their lives have experienced an uncomfortable sensation when crossing the road or going round a corner, as if they were dreaming in broad daylight and were about to encounter a familiar situation, and then acted automatically, even though they had perhaps never been in that part of the town before?

Foreknowledge is reason turned instinct, and it can save us in situations where our lives are in danger. Just because much of our life takes place in the unconscious, because with our academic 'higher' truth we spend our lives in a mindless daze, science is forced to posit an unknown sense. A body does not throw a shadow for a person who has died, just as a body does not throw a shadow for someone who switches off the light: that is the kind of equation that our limited sense of reality sets up. Our ability to get things wrong is the only irrefutable, generally valid law of reasoning. In suggesting the existence of an as yet undiscovered

sense, academic science is leaving itself a loophole and assuming
a source of human error which presents our ability to get things
wrong as a development in intellectual history. On that night all
those years ago my friend ran away. For a long time I bore him
a grudge for the word 'Liar!' he had shouted at me, simply
because, in an impossible situation, I had asked him to pull my
feet back down to the ground. There was no one else around to
help me, and I couldn't stay there forever hovering in the air, in
a logically impossible position.

My friend and I met again long after the war, in London
where the story which I had in mind to tell from the very start
took place. He must have been the only person there who made
an immediate impression on everyone. His dress and behavior
reminded me of Wilhelm Hauff's story of the bogus Englishman
who one day threw off his exaggeratedly correct suit, turned into
a monster from the primeval forest and cut off someone's head
with a razor. Admittedly, my friend was not quite that bad.

So one morning I went with him — his red hair had already
gone white and he had whiskers like an old English shipowner —
to see the famous greenhouse in Kew Gardens. The huge glass
house was empty at that time of the day. We walked up and
down the avenues of palm trees, many of whose trunks were so
big that a fully grown man could hardly get his arms round them.
Under the endless glass roof it was like being in a magic box, and
I was somewhat surprised, given the well-known English love of
nature and their exceptional talent for nurturing animals and
plants and cultivating perfect specimens, at the rather neglected
state of these famous botanical gardens. The uncared-for nature
of the display of plants only served to heighten my awareness of
the solitude surrounding us. So it was only when we came across
a table some twelve to fifteen feet square on which a miniature
Chinese landscape was laid out that my curiosity was aroused and
I felt our visit was worthwhile. In the foreground was water with
fish, from the bank of which, dotted with ancient but tiny
conifers, miniature bridges led across to the other side. This rose
up to a little cliff beyond which was a further rocky landscape
covered with plants which, with its paths, overlapping vistas,

heights and depths, made the artificial perspective a perfect
illusion encapsulating infinity, providing one was willing to
suspend one's disbelief. This has become instinctive for Euro-
peans, especially for the English, who even today measure the
whole world, as far as they want to comprehend it, according to
the length of their own stride and their own arms, by the
proportion of their own self to the cosmos. They haul themselves
up in the universe as if they were on a rope ladder, just like
Baron Münchhausen pulling himself up by his own pigtail. That
is why people who are happy with the proportion of this inner
truth we call experience enjoy contemplating such works of art,
allowing full rein to their remaining curiosity, like a grown-up
watching a child's activities in which he can see no practical
purpose.

On that morning there were no other visitors. My whole
interest was concentrated on looking into the tunnel through the
miniature mountain on the garden table, searching out things
more distant, things that were farther away from me, abandoning
myself, willingly losing myself in this deliberate and ingenious
deception. Once the eye had accustomed itself to the darkness,
the imagination could revel in a landscape that lay beyond it:
high meadows gleaming in a cunningly contrived ray of light, a
waterfall which splashed up in a few drops from the depths of the
valley floor, from a damp and mossy cavity which, in reality, was
perhaps the size of a hollow made in graveyard slabs for the birds
to drink out of. Here was gathered the whole freshness, the
whole dampness, the whole magic of nature which I had sought
in vain among the monsters of the Royal Palm House. I was
about to call my friend, to show him my discovery, when I saw
that he was sitting on a bench some way away in animated and
even, it seemed, somewhat flirtatious conversation with an
English nursemaid. The little girl she was in charge of was
standing there, forgotten and unoccupied, tapping the smoothly
raked ocher sand with the tips of her black, patent-leather shoes.
Then she raised her arms and spun round like a top. The dress
the little girl was wearing had a pattern of vertical lines and stood
out from her waist, falling down round her body like the bloom

of the flower called '*pretty-by-night*,' which in summer opens for one night in our arbors. She looked at me with her shining, nut-brown eyes, came up to me with that easy self-assurance English children have and asked me what I was looking at with such rapt attention. I had to lift the girl up a little so that she could see over the table into the tunnel, and I did it very carefully, for I could quite clearly feel her little heart beating against her ribs, like a fish caught in a trap. Once, when I was a boy, I saw at a theater exhibition, I have forgotten exactly where, a performance in which, by means of an optical trick, the dancers on a darkened stage appeared so reduced in size that you thought you were watching a ballet danced by Thumbelinas. Although I was not conscious of it, this impression probably contributed to the illusion, to the interweaving of dream and reality, that appeared before my eyes the moment I held this delicate little elf in my arms. The little valley had so bewitched me with its sense of remoteness that I was not in the least surprised to see it come alive. Having been picked out by the girl's eye, I now saw my little elf herself in this miniature Island of the Blessed, reminding me of the Thumbelinas I had seen dancing all those years ago. And I had not even noticed her slipping out of my arms. Now she was calling to me in her cold, high-pitched girl's voice, from the other side of the table, as it seemed. After one last glance at the dainty dream-figure in her red-and-white-striped bell of a dress, now only half an inch long, I ran round the table, looking for the original. The girl was not there. Nor was the miniature apparition there when I looked through the tunnel again. A game of hide and seek, such as children love, but an adult no longer understands. Meanwhile my friend, seeing me so occupied and having decided to leave, came over to me and looked at me with his too-light blue eyes, as he had done once before, many years ago in Vienna. I remembered the word 'Liar!' he had shouted then as he ran away from me, so this time I was cautious, and asked casually, 'It seems some other visitors came into the Palm House while I was looking at the Chinese landscape?' He, as I foresaw, replied, 'I haven't seen a soul.' — 'So you can't have kissed the nursemaid, nor seen the little girl,' I thought to myself, but I said, 'It's another of those electric days today, not surprising given how close to the sea London is. I think we'd better go now.' By not telling him how I had seen a child dancing for me alone inside the mountain in the miniature landscape, after she had escaped from the tiresome supervision of her nursemaid, who had been flirting with a gentleman, I had avoided another 'lie.' Good! 'Let's go,' I repeated angrily. What can one do with an audience that has neither the eyes to see the miraculous things going on around us, nor the faith to let the artist recount these miracles when his innocent heart is full of them?

The artist has long since known of the treasure that is there for all to see. But the taste, philosophy, and ethics of the age go out searching for it with their divining rod. And the artist alone has the courage to confess publicly that to err is human. It is a sweet mirage, this artist's mirage of keener reason. Some have been burned at the stake for it, because official, academic history persecutes them as liars and unbelievers. Today there are too few humans who are ready to risk error, and too many who banish this sweet experience from human sight as something not tangible, not quantifiable, not calculable, preferring instead to believe in dogmas that are prejudices.

(Prague, March 1935)

THE WELL

In the past Vienna was much more rural. On the periphery, where my parents moved before we children were of school age, our world consisted of a labyrinth of gardens. Beyond them began the fields and meadows, woods and vineyards. Schönbrunn, where the Emperor lived, lay in the woods over toward the blue hills which rose steadily up to the Semmering massif. On the horizon the peaks of the Raxalpe were half veiled in the shimmering heat-haze.

Running round the house one story below our apartment was a balcony where we could get some fresh air. We were invited onto it by a girl whose parents were foreigners. Unlike the children of the other families in the building, she was not allowed to play out in the street. We children were still so small that we had to stand on tiptoe if we wanted to see over the balustrade. Leaning over was forbidden.

My sister was a restless child, always buzzing around like a gnat, and once I saved her life. She was impulsive, and would immediately grab at anything she saw. Fascinated by the many-colored glass balls down in the yard, she rashly reached out for them, leaning out and losing her balance. By chance her feet were caught in the gaps in the carved wooden supports of the balustrade that represented two intertwined dragons. I seized my sister by her skirt and held on to her for dear life until the nursemaid arrived. The foreigners had a nursemaid for their daughter. My sister used to scream with all her might at the least excuse, probably to frighten people, but this time she didn't make a sound.

Although my memory of most things since then is fairly hazy, I remember life as it was in our street in those days. For example, drinking water was still brought to the house in barrels. I used to watch from the window when the man came to the house; he was given a copper coin worth four kreutzers for his labor. Water for washing in, on the other hand, was brought in a cart which, like the beer-wagons, was drawn by two heavy Pinzgau horses. I still bear a memento of them in the shape of a scar on my knee that I got when one of the powerful, long-haired horse's legs shot out backward, catching me on the knee. Full of curiosity to see a strange pipe that, in some unaccountable way, was growing out of the horse's belly, I had come too close while the horse was staling. That knee has meant that I have never been a good horse-rider. Then there was the poodle-shearer, whom I could follow from the middle of the road to the gates of the house opposite. In those days there were lots of poodles and they had to be completely shorn, apart from a frill round their legs and a tuft on top of their heads, in which they wore a colored silk bow.

Sometimes, when my father had gotten behind with the rent, I had to take it myself. However often I was sent, I never lost my fear of the old widow, who used to sit at the window of the ground-floor apartment watching everything that went on in the street and in the house. On her puffy hands she wore fingerless gloves, which she never seemed to take off. Her fingernails were affected by some disease. It turned my stomach to watch her feel the dreaded thick pancake cooking in a frying pan beside her armchair to see if it was done. Summer and winter the little oven glowed. Given that the windows were always closed, the heat alone would have sufficed to make me feel sick, but she insisted on popping chunks of the yellow substance, always thickly spread with butter, into my mouth, turn and turn about with her pug dog, which snored on her lap. I had to take it like a good little boy, since this landlady liked children, in contrast to other house-owners, from whom my parents had tried to rent apartments in vain. That pug pursued me in my nightmares until the whole breed had died out. It is said that all genera and species

in the animal and vegetable kingdoms have their allotted span,
just as individuals do. My beloved Maréchal Niel, one of the
hybrid tea-roses, has also meanwhile died out. Once, before the
Second World War, when I went round the best flower shops in
Paris looking for them, I was told, regretfully but firmly, 'Ça ne
se cultive plus, parce que ça ne se vend pas.' Instead they offered
me modern roses, which I don't like because they are stiff and
uniform. Above all, they have no scent. I knew of one single tea-
rose which was lovingly cared for by an old German gardener in
one of the many secluded gardens in the baroque city of Prague.
It was there that I thought for the last time that life in this world
was not that bad if one did not have one's head full of high
expectations. The gardener, like all German-speaking inhabitants
of Bohemia, will have been expropriated and expelled, perhaps
even have died of homesickness. Today Bohemia exports Pilsener
beer and, principally, weapons to freedom fighters all over the
world. The decision as to what freedom is does not depend on
the man who comes home tired in the evening from the factory,
wipes the foam from his beer glass and thinks, 'Producing
weapons all day is no joke, but it brings in enough to keep myself
and my family, as long as the bullet is meant for others and not
for me.' In Bohemia there are no longer any of those tailors,
shoemakers, and carpenters, who were famous all over the world
as long as they retained their pride in their craftsmanship. Nor
any building workers, even though fragments of the historic
palaces of the old town are always falling onto the sidewalk.
People there just avoid the sidewalk and stick to the streets, like
all demonstrators, keeping their clenched fists in their pockets so
that the police won't catch them. But to return to the pug dog:
if the scented tea-rose was a symbol of a civilization that has
disappeared, the pug was a symbol of gluttony. Nowadays we are
more restrained in our dietary habits. Whatever led to the pug
dog becoming extinct, I cannot say that it was progress, a
Darwinian step *up* the evolutionary ladder. It was simply a
change in fashion, which does not determine just our clothes, but
even more the environment in which we live and which we first
of all think up and then imagine we perceive as unchanging

immanent principles of a religious, ideological, or scientific nature. Our perception and our understanding are bound up with the age in which we live. The pug of the Victorian age is supposed to be descended from the bloodhound of the conquistadors, who bred it to catch escaped slaves. Although, despite the Puritans, negroes were still sold at market in England at the beginning of the nineteenth century, the bloodhound degenerated into a lapdog there since, after the Boer War, they went over to the production of barbed wire, which is employed to secure the forced laborers of many modern states. In Vienna they used to say of someone who had once ridden in a carriage and now went peddling his wares from house to house with a dog pulling his cart that he had gone to the dogs; nowadays progress is only worth the bone dogs fight over. This is an insight that came to me quite suddenly. Whole peoples are being murdered before our very eyes in the name of democracy, which is nothing but a transitional notion of our age giving the state that right, just as the pious Puritans of yore assumed the right to deal in human flesh because they considered it a legal source of income. We see what we do, but we do not understand.

We understand institutions, principles, and ideologies as if they existed outside living nature; they have so far become second nature to us modern realists that, as in the case of the concept of property, we abandon our human rights, becoming ourselves the property of the state that, constitutionally, ought to be protecting those rights. It might be considered inappropriate to discuss politics in a story about dogs, but when humanity is going to the dogs before our very eyes, the narrator cannot really be accused of digressing. It is not dogs, but human beings who are out of character. Is not the only freedom of which we are still capable of dreaming the illusion of those who are today behind barbed wire that they will be tomorrow's prison guards? No, there is no other illusion left we can rise to, neither that of a Darwinian step up the evolutionary ladder, nor that of grace, which is timeless. Wars, revolutions, social reforms, and the sweeping pace of progress have all left us in slavery from which there is no escape because our imagination is drying up and withering away. Our horrified eyes can see the end, but we accept it fatalistically, as a fact we cannot change. In the past men used to crown the victims they were sacrificing to the gods with garlands. With roses they begged for grace from the gods to whom they were bringing human sacrifices.

It is not without reason that I chose to relate the history of the pug dog here, which the Chinese still supposedly breed as a delicacy. In its not very sublime end it is a mirror to mankind, which today can do no more than snap and bark. This world no longer has the strength to ward off the sword of Damocles that hangs over us all, nor has it the imagination to envision divine intervention.

With every morning of every day until death, new and incomprehensible things are happening in the world which, although they will ever remain mysterious, we try to understand according to the capacity of our individual intellectual faculties. I, for example, observed that soon after she had been born, my sister started to grab at her own toe because it moved of its own accord. Life is full of mysteries and remains a mystery. As a child, I for my part found it puzzling that when there was anyone I was interested in, anyone I had my eye on, I had to walk round them, otherwise I would only get to know one half of the person, the half that was facing me. If, however, it was an object, and small enough to hold in my hand, then I only had to turn it round and round for the whole to become visible. That is not a mystery nowadays because we no longer look, but think in facts and have lost our capacity for puzzling over things.

As long as Lala, my friend from the floor below, was sitting at the mirror tidying her locks, which had become disheveled while we were playing, everything was simple; I looked into the mirror with her. She was like a picture in a frame. Then something new, unexpected happened. The Lala in the mirror, who seemed to me like something from a fairy tale in a dark forest, started teasing and mocking me by pulling faces and snickering like a spiteful goblin. I quickly turned my eyes away from the mirror — how calmly she was sitting there! Everything's fine, I thought, perhaps she'll come round to see if I can play tomorrow. I never want to be alone. This decision had come suddenly, just like that. I made it under compulsion, almost against my will, in a terrible access of fear even. I could not see that I was making a mistake when I kissed her on the lips. She went bright red, her eyes flashed, she turned her back on me and vanished, not only from the mirror, but out of my life, for good. Her family had come to collect her.

There was a picture book in the hall. Actually, I didn't really want to have it, but the nursemaid brought it to us the next day. A book with a picture in several colors on the first page, the other illustrations were printed in black and white. The nursemaid said the family had gone away. They hadn't taken the book with them.

I would like to add that if we look closely enough we can understand much of what is happening in the world, we can get to the bottom of things. Naturally we can also learn much by listening carefully. And tasting, smelling, touching too each reveal a world of their own. But it is with our eyes that we discover the basic truth, the truth on which life is grounded, so to speak. What was so attractive about my first playmate was that at that time everything was grounded in her, she was the background to everything, more even than a frown flitting across my mother's face. I saw her image in the bird in the garden which, so to speak, flew into my arms. Oh, I remember that she was simply the first thing I perceived with my whole being. It was no use my repeating her name to myself over and over again, I was still surrounded by empty air, she did not appear to me in this world. Rather, I had to kneel down and, closing my eyes as in a dream, look inside myself — however ridiculous that may sound when I try to put it into words — then she would appear to me and my child's heart would rush wildly toward her in passionate greeting. Every person has the right to observe life with their own eyes, like the pattern they alone have created, to the best of their ability, in a carpet. Life allows both sacred and boorish dances. What carries some people through the air to the Orient, like a carpet, is used by others as a bedside rug. And it is just the same with the things we see.

Sometimes my attention was attracted by an infernal commotion out in the street: a herd of cattle being driven into the city. From their massive white chests, from their parched throats came a heart-rending roaring and groaning. The cows had not yet forgotten their pastures. They staggered along blindly in the shadow of the buildings, which grew more and more densely packed, the green spaces between them less and less frequent, as the suburbs merged into the city. The beasts were running everywhere, pressing up onto the sidewalk, along the walls, pushing each other forward; they were so cramped for space they climbed up onto each other's backs. Immediately the butcher boys would come running to sort out the tangle of beasts and drive them back into the road with their bullwhips made out of plaited sinews. Whenever I thought the many-horned procession was slowing up I would dash over to the window. Every time the moving street came to a standstill I immediately imagined the twitching, roaring flesh was piling up, rising up the wall to the first-floor balcony. But I had to lean out to see this horrifying sight.

During the summer evenings the windows were covered with gauzy material stretched over wooden frames because when the kerosene lamp was lit it attracted the moths. Then I would open the picture book that had been left to me. Since I knew the descriptions accompanying the pictures almost all by heart, I colored in the illustrations from a little box of colored inks I had been given for Christmas. The black-on-white prints needed, as I thought, colors to bring them to life. With the paint something like a faint odor came to hover over the illustrations, and from then on a taste of honey clung forever to the Greek myths. Thus the city of the Greeks with its white marble temples arose beneath a cloudless blue sky and olive-green hills. The Greek heroes were sacrificing a virgin and the high priest had raised his glittering ax over her head. An earthquake accompanied by a terrifying roll of thunder had split open the ground from which red flashes of lightning came shooting out. The blue bays and the rosy cities on the shore mirrored in the sea were enveloped in a menacing cloud. With my paints I followed the tiny figures printed in black all the way into the cracks in the ground that swallowed them up. There was an Aeneas, the founding father, who was carrying his own father on his back and from whose children the Romans trace their ancestry. Men were carrying women wringing their hands, others were riding off on donkeys with all their goods and chattels. Old women were staggering along with anything they could save from the ruins wrapped up in their togas. Perhaps it wasn't an earthquake, no, war had ravaged the countryside. Achilles drove his fiery horses, dragging Hector's corpse in triumph round conquered Troy. Heroes in gleaming armor killed other heroes, packs of fat rats emerged from their hiding places into the light of day. The last picture in the book showed the goddess with the half moon in her hair appearing from the cloud, saving my playmate from the high priest's ax, and taking her up with her. That was why I dressed her in a kilt such as my friend used to wear. As I have already said, I could read, but I found it easiest to communicate with Lala by signs and looks, since she spoke English.

If, when we children were still invited downstairs to play, we went round the gallery — 'faire le tour du patron' as Lala, who had French lessons, once said — we could see the sun almost all day. It rose and set over the gallery. There was a railing with gilded spears separating the yard from the garden. Among the roses in the beds were colored glass balls on posts. But when Lala threw her ball to me in the garden I saw many more colors than there were. Now my heart was sad, especially in the afternoon; the garden was closed to us since she and her family had left. The garden with the lawn that was just made for playing on, with the large green trees and the colored balls, was empty, was gray in gray.

Now we were allowed to play in the yard. The yard was cobbled and our footsteps echoed round the well in the middle, and that was strange. You could well imagine it wasn't children's steps but giant's feet crossing it. In the middle of the brick-built well was an upright post with a circular winch at the top. A pail on a rope went down to the bottom of the well through a square hole that was left open in the boards covering the well. Because the wood was already rotten and broken in places my little sister and I had been warned not climb up onto the boards, never mind jump around on them. What we did dare to do was to lie down on the boards and stick our noses in the square hole to smell the musty odor coming up from the dampness below, while the upper surface of the boards had been dried out by the sun. In the cracks and crevices tiny mites dashed to and fro like little silvery fish, ants came and went through the hole. How they scurried about, constantly waving their feelers, with which they would prod each other as if they were talking! And then the mysterious noise of the drops of water in the depths below, farther than we could see! Whenever a few particles detached themselves from the wall inside it took a while before they hit the water. And we could only hear it if we were on top, over the middle of the well. We could not see this underworld, only hear it. I once heard someone say there was a toad at the bottom of the well. I never saw it myself, but some nights I made a special effort not to fall asleep so I could hear it croaking, but I couldn't stay awake that long.

One day the nursemaid disappeared for good. The incident has stayed in my mind because on that day they got the janitor to close the huge front door, which usually stood wide open, winter and summer. No one was allowed out in the street. People were standing in the entrance saying the bull had escaped. In my picture book there was a woman riding off on a bull that had emerged from the water. None of the people were around when the nursemaid disappeared, not even my sister. I knew her well because she often used to give me candy since I had started school and went past her shop. Usually she was crying. Once I was almost caught sitting on her lap. They were looking for me in the shop where she had been working since she lost her position. I was late coming home yet again. They said she couldn't go on like that much longer. The last time she took me secretly to her bedroom behind the candy store. Why did I follow the nurse-maid, even though I had been forbidden to go into her shop ever again? My curiosity was too great. She showed me a plant in a pot that was in flower. These plants are called nightshade because they are closed by day and only open at night. Such flowers give off a dangerous odor and if you have them by your bed you will get a fever. The nursemaid said that she was going to die young and that was why she had the flowerpot in her bedroom. But that was not why I had gone there. Her sin was buried in that pot, she said, which was the reason why she had lost her position. But there was nothing to see because there was soil over it. That was why it didn't make much of an impression on me.

I'm sure the bull carried off the nursemaid. On the day when the bull escaped I was in the courtyard with the nursemaid and saw exactly how it happened. I think I can reveal it now. Her headscarf had slipped down onto her neck as she put up the lines that criss-crossed the yard and then hung out the wet washing with wooden pegs. She did the washing for the landlady with the snoring pug. Her hair must have got into her eyes, which was why she kept on wiping away her tears with the back of her hand. Then she went to fetch the watering can to spray the linen. That was the custom in Vienna so that the bed-linen would come out beautifully white. She climbed up onto the well-cover, cautiously at first, just on the edge, her legs wide apart. But as she was winding up the full pail on the rope, the winch on the wheel gave a screech and came to a stop. She turned round on the rotten well-cover with the washing in her arm in order to free the rope that had come off the drum. She hesitated for a moment when I shouted out that the cover would break. Then the blue sky darkened. Her blue dress flew up in the air for a brief second, and she was gone. In the black hole the depths yawned. Although now I could have seen the toad sitting at the bottom, it would have been impossible for me to look. Perhaps I would have done better to look for the bull, since no one was paying attention. Without that silly order forbidding us to go out of the house there would have been people outside. They had locked the main door. I shook it for a while, but in vain. There was a crowd in the landlady's apartment, and even in our corridor there were some people talking who did not belong to the house. I heard someone remark that the bull's horns had a spread of over six feet. It was said to have speared someone with them and dashed off with the person still stuck on its horns and no one had dared go to help. Everyone was listening. Finally they were relieved to hear the butcher boys run past in pursuit. Whether the bull was caught or not, I can no longer remember.

Finally it was all over and the front door was opened again. I immediately told the people what had happened out in the yard, but no one was interested in my claim that the bull had come up out of the water and carried the nursemaid off. They could easily have checked: from the corridor window you could see that the cover over the well was broken. The lady who owned the house — she never moved from her armchair, I think she even slept in it — said the old cover was no good anyway and needed renewing. For a while I wasn't allowed down in the yard.

An event occurred for which I could not find a satisfactory explanation and which occupied my thoughts for a long time. There was a silver and glass coach waiting outside the house. It couldn't be Snow White in the glass coffin they carried out of our house because she was just a fairy tale. The main thing was to stop myself getting bored by watching out for the moment when the black horses with the sky-blue ostrich feathers on their heads started pulling and the coach drove off. A stale smell of candles lit in broad daylight floated up like a cloud from the street to my window. Then the two horses trotted off in step, pulling the glass coach toward the fields by the highway in a shimmer of dust. I could see the wheels of the coach clearly as they revolved, at first as big as a house door, then growing smaller and smaller, until finally the whole thing was no more than a spot gleaming in the sunshine at the last twist in the road. Then there was nothing left, nothing at all.

'She's dead', they said. What 'she' would that be, I asked. Lord, how simple can you get! He doesn't know it's the nursemaid! I just thought they were making it up again. Didn't I tell them often enough that the bull carried the nursemaid off on its back? They shouldn't have been in such a hurry get rid of the black box, there were enough people standing around to see what was in it. That is how you put away a doll you are not playing with, but a person who is sleeping will surely open his eyes again in the morning? What does it mean, dead . . .

CHILDHOOD ILLNESS

After the mysterious disappearance of the nursemaid in the well my parents managed to procure permission for us to play three times a week in an isolated part of a park belonging to a Polish prince. In fact, the park was a hill crowned by a mausoleum. It was called Galizin Hill after the noble family that had lived in Vienna since the partition of Poland under Czar Alexander I. My memory of the park has been contaminated by an illustration of the former Russian imperial palace in Tsarskoye Selo, which I later cut out of a magazine. However, this reproduction of my childhood experience was nowhere near the splendor of the original. All the things that worked on the imagination — the spirits and demons of the painted and sculpted allegories which were on an equal footing with the lords of the castle, even the marble group with the Hound of Hell — together with the exaggerated dimension of a child's vision, I have since found in the theater alone. Indeed, it was probably this perspective, in which everything is seen through the imagination, which made the whole attraction of the theater for me. In reality, that was the time when parks and castles began to fall into ruin; the grounds were divided up into building plots, the castles converted into hotels. Wherever you went to see a ruin there was a pensioned-off sergeant selling tickets and picture postcards. But for all that, this aristocratic world remained the basis of the world in which the Austrian of the nineteenth century lived in his imagination. As the Englishman says, 'My home is my castle.'

This was the magical world in which Ferdinand Raimund placed the characters of his fairy tale comedies and farces, tragicomic characters because they try to climb the social ladder until they bump into the spirit world. Each one of them was a baron, or at least a 'Your Honor'. The shabbier the age, the more threadbare the umbrella, the duller the stovepipe, the tall Sunday hat the good citizens doffed with a wide sweep to greet each other. While in Germany after Goethe and Schiller classical plays had driven popular theater from the stage, it lived on in Vienna in the works of such writers as Raimund and Johann Nestroy. As well as the spirits and fairies in Raimund's *The Spendthrift*, strutting along arm in arm with the ennobled parvenus comes the buffoon, a figure from the Viennese tradition (a conservative tradition, going back as it does to the plays of antiquity), as witty and garrulous as the respectable ladies and gentlemen themselves, parading under the Corinthian colonnades of princely porticos, painted on canvas, looking straight up to the gods.

In reality the castle was probably only the kiosk for the park-keeper, who also ran a tobacconist's. The sun of the myths of antiquity must have bleached his bushy beard to marble, which, in my eyes, transformed him into Hercules. The Deliverer who chained up many-headed Cerberus! The bicycle belonging to this park-keeper and tobacconist was leaning against the dog's kennel. My sister did not really trust the legends of antiquity because she felt I was giving myself airs among a circle of acquaintances from which she was shut out. I felt I had to prove to her just for once that I was no mere braggart. Constant caution had become second nature to her. She had acquired cunning and craft in order to escape my supervision or, rather, my perpetual tormenting. As the older of the two, I had to keep an eye on her. She was supposed to take a lot of exercise in the fresh air because she was shooting up and was slightly anemic. So we played at horse and carriage. I used her plaits as reins and hit her with a stick to keep her going at a lively pace. Like a coachman, I clicked my tongue and had a self-satisfied look on my face. 'Stop kicking up such a fuss! Every coachman gives his horse the whip, it's all part of the game. If you cry just because of that you're nothing but a spoilsport.' My sister kept on crying, so I gave her a wink and, pointing to the tobacconist with my outstretched finger, whispered the magic formula that never failed to work, 'I can see something you can't see.' With the sudden rush of confidence of a lost soul hearing familiar tones, she stopped crying and looked up. We both saw him, Hercules, both at the same time. Only a moment before, I myself had not seriously believed that the owner of the bicycle was Hercules, the mythical hero. But already I could see a glint of mockery returning to her eye; even panic, which paralyzes people who find themselves in a forbidden region, cannot stifle a child's quick spirit. It looks on fences and frontiers with scorn. 'I know you. I won't believe you until you ring the bicycle bell.' I would have preferred not to have to submit to this ordeal, but then she would have told our parents that I had bullied her. If she made stipulations, then it was essential that I should gain some advantage from the deal, on which I had to stake all my courage. She knew my weak side and knew well that I only pretended not to notice her mockery. Mockery strikes the spot where you are naked beneath all your clothes. If, on the other hand, I willingly submitted to her will, then she was mistaken in believing she could break my will; she could just bend it to her will.

I had forgotten our Hercules. Was I not close enough to being a hero myself, ready to brave all dangers to stop her laughing at me once and for all?! We peered through the branches that hid us from the park-keeper. 'Don't just keep on saying you know no fear', she urged me, 'just stretch out your hand and ring the bell.' So we shook hands on the agreement that would stop her laughing at me for ever. I spied out the land again. A customer was about to leave the tobacco shop, so I leaped out of the bushes and rang the bell. The guard-dog was even quicker out of its kennel. My sister collapsed to the ground, stiff as a board. Her usual trick! She had often employed it successfully in church when she couldn't find a way out of the crush of grown-ups. How crafty she was! Everyone came running to help her, while no one came to help me when the guard-dog had me in its teeth. 'You idiot! Can't you read? It says "Beware of the dog" on the sign. And there goes the baron, getting away without paying for his cigar again.'

The park-keeper swore and cursed. Once more I could hear my sister laughing . . . I was lying in the grass with a strange feeling, as if people were playing ball with me. The wind rustling the leaves of the tall trees gave a comforting sense of security. I had the feeling the air, with a white dove flying to and fro in it, was the safest place to be. To help me recover from my fright, the park-keeper had treated me to some of the schnapps in which he preserved his cherries. Afterwards he even sat me on his bicycle. He was fond of children. In a circle all around me the birds, butterflies and flowers were gradually awoken one after the other by the eternal light. The dove was the first to fly out of Noah's Ark, the olive branch of peace in its beak. It rested on Mount Ararat, after the Flood was over. A long white beard was hanging all by itself above me in the air. I could not see clearly, I was still too weak and my eyelids were too heavy to open. That was how I came to see the spirit of God in the mysterious green light that shines through your eyelashes when your eyes are half closed. A piece of luck that God exists, I thought, for there was something I wanted to ask him about. It is obvious that in its dealings with the stronger sex the weaker willingly subordinates itself. But girls seem to be marvelously adept at developing their powers of reason so that they command my respect. I will marry my sister. A twitching at the corners of the mouth hidden under the flowing white hair became a divine smile. The company of the Omniscient One was so inviting that I wanted to ask him why the Almighty is alone, for ever and ever, amen! There was a soft humming in my ears. God was standing alone among his stars, just like the park-keeper in the big flowerbed. There must be angels, looking like girls with wings, singing in the heavenly spheres and playing their harps, and the Lord God remained unmarried?! But my weakness returned and I decided to leave the matter to another day.

'Just look at the lad, he's drunk,' came the voice of the park-keeper out of a cloud of rather strong-smelling incense. 'It was that kirsch!' He lifted up his cat, which was wearing a black collar. 'I've spoiled him, just as I spoil my cat with rolls soaked in milk every day. The good-for-nothing! He's going to fast today. He'll have to wear that black collar for a week because he tore the feathers out of my angel of a canary, just as if it was any ordinary bird. He sings like an angel does my canary! But to make up he'll get two white mice from me tomorrow.' As he walked away, the park-keeper was still muttering that he could not stand white mice. He could see them in front of his eyes everywhere. But I didn't like the smell of the schnapps, so I got up and went to the Hercules fountain to wash my face.

Recently two girls had started coming regularly to the park, accompanied by their mother. While the lady read a novel, her children were allowed to play with us. The older girl and I were soon inseparable friends. At five o'clock, following the English habit, a tartan rug was spread out on the grass and tea taken. I didn't care for the bitter brew, that was kept at boiling point under a padded cozy so that you were sure to burn your tongue on it. All I could see in the custom was an invitation to join in a party game, the rules of which required you to behave as if they were inborn. During the tea ceremony I forgot what my new-found inseparable friend had impressed upon me, namely, that I was to behave like a grown-up. Sitting opposite me on the tartan rug, she kept her eyes modestly fixed on her lap, like the ladies in Schiller's ballad, 'The Diver,' which we were just doing at school! 'May I pour you some more hot water?' I was asked. According to the rules, I knew I was supposed to say, 'Yes, but please serve the lady first,' which was why I snatched my cup away and the hot water spilled all over. The lady said reproachfully, 'Please use your saucer, otherwise the next thing we know that valuable Japanese cup will be in pieces.' It was time for us to get up and leave the lady to her French novel. Was my face red! Never again would I accept an invitation to tea. My friend forgave me the wet patch on her dress, but I didn't. I refused to play the parfait gentle knight, however many crowns her mother had embroidered on the tablecloth.

I was used to coffee at home. Anyone from Vienna who, in the good old days, had not learned to distinguish up to twelve different ways of preparing it cannot be taken seriously if he insists on expressing his opinions as to why the Austrians in particular and Europe in general have gone to the dogs. The real reason is that in Vienna, even before the world wars, instead of this oriental magic potion that brings people together and gladdens their hearts, they had a poor substitute made from roasted chicory, as they have in France. Up to the War of the Spanish Succession people in Europe drank chocolate. Nowadays tea is the fashion everywhere.

England, as is well known, has a damp climate, more rain than sunshine. It is an island, surrounded by the sea, a breeding ground for rheumatism, which is the reason why they brew tea in boiling hot water, tea imported from India. England had colonies even before the Congress of Vienna. How did coffee, which since the Congress has been displaced by tea, originally come to Vienna? A brief review of history may be in order here. Nowadays, when package tours to the moon are no longer merely a figment of Jules Verne's imagination, we should try to view history in relation to what determines matters in the real world and what is simply imagination. Palmerston in his own day could say that the British made pacts with other nations in order to counter threats of war which existed more in their imagination.

Even today history books tell us that the Jacobin coup in Paris, the French Revolution and Louis XVI's miserable end on the guillotine so horrified the English that they started meddling in European affairs. That is not the case. England had already beheaded a king of its own, and it was the crowned heads of Europe that were filled with panic at the invention of the guillotine, that first dangerous child of the dawning age of mechanization. This period of the Jacobin reign of terror is still, for the English, the age of the philosophers of the Enlightenment.

The Corsican condottiere, Bonaparte, took only few years to deal with the revolution in France. Even the fact that under the brilliant leadership of Napoleon, as he was now called, the French revolutionary armies were laying waste to the continent, did not perturb the English unduly. It was quite understandable; France was starving, people didn't revolt against a God-given order by accident. Austria had to cede its rich Italian provinces,

France needed Holland, Belgium, and the German coast as a shield against England, but Wellington barred the road to Spain because of the port people take after dinner in England. Now the French revolutionary general had a plan that won the approval of the Directoire: Egypt. Since Louis XIV, since the Crusades even, the legendary treasures of the Orient have occupied the French imagination more than the liberation of the Holy Land from the infidel. This had already brought Louis XIV into conflict with England. From Egypt it was only a short step to India, where the English had wrested the East India Company from the Dutch; it would be a simple matter to overthrow British global power. England remained calm, and with good reason. In the shadow of the pyramids, Napoleon said to his men, 'Soldiers, from the summit of yonder pyramids forty centuries look down upon you,' but when the news came that the English had sent their warships to the Mediterranean, he decided he would be better off at home. He left his army behind, was received with open arms in Paris, was appointed First Consul — dictator — and, five years later, after brilliant victories on the battlefields of Europe, proclaimed emperor by the French, who had tired of their revolution. He was consecrated in Notre Dame by Pope Pius VII in person. Now even the emigrés recognized him as the legitimate ruler of France and, overcome with homesickness, returned contritely. The former field-marshals of the revolution became princes. Napoleon understood people, and it was not for nothing that he had started his career as an artillery lieutenant. He knew one could gain victories with children; the old guard had been gradually wiped out. If young people were armed with the latest inventions of the technological age, rapid-fire automatic rifles and long-range artillery, perhaps Napoleon I might have succeeded in uniting Europe (a dream as old as the history of Europe) by force, if not in harmony. The Russian Tsar, Alexander I, even offered to divide up the world with Napoleon. Napoleon was a sceptic, he would have been quite content with Europe. Not so Alexander, a product of the Russian Orthodox Church's mystical mission to convert all mankind and unite them in the bosom of the Orthodox faith. This faith lives on in various forms: as a religious, political (in imperialism), or communist mission.

Napoleon did not trust Alexander. Since even his old revolutionary marshals, after such successes in Europe, believed it would be possible to gather reinforcements from the occupied countries and conquer Russia, Napoleon invaded Russia. In so doing he was following his old plan of breaking England's power by marching through Russia to India. For that he would not need a fleet. This time, however, England did become uneasy, and took Copenhagen. An alliance — a 'Holy Alliance' in keeping with Alexander's outlook — was concluded to attack Napoleon with united forces. Alexander had broken with Napoleon and had persuaded the Prussians to combine with England and risk a war of liberation against the usurper. Austria armed its militia. The Russians set fire to Moscow and Napoleon's army froze to death in the icy wastes of the vastnesses of Russia, a fate which centuries ago befell the Tartars and more recently the German army. Once again Napoleon had to flee and was forced to abdicate by the French. With Louis XVI the legitimate Bourbon dynasty was put back on the throne and at the Congress of Vienna that skilful negotiator, Talleyrand, had managed to save not only France's frontiers but also part of the conquered territories when the terrible news of Napoleon's escape from Elba struck the gathering of sovereigns like a bolt of lightning. Napoleon's second empire lasted one hundred days. The united armies of the great powers under Wellington dealt him a crushing defeat at Waterloo, and he was sent on an English cruiser to exile on the far-off island of St. Helena, where he wrote his memoirs. Perhaps his liver had been affected by the Russian vodka, to which Alexander had introduced him during the days of their friendship. Perhaps he was not the strategic genius he is still considered today. To bring this long story of a turbulent era to an end: England had no need to worry about her supplies of Indian tea, which kept revolutionary ideas out of the heads of her population. That had been the prime concern of politicians there. We are what we eat and drink.

'Everlasting peace' was the slogan of the Congress of Vienna;

the Russian soul seems to have been enmeshed in an everlasting dream since people in Byzantium thought they had found the cross on which the Savior died to unite mankind. Everlasting peace remains the favorite goal of idealists the world over. But a rational man like Prince Metternich managed to convince the Congress that, while everlasting peace was perhaps a possibility in the next world, all that was realistic in this was a temporary balance of power in Europe. This balance survived until the middle of the nineteenth century when the great powers forced the sick man on the Bosphorus to abdicate, at which the peoples in the Balkans, and then almost everywhere in Europe, adopted the old slogan of the revolution, 'liberty, equality, fraternity.' That was the end of a united Europe. Prince Metternich found it easier to deal with Tsar Alexander. The latter had often threatened to abdicate and Metternich had encouraged him in his intention; the rumor of the Tsar's death was spread, and he is said to have lived on for a long time as a mystical hermit in a monastery near Tomsk. I repeat: that was the end of a united Europe, but it was also the end of good Viennese coffee. That is why I would like to say something here about the way this oriental magic potion, which, as Metternich said, was known for bringing people together and gladdening their hearts, came to Vienna. To do that, however, I shall have to go back in history a little.

Tu felix Austria nube. There was a time when Habsburg power had been so increased — less by wars than by marrying into royal houses — that it aroused the jealousy of France and led to the War of the Spanish Succession under Louis XIV, who wanted to place his grandson, Philip, on the Spanish throne by force. As a result of the long war, France — and Spain as well — was almost reduced to beggary. So the Most Christian King, Louis XIV, called the Turks into Europe to bring down the House of Habsburg. The Turks got as far as the ramparts of Vienna, and everywhere they passed through on their victorious advance they left behind them ruins and devastation, starvation and ashes. In conjunction with Jan Sobieski of Poland, Prince Eugene of Savoy, whom Louis XIV had scorned because of his puny physique, inflicted such a crushing defeat on the Turks that their commander was forced to flee for home, abandoning all his prisoners, jewels and gold. The victors even captured camels and wild animals; the camels were put in the imperial zoo, the first in Europe. The only thing they had no use for were the sacks of coffee. A Viennese woman who had been freed from Turkish captivity had married a Turk. Together they opened, with the permission of the authorities, the first Viennese coffee house. For the population of Vienna, decimated by hunger and disease, one coffee house was sufficient.

Viennese coffee became fashionable, until Russia lit the fuse to the Balkan powder-keg, which led to the First World War and, of course, to *ersatz* coffee.

To return to the mother of my friend: we heard that the lady's father was said to have been one of these respectable Viennese coffee-house owners. The coffee house went well, and she married a man with the noble *von* to his name. One of her daughters spent most of the time on a swing which was fixed to the branches of a tall tree in the park. Her sister, my special friend, often had to use more than tender persuasion to drag me away from the tree. Angrily, she would shout up to the sylphide to pull down her dress. My friend could see enough, in spite of her shortsightedness. She had delicate eyes, which were shadowed by long lashes. She was someone I could rely on implicitly, she was always ready to help. I gave her all my school homework to look through.

No one who has outgrown the age in which the first — inexpressible, unadmitted — stirrings of sexual maturity appear is ever again so exclusively influenced by lethargy, submissiveness, little misunderstandings, vanity, by an undeveloped mind lacking experience, by fluctuations in their state of health, that they would head open-eyed for the abyss to which this chain of circumstances has led them.

For that reason it is more honest, in this portrayal of my youthful experiences, to refrain from seeking out bizarre or unusual circumstances for my case — which would anyway not be verifiable — from the state of childish innocence. It is an elemental occurrence, sometimes making no more than a tiny splash in the still waters of time; a gnat falls into a pond and, as the ripples spread across the calm surface, becomes the harmless agency that stirs up the depths.

My friend had gone away on a little errand, looking for a bottle of smelling salts that the lady had put down somewhere and could not find. Scarcely was she out of my sight than she was nothing more to me than a memory of a childhood gone forever on that very day. A rolling stone gathers no moss. I had become aware of the contradictoriness of nature as of a mystery abruptly and nakedly revealed in the girl on the swing. Things that must be the way they are and things that can be different both disintegrated along with innocence. Things one ought to do and things one ought not to do. But the contradiction, the indecent thing about it even, was that I craved the fruit of the tree of knowledge. I did! I did! I did! The girl did not pay the least attention to me, lying underneath the tree. My heavy heart probably meant as little to her as the devotion of her pet dog which, for once, was not scolded and sent away when it jumped up at its little mistress, crumpling her dress. A butterfly was silently fluttering round her, kept coming to rest on her. Nothing betrayed to her the mixed feelings that made me laugh and sob, as when reason, sunshine and the breeze spreading pollen combine in an April mood; or when you have discovered the first violet among the dead leaves and just have to tell someone else.

Before I go on, I must tell you about a snow-sweeper whose acquaintance I had made the previous winter during the preparations for the carnival procession that was to pass through our district. Day after day I watched him pile up the snow in high walls on either side of the slippery street. Everyone had gone out to see the decorated floats of the procession which were preceded by a crowd of people in fancy dress: chimney sweeps and hunchbacks (it brought good luck if you touched one), soldiers dressed in *biedermeier* costume with red noses, bandoliers and puttees, a giant with rolling eyes, ghosts, negroes, men dressed up as women, magicians, all carrying rattles or throwing paper balls and streamers. If any of the spectators got annoyed at being hit, there was immediately a great to-do and the whole company of clowns would fall upon them with coarse pranks and rude jokes until the floats had to continue on their way and the fools looked for new opportunities to amuse the onlookers.

The snow-sweeper had covered his head in sackcloth. Not, however, because he wanted to demonstrate his repentance to Jehova, like the Jews of old in the Bible. In Vienna in those days the ashes were still collected in sacks from the houses by the ashman. The weather was foul, that was why the snow-sweeper had put an ash-sack over his head and wrapped others round his legs. He didn't actually need to wrap up both legs, like his friends, because he had lost one in the war and it had been replaced by a wooden leg. I felt flattered when the man with the wooden leg invited me to go with him to Herr Borowitz' schnapps-shop. That was at midday, as I was on my way home from school. In the morning the snow-sweepers would gather outside the taverns to pour off the dregs from the almost-empty beer-barrels. For this purpose each carried a rusty pan tied on a string round his waist. In the schnapps-shop this man, whom his friends called the 'Gentleman,' encouraged me to spend the kreutzer I had in my pocket on a kümmel. The coin was meant to pay the school janitor for the roll I had during recess, but the young master just had to try that kümmel.

In the spring, to my delight, I met the 'Gentleman' beside the park gates with a hurdy-gurdy. He was wearing his veteran's tunic with a glittering medal for bravery in the face of the enemy pinned to his chest. He was so proud of the emperor's uniform! He had had to wait a long time for his hurdy-gurdy, had had to keep on sending in petitions to the War Ministry because there were so many who had lost eyes, arms or legs in the Bosnian campaign. A hurdy-gurdy was the standard compensation for common soldiers, noncommissioned officers with a long service record were given a position as park-keeper or watchman, prison guard or foreman in the state-owned brush and cigarette factories, school janitor or doorman outside one of the ministry buildings; officers received a store selling tobacco or lottery tickets. Thus I came to receive instruction in Austrian history from my friendly veteran. Who had the enemy actually been? I wanted to know. The Bosniaks, who carried long knives between their teeth and tried to cut off from every honest Christian parts which, for decency's sake, he could not mention by name. Had he suffered that misfortune as well? I asked, somewhat hesitantly. With a great show of indignation he refused to answer such a question from a silly schoolboy. If that happened, a man would have no fun at all to look forward to in life. He had just lost a leg. Yes, he had been left for dead on the battlefield; the next morning the medical orderlies had come to fetch him, galloping right through the middle of the enemy ranks. Orders are orders, and his name had been put on the list for a hurdy-gurdy. Since it had already been chopped off, they left his leg there. Yes, those were the good old days, he said, and he had had to wait more than twenty years for his hurdy-gurdy. He played the only roll he possessed for me, the song of Prince Eugene, the noble knight who:

> Across the stream a bridge did throw
> So his bold men could swiftly go
> And take by storm the town and fortress of Belgrade.

In those days so-called 'real facts' were given preference over instruction in dead languages, which could only be of interest to philosophers, philologists and pharmacists. Just as a magnet attracts iron filings, so I went to the high school for science and languages, called the *Realschule* at a time when the future belonged to the 'real world.' It was progress that had brought about this revolution in outlook.

Excellent, really excellent! The study of 'real facts' guaranteed a deeper insight into the nature of progress than lessons in classical languages. Looking back today on the reasons why I was somewhat skeptical about this scheme, I am sure it must have been the replacement of horse-drawn trams by electric ones in our district. We schoolboys were in the habit of jumping up and hanging onto the back of the car, unseen by the conductor, and getting a free ride part of the way. But when I tried the new means of transport I found I had reckoned without the speed of progress. My strength soon gave out, but I could not jump off, as I used to when I had had enough. I was hurled off and taken home with a bloody head. That made me think. Perhaps progress did go a little too fast after all.

The two great inventions — the printing press and gun-powder — must have made the history teachers of my youth very uneasy. Since they did not know how to deal with the period ushered in by these inventions, they simply ignored the modern age in their lessons. If, as far as the printing press was concerned, I felt that something that facilitated the production of more and more schoolbooks was a fiendish invention, the other was, if possible, even less to my taste. However plausible the teacher's explanation of the laws that led to pressure in the carburetor producing motive power, the only way I could get to the bottom of things was by practical experiment. I managed to get hold of saltpeter, sulfur, soot, sawdust, and some iron filings. I took it as the hand of fate that my friend, the veteran, had served with the Imperial and Royal Bombardiers in the Balkans, where he came from. Loyalty to the branch of the armed forces in which he had served may have kept alive his interest in explosives, as well as his friendship with fellow-countrymen who called themselves anarchists. In his willingness to help me in this, one must make allowances for our war-veteran's impetuous Slav temperament, especially considering that a scientific mind such as Alfred Nobel's was strong enough to feel no qualms at all about possible side-effects of his invention of dynamite. He washed his hands of them with the foundation of the Nobel Prize for Peace. The veteran on the other hand was untroubled by such compunction when he made the primitive bomb I wanted, a simple child's toy.

Only the two daughters of the noble *von* knew about the bomb buried below a tall tree in the park. The veteran missed the great day, since he was not allowed in the park with his hurdy-gurdy. The task I had set myself, in accordance with the scientific method I had learned in physics and chemistry, was to blast a large anthill under the tree sky-high. My friend, the girl with the gentle eyes, was very concerned about the fate of the ants, but her sister said they were a nuisance when she was lying in the hammock. My friend's reproaches that my experiment would cost the lives of other living creatures did nothing to persuade me to call it off, especially since, as I have told you, our relationship had cooled. Hadn't she watched when a frog was galvanized in the physics lesson? You just have to put a woman in uniform and she'll do whatever you want. I sent her to fetch the smelling salts and had a Red-Cross armband ready for her, so that she could be the voluntary medical corps. As you can see, I'd thought of everything. Everything was ready to set the world alight according to the instructions in my textbook. Let those of riper years, who have more freedom to determine their own actions, condemn me. At that age I had no real idea I was committing a rank misdeed that smelled to heaven. I had intended to light the fuse with my magnifying glass. But the sisters' embarrassed silence when the sun disappeared behind a cloud persuaded me to abandon further attempts and to set the catastrophe on its way with the help of ordinary matches. It was, unexpectedly, my nurse who was now urging me to get on with my explosion, since the whole affair had already given her *une mauvaise tête.* Her younger sister was up in the tree, intending to time it with the pretty new watch her parents had given her for her birthday. After a brief discussion with my medical adviser, I came to the conclusion that it would take forever for the flame to creep along the fuse to the tree beneath which I had buried my petard in the anthill.

'An accident could happen, just as in a proper war.' I answered, 'God is with us, that's what they're always saying in the newspapers.' The girl: 'Who knows whom the ants believe.' Me: 'A bomb that kills others is only a game if you keep at a safe distance.' The girl: 'I'll look at my watch and count the minutes to the explosion. Will you be brave?' Me: 'I know what I'm doing, I've learned about experiments at school.' I told her I was going to light the whole box of matches, throw them onto the nest, and retire to a safe place as quickly as possible. I was often capable of doing unexpected things when my personal courage was called into question. With a crash like thunder a huge cloud of smoke billowed up, sending the burning city of the ants shooting into the air. What a gruesomely splendid sight! The survivors, wings and limbs scorched, dragged themselves across the ground. Just like a soldier with his leg shot off trying to escape from the hail of fire on the bloody stump — in vain, the last way out is already on fire! The way the poor demented creatures pulled their larvae from one burning part of the nest to another, which was also ablaze! Quite human really! Just like mothers, in a war in which both sides believe they are fighting for what is right, trying to save their children from the destruction a higher power has already decreed. This particular higher power was hopping irresolutely from one foot to the other, remembering that the explosion had occurred at five o'clock precisely, the time when the warmed basket with the tea-things was brought by the maid. An unfavorable omen, rendering any attempt to approach the source of the confla gration impossible. It was easy for my medical orderly to weep at the fate of the ants, my morale was in tatters for quite different reasons. The lady was hard of hearing and so had not heard the explosion, but the clouds of smoke drifting across the park brought on a terrible fit of coughing. Knowing well there was no smoke without fire, she immediately started questioning the park-keeper as to the cause of the noxious fumes. The smelling salts were nowhere to be found and the result was palpitations and attacks of dizziness.

Forced to the conclusion that I was the vilest reptile to sully the earth, I felt sick. There was only one occasion when I thought there were other evildoers apart from myself. That was during the Second World War when I heard of the destruction of the city of Hiroshima. The name of the hero who, by dropping a newfangled bomb, had incinerated hundreds and thousands of mothers and children in one fell swoop, was on everybody's lips and printed in large letters in special editions of newspapers throughout the world.

'We're lost,' I whispered to my friend, 'your mother doesn't know the worst of it yet.' Her mother had fixed us with a steely gaze and was asking what had happened to her younger daughter. As the smoke had now cleared we could see the girl lying motionless in the hammock. I had murdered her! The lady gritted her teeth and, with the aid of the park-keeper, did the only sensible thing and lifted the lifeless body down from the tree. An ambulance was called, very soon a doctor was administering first aid, the girl came to, and was immediately sick. 'I'm not a murderer after all!' I cried with such heart-rending sobs that I could have done with a whole bed-sheet to dry my tears, as the object of my tender passion emptied her stomach of the poison she had inhaled. Should the reader find this not entirely convincing, I should add that, out of despair at my expulsion from the Garden of Eden, I failed my final examination in chemistry and physics.

From now on, whenever I tried to enter the park I was confronted by the park-keeper brandishing his curved sword, as unyielding as the Angel Gabriel.

The moated castle formed of crystal jets, in which I had dreamed away my childhood, had evaporated. All that was left of the sacred fence of innocence was the park gate, now closed to me forever. In the circus, where I was taken to cheer me up, I saw a clown — the fool who is there to take the beatings he has done nothing to deserve — one of whose gags was to bring his own garden gate. He took great pains setting it up in the middle of the arena, unlocked it, went through, and carefully locked it behind him with a huge key. Could he not just as well go around the barrier? And why on earth did he produce it in the first place? The whole audience laughed at the clown, and he gave me the idea of not letting myself be fooled by a silly park-keeper when it was easy to get into the park from the rear. People laugh at a clown in the circus who makes heavy weather of going to fetch his conical hat lying in the sand on the other side of the gate, which he could very easily go round, instead of spending all that effort unlocking it. Of course, he knew that just as well as the audience laughing at him. Something that grown-ups find funny is not amusing to a boy who has a girl waiting for him on the other side of a park wall, even if it did have broken glass along the top and I had been told by my mother to sit still until the end of the performance, which would not be long.

The moment my mother got up I pretended I needed a breath of fresh air, and as soon as her back was turned I dashed off to the park and around it to the spot where there was no park-keeper to deny me entrance.

The people living by the park used the place to dump garbage. 'My kingdom for a horse!' Richard III is supposed to have said, according to Shakespeare, in a similarly desperate situation. The English words I had learned at school came back to mind as I climbed over the fence. Let kings rack their brains. But when I reached the top and found nowhere to set my foot, all my strength vanished. I could not hold on with my hands any longer because the wooden slats were bristling with rusty nails. I must admit that the yearning for my beloved, which had given me wings, seemed unfortunately to have vanished, since the loftiness of spirit, which should have accompanied my elevated position, was conspicuous by its absence. I was being dragged irresistibly down into the void. Would my endeavors have found such high-minded fulfillment on a dunghill in an era in which, instead of a ninth symphony in which all mankind embrace each other, the sun is split by scientists, as I had learned in physics?

I had taken a terrible tumble onto the district garbage pit. It was a real cesspool, teeming with all kinds of voracious creepy-crawlies. The yellow sludge spurted up in a stinking spray. A cloud of stinging flies rose from the bloated, rotting cadaver of a long-dead pig. The doctor had to be sent for. I spent a long time in bed because I had pustules on my eyes. All the time I had a temperature, the sun, which is constantly hatching out new life and hastening its decay, was blazing down on the wallpaper, so that I could not manage to open my eyes. There was a fly sitting on the back of my tongue endlessly rotating, laying its grubs in a circle around it. It cut into my dry throat like a red-hot iron disc. My tongue had become short and fat, and I couldn't move it. The fever forced all the moisture inside me out through the pores of my skin and was hammering so violently at my ribs that it was suddenly all over with me. The wallpaper was now covered with red and green suns whirling round and round. My brain had dribbled out of my eyes, nose, and ears in a vile, gray liquid, and was evaporating in the room. I was lying under hot, heavy sheets, and there was not a sound to be heard. Then my dry skin began to burst, to peel off in whole strips. Like strange, white worms leaping into the air and rolling up, the sinews detached themselves from the black lumps that were all that was left of my flesh. Now my body was like a frame carelessly tied up in rags, or an empty basket made of ribs. My bones gradually crumbled to dust on the linen and then, finally, the many little whirling suns, the hot ones that had stung and burned me, turned into one single, smiling sun shining high above me, not hurting me any longer and unshakably still. What was left of me was more like a photograph than anything else. The patterns made in powdered rosin on a plate of glass when you run a violin bow firmly along its edge are not dissimilar. Only the process was much simpler, much simpler than in our physics class, more like the way music from heaven resounds in a child's ear, before you grow up. It hardly bears thinking about!

While she nursed me day and night, my mother kept looking at the little picture with the pierced heart of the Virgin that my religious instructor placed on my breast when the doctor was at his wit's end. And my eyes recovered because my religious instructor prayed for a miracle. My mother gave me almond milk to refresh me and, as far as food and drink are concerned, nothing has ever tasted as good as in childhood. Nothing was more delicious than the first cherries in May, tied together in pairs with green leaves on a splinter of wood.

GYPSY WOMEN

I

Some distance from the village in which I spent the school holidays, at the place where the stream ran along the boundary of the communal fields and the track led off to the station, stood a lonely cottage. The village lads who had been drafted used to point at it on their way to the station to report for duty. Toward evening you could hear the long-drawn-out notes of a trumpet from the distant cavalry barracks where the moon slowly crept across the fields to the willows beside the stream. In the moonlight, as if caught at some secret deed, you could see the pale cottage where two female vagrants lived. Sometimes one or the other would be leaning out of the window; she might be biting open sunflower seeds and would laugh as she spat out the empty husks at the recruits as they passed. Her teeth were so white they made you think of sugar. They always seemed to be half dressed in their brightly colored things. They had a bad reputation. I was spending the holidays with my aunt, and my cousin was older than I, already a real student. He had crossed rapiers on the wall of his room and tried to smoke from a long Turkish pipe. He often took me out with him in the evenings. We would creep round the cottage and, even if there was no sign of life, open the door to have a look inside. There was one single room with whitewashed walls and a large bed in the middle. Beneath the picture of the black Madonna an eternal flame was burning, and in a niche in the wall little gold and silver posies, such as recruits wear in their hats, lay like votive offerings. I used to jeer at the gypsy women from a safe distance, shouting that they stole little children, as I had heard other people say. There was no crime they were not accused of, the way the simple souls in a village make things up out of an imagination still fueled by primitive instincts, before a false sense of shame spoils the triumph of naked spite over helplessness for us. My passions had grown inflamed, so that I had come to believe the village gossip, made up to pass the time, to be the literal truth.

My cousin must have continued on his way, but I just stood there, spellbound, because the younger of the two gypsies had suddenly appeared as if from nowhere in the middle of the sun-flowers, squatted down, her back to me, pulled up her red skirt and relieved herself. I would have preferred to see anything other than this confirmation that Eve was made of the same clay as Adam. Immorality, vice, and shame gave brothels a romantic aura and were fundamental to the legend spread about whores. Anyone who had heard this legend was himself infected with it, as if with some insidious disease. To forestall any expectation of confessions of debauchery, I must say from the outset that it was simply this naked fact that the gypsy girl was a human being like others that caught me completely unprepared. One can discuss immoral things in a familiar tone — one does not, for example, have underwear in mind when one says someone is washing their dirty linen in public. It is not improper to write at great length about the lingerie of a lady of easy virtue, but the naked truth we find disconcerting. All the themes of all the masterpieces of literature such as I was reading at the time, from Oedipus to Maupassant, could not have offered such daring revelations about human nature, even if, to improve my understanding of them, the Freudian interpretations had been available to me at the time. I hurried away, deeply disturbed by the event I had witnessed. Stopping to draw breath, I looked back over my shoulder, and the gypsy woman's calm gaze caught me in an embarrassing situa-tion, as if I had been watching her deliberately. Her thick eye-lashes fluttered, she crossed herself and went into the cottage.

I can't find the right word in my own language. You can't translate *une situation louche* into German, so I had a blindfold over my eyes as I tried to return to a way of looking at things that you don't have to run away from. I felt homesick for the

village with its houses full of worthy people, where you know
for sure to whom each one belongs: this is the burgomaster's,
that the butcher's, the shopkeeper's, the schoolmaster's, the
postman's, the farmer's, and the roadmender's. The village is a
world of its own where you know what is right. A world that
holds together owing to the very cramped compass from which
other possibilities are excluded because their existence is simply
not recognized. A world of clear views, solid facts and clearly
defined tasks. Even the animals know what is expected of them,
or at least have to act as if they did, which comes down to the
same thing. The cow provides milk and butter, the hen eggs, the
dog guards the property from thieving riffraff just as the
burgomaster has to legalize marriages, and the new-born child
only starts to exist officially when it has been registered. There is
no state where officialdom does not levy taxes and troops. That
was at a time when there were still a few years to go to the
outbreak of the First World War. The pig provides us with juicy
ham. Popular wisdom associated the animal with St. Anthony, to
help us understand the nature of the temptations of that much-
tormented man. Do we not laugh ourselves silly when the man
beside us in our neighborhood bar gets drunk and behaves like a
pig? The element of surprise is the essence of comedy, the chair
being whipped away from under our own backsides, so to speak.
We are satisfied with our own truth from morn to eve, all life
long. It explains why the bed creaks, why the bar of the well-
hoist squeaks, why the key fits in the keyhole, why this person
has reason to laugh, that to die, or why one was born for wine,
women, and song while another, a poor man, is a burden on the
local community. For everything there is just one quite specific
point of view, one reason things are the way they are and not
different, the sign, the password to mutual comprehension, which
also distinguishes us from foreigners. Every village, every nation,
every age has a monopoly on truth, its own truth. Even a child
realizes what is going on when a foreigner can't understand our
way of looking at things because he can't speak our language.
This was true from the Ark to the First World War.

While I maintain that a whore is a human being like one of

us, some of the unmarried village lads were known to say
something else about the whore, namely, that she got under your
skin. On the other hand, people used to say of those lads that
what they sought in 'that kind of girl' was being withheld from
one of our girls, to whom it belonged by right. Where would we
be if we did not stay within our allotted bounds? If you live on
the moon, then you need observe no bounds! Everything must
have its point and purpose to take us from the cradle to the grave.
A truth which is naked is simply indecent; we do not wear
clothes only when the weather is bad. Where does our cramped
little world end? Wherever someone appears who has the
openness of mind to demand more of us than is his due;
someone, to give an example, who comes to complain of his
misfortune to us, instead of to the Good Lord. Indeed, if he does
it too often, he awakens our suspicions. Our mockery is stirred,
scandal seeks out its victim, abandoned by the gods. Does our
religion not tell us that the God whom we adore does not strike
down his creatures without reason? We dissociate ourselves from
the neighbor the gods seek to destroy, even though, on the other
hand, we have never seen anyone come back from the grave who
was with God in this life. Be reasonable, o children of men, a god
cannot remember you all!

The big fir at the entrance to the wood was where this bewildering world, this other country, everything, that is, from
which the stream separated the village where I spent my holidays,
really began. Everything has to have a beginning and an end, and
that goes for foreign parts, too. The first fir tree I had seen actually growing in the ground. If you cut down a fir tree and transport it into the city, then it becomes the Christmas tree which is
decorated with stars over the festive season and then chopped up
for firewood or thrown on the garbage pit. A sad end, balancing
out an excess of glittering candles on a wooden cross. The
Christmas tree is no longer a proper tree. No more than giving
ourselves presents is a true festival in a world where everything
has its price. All the talk of 'men of good will' is no more than
just that — talk. What is still moving, though, is the scent of resin
drawn out of the felled tree by the heat of the candles.

I feel obliged to apologize for the fact that I was suddenly seized with such an intense tenderness for my fir tree that I embraced the tree growing on the boundary of the village and tried to squeeze myself to death against it. My world was too cramped, seemed not to have enough fresh air. That resin did smell good! I just had to fill my lungs with air, I could not get enough of the pure air. My hands could actually feel the sap rising in the tree, just like the blood quivering in my heart. I knelt down before the tree and, weeping tears of joy, kept kissing it again and again. I was in love, I could do nothing about it. How had it come about that I was overcome with this bewildering feeling for another being, for something alien? I must leave it to the imagination of the reader to explain why fate had paired me off with a tree. I could not breathe a word of it to my cousin, I would rather have cut out my tongue. He would have been embarrassed. As a thoughtful person, he could appreciate tragedy, of which even science takes account when it is a matter of the attraction between the sexes. And it is indeed tragic that, while every living being is assigned a specific number of characteristics of the species by fate as if in a lottery, finding another being to complement this allocation from heredity is, as is well known, left entirely to chance. Two beings that belong together in some romantic way. It's what is at the basis of all novel-writing. No, I couldn't talk to my cousin for, like all the others of his age who were due to be drafted for military service, he was a man who had already, as he put it, graduated from the brothel. I, too, would probably have followed the same route as my cousin. The herd instinct is deeply embedded within us, and it is wrong always to blame the social order for its reactionary policies. Why does every army command have to set up field brothels? Not, one would imagine, simply because the supreme command enjoys channeling normal instincts. As in moral matters in general, so there must be order in matters concerning health. What would human life be like without the medical service? How could one distinguish friend from foe in war if any pimp could takes his wares back and forth across the frontier, as if universal peace had broken out? That is one more reason for setting up military brothels. After all, it's not the supreme war lords themselves who recruit the prostitutes as the army invades a foreign country. I'm sure there must be laws to ensure that in wartime the experts in the white slave trade fulfill their duty to the nation to the best of their ability.

Some chance or other led to my amorous inclinations finding their object in a tree, which stood in the way of my normal development at the time. I'm afraid readers will find my record of this brief lover's whim somewhat improper, the portrayal of a sexual perversion even. I myself had no idea how to explain it to my cousin. I probably said, 'Love is like the night, when the animals come to the spring, and even then we are only talking with one of the many voices of nature in order to sip from the fount of knowledge.' That our thirst for love is not quenched by knowledge of a woman was something we would have to talk about some other time. I ought to read books on sex education for the young instead of using such high-falutin' expressions, which had nothing to do with the case. It was simply outrageous that my cousin thought I had been carrying on with the whore behind his back. One has a duty to oneself and to one's race! 'Out with it!' He'll learn nothing from me, I thought stubbornly. He'll not let me out of his sight, to prevent a repetition of any such adventure. Just let him try to shadow me! But I had gone bright red. This cousin of mine made me furious at the mere idea of his profane eye prying inside me, so to speak, where I love the tree with no false sense of shame, when the wind blows through the grass, scattering its pollen in all directions. Had my cousin not been so thoroughly normal, I might have told him my secret. And if I was preoccupied with my idea, he became obsessed with his. He took my pulse and muttered, with a serious expression on his face, 'No doubt about it, you're in seventh heaven, even if you die without confession. Every man gets his first dose some time, but from a gypsy woman! Yeuch!' I felt like hitting him in the face with both fists. 'That kills off any desire for further conversation with you.' He didn't flinch, but just said casually, 'When someone's head over heels in love . . .' He was closer to the naked truth with that. 'You people who have your feet planted firmly on the ground of fact, your whole world collapses when you come across something you can't prove.'

But the next day we were inseparable again. Hadn't we made a pact, signed in blood from our fingers? We still got on excellently together, even though he was in his first year at medical school. We had bound ourselves to help each other, if one of us should ever be in need, all life long and in whatever part of the world the one in need happened to be. The next morning, a Sunday, I had to borrow his lily-scented soap. And my white gloves were still not white enough. My cousin was suspicious, he noticed everything. Especially the fact that my cheeks were glowing with happy expectation. 'You just dare go to that gypsy woman again! In love and still a schoolboy! Those girls are not subjected to medical checks. You'll find a nurse with a great big syringe waking you from your dream.' There was nothing I could say. In love? And with whom, might I ask? But when the mythical fire starts burning in your heart, you just have to talk to someone. However, I also wanted to tease him a little. 'You'll have to guess my secret. It's a bit like a locked door behind which there's something that wasn't there before. In my riddle there's room for a whole world that will remain alien to you. The shepherd takes his lambs there from the meadows, it's a house for the most beautiful birds, it's wreathed in sweetness and light once it no longer has its leg firmly on the ground.' It meant nothing to him. 'Standing on one leg, I said.' — 'On only one leg, you say?' he repeated. Until just a moment ago I had felt inseparably bound to my cousin, no secret could divide us, for all that business with the tree was over. But now something even I could not explain had come between us. My thoughts had gone to Miss Marie Louise, the only child of the old village school-master. She never went to the shop, never went for a walk along the village street in the evening like the rest. If there is anything that will make me never forget that morning in the church, then it was her, the Miss Marie Louise whom I had seen in my despair as, kneeling in her white first-communion frock, she looked up to the choir when my voice broke. It made me hard. I couldn't care less about my stupid cousin, even though he said, 'You know, your voice is breaking. I've been expecting it for some time.' And indeed, my voice did break, right in the middle of the solo I was supposed to sing during the consecration. When my voice cracked I had the carved white dove above the high altar in mind, in which form the Holy Spirit circled over the congregation, as if it were in the air, swaying in the wind. I wanted to run away when, at that very moment, Miss Marie Louise looked up at me. It was her look I couldn't resist, never mind anything else. Wasn't everything about her affected? The heavy weather she made of sitting down, the way she grimaced when she had to get up? The ridiculous way she preened herself, as if the bishop had come to the parish solely for the purpose of conducting her first communion when this was the very church where he had said his first mass as a newly consecrated priest. Of course, she was only trying to hide her missing leg. Miss Marie Louise is a cripple, I thought. My cousin shook his head. 'You can't keep still even in church. We'll never make a real man of you, even if you don't fail your final exams at school. Anyway, I've more important things to do than keep my eye on such a worthless customer as you, devil take you!' His draftee's suitcase in his hand, he made his way to the station alone.

II

So I was worthless, was I? Worthless? Did I show such contempt for others because I was worthless? Even while the bishop was celebrating mass, although I was involved in the service with eye and ear and voice, there was something missing, though I couldn't quite say what. The choirboys were different. Their voices came from the heart. When my voice broke it became clear that I was not one of them. I sang with them, but not from the heart. That made me so angry that I kept repeating with relish, 'Marie Louise is a cripple.' Of course, I also had religious instruction at school, but that had simply left me in a state of indifference. When our religious instructor explained that suffering came from original sin, from the fact that our bodies were sinful, forcing us to do evil, to listen to and look at things an inner voice warned us against, I thought of what I had looked at when the younger of the two sisters had sat in the tree in Galizin Park. Even the incident with the gypsy woman just made me laugh. All that was left was the fact that I was worthless. Thinking about the temptations of the Evil One was simply not worth the effort. The best thing would be just to put the fact that you were worthless out of your mind. If you have no opportunity to be good, then being worthless is something you have to come to terms with. Quite simple! I already despised myself, and even derived a malicious glee from it into the bargain. Reason enough when a nobody such as me shows himself to be what he really is, a complete nonentity, in which case even a magnifying glass is no help. The cripple is making me spiteful. If only I weren't so unhappy about it! No amount of reasoning will get you anywhere against love. Self-love, of course. It's nothing but wounded self-love! 'Why all this tragic posturing?' I mocked myself. Just imagine someone being forced to put up with the society of a person like me from morn till eve, a person with whom they had nothing at all in common. A girl, maybe? Marie Louise? Did not the reason I despised myself lie in the fact that I could not avoid myself, as I could any other person, that there was no corner of the earth where I would not find myself confronted with the naked truth of my own worthlessness. This solitude that makes your life almost impossible is a terrible, unthinkable thought.

The first premonition that you are alone gives you a shock, and after that you can't stop thinking about it. How can you exist once you've lost your inner peace? Once you've lost your peace. And we receive no help from within, from our dull, obdurate hearts which would dearly love, with every breath we draw, to deny the existence of this torment. The Devil's vestibule must be filled with such a damned silence. But everyone invents a little white lie to deny the existence of facts that don't suit them. And we're poisoning the well we drink from. However much we may tell ourselves we're as alive and kicking as the next man, we're dead, cold at heart. I was filled with dread at this inescapable entanglement, which turns loving to hating. Is not love-hate, an expression I came across recently, the right word for it? False truth, or true falsehood would be just as good a way of describing this wretched state, the Pharisee who prays, 'God, I thank thee, that I am not as other men are.' Are the people in this great, wide world of ours any different? Why would a writer have bothered to unmask them? They just happen to be better at concealing it, otherwise I would have seen it for myself. Or they are simply too stupid, and resent facts for not being as they would have them. All men are equal and the world is evil! Thus remonstrating with myself and life, I managed to work myself up into a fury of despair. I had been deceived in this 'as-if' world, where people try to get round the truth somehow or other, in order not to have to admit they are rogues. Were they not all, all honorable men, these grown-ups!? I could hardly breathe in this shameful world which is like a clouded mirror which does not show people their true face. I could throw a stone at the glass, even if only to demonstrate that, for me, facts are still facts. I will prove that I am as old as my age says. If goodness doesn't work, then I'll show them I can be evil. I will play with this Miss Marie Louise as only a stage villain can. I will torment her and make her cry, and I'll laugh. God! life would be so boring if there were no baddies! What could be a better reason for laughing and crying than to cry because one is a cripple and to laugh at other people? Long live villainy! Kept within permitted bounds, of course; that is, being careful to make sure you are not on the receiving end yourself.

Once again the children in the neighboring garden were drumming with their little legs like rabbits, bleating like baby lambs, their clapping sounded like a salvo from an army of dwarves. When the noise had roused me from my thoughts, I took the fact that Marie Louise was playing with the children and not with me as disparagement. She'll soon have nothing to laugh about. I'll have a closer look at this Marie Louise who thinks I'm such a worthless individual. Quietly I worked my way up the wall separating our garden from the schoolmaster's. 'There she is, surrounded by the children, a regular guardian angel,' I silently mocked. Then the metal garden gate, which, as I knew, was always kept locked, silently opened and the old schoolmaster, whom I only knew from hearsay, was standing in our garden. 'This is the way to go, if you want to see our house,' he said reproachfully. I fell off the wall like a sack and landed right in front of him. Furious, I stuck my bleeding fingers in my mouth — the top of the wall had broken glass on it. I had no idea what look the old man had on his face, since I turned away with a grimace. The schoolmaster gently closed the door behind him, but not before adding softly, 'You can visit Marie Louise after you've washed the blood off your fingers. It's just the spying I can't stand.' I thought of putting on my white gloves. But why all this fuss now I had regained my peace of mind? It's good to know the door is not locked. Then, while we were having tea, I felt very hot and was so thirsty I asked for a glass of water. It's a disgrace the way a girl like that throws herself at you! She immediately stood up to get it herself. 'It will be a pleasure,' she said with a smile. And then there were the children's games. In a serious tone, to conceal my mockery, I asked whether she was not too grown-up to be romping around with children. Like a saint, she simply ignored my mockery. 'There is only one way to win the heart of another, and that is . . .' — '. . . and that is?' I was foolish enough to ask. '. . . to be like those one wants to be loved by.'

I refused to be won over. How bright and sunny she was, how unaffected. I listened to the vividness with which she described subterranean caverns; it was the story of Ali Baba, and the jewels sparkled until the children's eyes were popping out of their heads. You can't catch me like that! At the magic words, 'Open sesame,' a rock in the cliff face opens, revealing the entrance. The children clasped their hands together and formed up in two lines, the boys standing on one side opposite the girls; when Marie Louise went past, their hands flew up into the air and, one after the other, the children followed her. As they did so, the two rows, representing the entrance, sang, 'And then the forty thieves, marched into the cave. The last one stays outside, he is an arrant knave.' The last one has to forget the magic word so that the game keeps on going back to the beginning again.

They seemed to have forgotten me. I bit my fingernails, for it was easy for me to imagine more entertaining company than mine. But from the line of girls she called out to me, 'Why are you standing there all by yourself? The game's easy enough, you just need to forget the magic word.' I suppressed a loud oath.

Then I had a brilliant idea. The devil himself couldn't have thought of a better way of sowing the seeds of evil in these children's hearts. I had my cousin's penknife in my pocket. I called the children to gather round and told them I had seen the children in the city playing a splendid game. Using all my powers of persuasion, I explained 'Mary sat upon a stone' to them. It had the advantage that Marie Louise didn't need her crutches. The little brats were very interested now. I said I would like to join in, too, and organized the game. Marie Louise, who was a little tired, sat on a stone, just as the children dancing round her were singing, and then I jumped out from the circle at her with the opened pocket knife. 'Up came her evil brother Karl, brother Karl, and stabbed poor Mary to the heart, to the heart.' Marie Louise had to hold a white handkerchief in front of her eyes, and not for nothing, as I saw to my delight. Although they were only supposed to be pretend tears, the seeds I had sown had borne more fruit than I could have expected. Real tears! While the children were singing, 'Mary why do you cry, do you cry?' lo and behold, the young lady really was crying, her shoulders shaking with the sobs, serve the little goody-goody right. Just what I had been waiting for since church that morning. All the following verses, about a lilac tree growing on her grave and so on and so forth, I just found irritating. It wasn't right of me, she sobbed, to corrupt the innocent children. I for my part gleefully wished her a speedy resurrection in paradise, as it said in the song, since she did not have long to live anyway. Once in Heaven — I couldn't resist this final mocking twist — she would be freed from her affliction, since she would have two wings and could thus dispense with her crutches. Nor was I afraid, I added, of the end when 'Her evil brother Karl went to Hell, went to Hell.'

By now everyone was in a bad mood, the children were

hungry and went off home. Although I was pacing up and down like a sick wolf in its cage, I regretted nothing. Thanks to my brilliant idea, I had clearly wounded her more deeply than I could have with a real dagger. My conscience would torment me, she said, however much I might mock the idea of a Hell full of little devils with claws at the end of their arms, like huge lobsters, and funny animal faces that made me laugh. And the poisonous sting, like a scorpion's, would stay inside me, I couldn't escape it, she said. It was my bad conscience that made me pace up and down like that, instead of sitting still. Day after day my whole life would be a purgatory in which I would find no peace until I had passed the test. And the fact that I enjoyed such good health would only serve to lengthen the test. The idea of tests reminded me that my holidays would soon be over. How unpleasant! There was something in what she said. And she was eloquent, argued clearly and skillfully, sitting there in the white dress of some church girls' organization, playing the devil's advocate. I sometimes wished I could have a lock on my lips, like Papageno, to stop me saying the wrong thing. Anyone who intends to write a play should learn from female casuistry, it would be difficult to do it better. Now her delicate health seemed more like a loss for me; all the time she was speaking I would not have been disinclined to start a new life, but only if she would throw in her lot with mine. 'No', she said with a gentle smile, 'I won't live long. You said so yourself.' But, she added, she intended to devote the short span allotted to her to make my heart receptive to goodness. For herself, she could feel the onset of grace, as if her guardian angel were bearing her up higher and higher to the peak of a snow-covered mountain, to the light. By this time I was not even laughing at her affliction anymore. 'There are fine days and rainy days, as you know', she said, 'and I would be sorry if until now you had only noticed the bad days.' To show that she bore me no grudge for the errors of my ways, she concluded her exhortations, to which I lent a not unwilling ear, with a kiss — for evil came when our understanding was not warmed by love. By now I was somewhat apprehensive as far as life was concerned, which seemed to be a regular purification zone one had to pass through. And it took on great significance, not just with respect to my future salvation, but rather with regard to my general well-being, on my own and faced with the task of making the most of life. It wasn't true contrition which made me grasp the hand held out to me, it was the prospect, which in those days was more important to me, of getting what one might call the correct rules of behavior from an authority, of learning how to take care of myself, so as to avoid suffering. Above all to avoid suffering.

Marie Louise had to promise to appear to me immediately after her death, or at least to write to me as soon as I was back at school. For the brief time, however, that she intended to spend together with me here on earth, or at least during my school holidays, I had devised a test of courage to toughen me up for the conflict with evil. Life is a battle. I had realized it was not a bed of roses. Since in this small village there was a decided paucity of dangerous situations, I set my eye on the communal pigsty outside the village. It was a calm evening, the smoke rising from the chimneys where soup was being made. There was a good smell of wood and trees mingling with the dampness coming down from the mountains which, cooled by the night, turned into mist hanging over the valley like a white shroud. The church bell was sounding a quivering Angelus as I clambered over the circular fence made of willow hurdles with a roof in the form of a gigantic straw hat to give protection from bad weather. That evening the stars were falling down in clusters, as if they were being shaken out of a sack. The gray pigs, which had been biting at each other, whistling and squealing like huge rats, froze as I suddenly appeared in their midst, brandishing my cousin's rapier, ready to do battle. The only sound was the cry of the owl. The pigs took fright at one who brought them no peace, and began, first one, then all the rest, to dash wildly round and round the ring. I knelt down, drawing my cousin's rapier from its sheath in my white-gloved right hand. To fortify myself, I took one final sniff of the toilet soap in my breast pocket, for I felt less afraid when I thought of the lilies in the hands of the bride of Heaven, with her blue sash round her, two gold braids falling down her back, and shimmering wings at either side. Her wooden leg was concealed by a long white dress. 'Back down to hell with you, you unclean seed of Satan!' I shouted at the pigs. I fought with the black pachyderms, sending them scurrying round in ever more frenzied circles, farther and farther from the center where I stood my ground, a picture of heroic defiance. In the end they almost knocked the fence over. The urine flowed and noxious devil's dung spurted up to high heaven, spreading the reek of hell all around. There was a stench like burned hair, sulphur and pitch, and I felt hot, as if I were standing in the middle of flames. I wiped the sweat out of my eyes and, lo and behold, my enemies had fallen asleep with exhaustion.

The architect, Adolf Loos, was a good friend to me during the days when I was starting out in Vienna. He was the first person who believed in me and tried, in his brusque manner, to create opportunities for me to paint. Whenever he had found someone, he would say, 'You're going to paint this or that person, off you go.' And off I went, and Loos got the painting, because he had started paying for my upkeep. It was a very long time before my first paintings found a place in public collections. Later on, all Loos' pictures went to museums and galleries in Germany.

One fine day he appeared at our apartment and said, 'Pack a few things and tell your people you're off to Vevey. My wife Bessy's there, you're going to paint her.' My mother was concerned. 'The boy's never been abroad,' she objected, 'he's well fed here.' Loos was imperious. He knew the world, he told us and, anyway, Bessy would be there. Bessy had tuberculosis and was in a sanatorium in Les Avants where there were some English friends of hers as well. 'He'll make his name there,' Loos said. My feeble protests were brushed aside. My mother gave me a gold coin she had been keeping since her sister had given it to her for me at my christening, and I set off with a little suitcase and my box of paints. Loos came with me. For the first time in my life I saw an electric railway, the high mountains, people speaking French, elegance. His wife met us at Vevey station, and I was found a room in the hotel where she was staying. Loos arranged demi-pension for me, which meant only one main meal a day, but I was young.

Loos paid the bill every week. The next day he left me on my own in this foreign world.

The first picture I painted in Switzerland was the Dents du Midi, also my first landscape. At the railway station in Vienna there had been huge posters with photographs: the Alps, snow. I had studied them carefully. But when I saw the Dents du Midi in reality, there was an immeasurable depth to them which wasn't there at all in the photograph. I particularly noticed this as Loos was setting off. I was apprehensive at being left there on my own. I looked down from the window of my attic room. There was the sleigh. I could see the horses, with the steam rising from their nostrils. Loos turned round, looked up. His remarkable, eloquent eyes were looking for me, but could not find me, although he had been in my room a short while before. Then I hear the crack of the whip, the sleigh slowly starts to move, grows smaller and smaller. The track meanders through the landscape, the bells jingle. Then all I can see is a dot disappearing in a glitter of snow. But in my mind's eye I can see Loos clearer than ever. Where is there room for the mental image in the optical appearance which had swallowed it up? Between me and the view of the Dents du Midi something had happened; something had disappeared that I must carry round within me for ever. To restore the equilibrium between the inner and outer world, to bring the spirit of contemplation into harmony with physical reality: that was why I painted the picture. The spatial dimension has a spiritual as well as an optical significance.

That is a different perspective from any rational artistic program. It was a task that involved my humanity. When I had painted the picture, my fear disappeared.

In Les Avants I painted a portrait of Bessy Loos and was introduced by her to the marquise and marquis of Rohan-Montesquieu. She was a marvelously thin, tall, pale creature and wore a black velvet two-piece which made her look even thinner. She was consumptive and seemed to me so beautiful that I immediately fell head over heels in love with her. Her husband looked very degenerate, a tall, effeminate man with a hook nose and a reddish mustache who wore a lacy frill collar. With his yellow complexion he looked like a figure from a waxworks. There was a rumor that he was at times rather rough with her; she herself once hinted at something of the kind when she did me the honor of showing me her room. With its quiet, sad atmosphere and yellowing photographs on the wall it suited her well. I painted both of them, though today I have no idea where the two portraits have got to. That was also the time when I painted the Comte de Verona, a little Italian who was keen on ice-skating and sometimes coughed up blood.

All the people in the hotel were ill. Originally Bessy Loos had been one of the Barrison Sisters, the English dance troupe that appeared at Vienna's first night club, the Casino de Paris. Most of them married bankers or counts. Poor Bessy married Loos. He wanted to save her life and sent her to Switzerland. She was supposed to stay lying in bed in her room, but at night she would slip out of the hotel through a window and go down to the town to dance.

Bessy introduced me to a wealthy aristocratic family in whose house I was to stay while I was painting the wife. The day before I was due to leave, there was a heavy snowfall. It was freezing cold. I was oppressed with a feeling of hopelessness, which lifted slightly when I thought of the gold coin which I kept in a knot in my handkerchief in my pocket. When I took out my handkerchief, the coin fell out and vanished in the snow. I started looking for it feverishly, the train was due any moment. The more people who helped me in my search, the more the snow was trampled and the less prospect I had of ever finding my gold coin again. I was penniless. A stranger took pity on me and paid for my ticket to Vevey. That was how I came to Lake Geneva.

The lady I was to paint was a follower of the Rudolf Steiner sect. I felt uneasy from the moment I arrived. Also, I kept thinking about money and how I was at the mercy of fickle fortune. The lady went round in a riding costume, complete with riding crop and a hat with feathers. She was divorced from her husband and lived alone with her small son. There were lots of bedrooms in the house, all of them decorated in harmonizing color schemes. Mine was painted gold and silver. Presumably it was meant to relate to the sun and moon, but the result was a chocolate box effect. The house was surrounded by a whole detachment of police. They were there to protect the mother and her child from the father, who was threatening to abduct the boy. It was all concerned with an inheritance or the right to bring up the child, I can't remember which. One night there was noise and disturbance in the house and garden, I could hear voices and see lights moving around outside. I emerged from my room, where I preferred to lock myself in, to be told by the agitated lady that her husband had tried to have the child abducted, but that the police had managed to prevent it. To cut a long story short, she poured out her heart to me, all her fears and woes, and turned out to be a worthy successor to Potiphar's wife. She frightened me. What should I do? I had already started painting her portrait. Whenever she came too close my only defense was the Prussian blue which I had deliberately smeared over my fingers. This went on for several days until I could stand it no longer. I fled from the house, abandoning my picture, easel and paint box. I managed to get a telegram begging for help to Loos, who, by the way, had to pay for it. Loos sent me money and Bessy came to rescue me. I returned to the hotel.

One marvelous day in early spring — the sun was blazing down on the snow, which lay there calmly, with its beautiful reflections — I saw a girl on a wall. She was about fourteen years old. She lay there without moving, enjoying the warmth. She gave me a long and strange look through her eyelashes. There was a fig tree close by, it was just like in a fairy tale. I went up to this delicate apparition and asked her what she was called. She said Virginia. Years afterward she was to be the dream daughter in my starvation fantasies in Berlin. I will come back to those later.

One morning I heard shouting outside the hotel, doors being slammed, commotion. I looked out of the window. There was the woman from Vevey in her feathered hat and riding habit, carrying her riding crop. She wanted to give me a flogging and carry me off. She demanded that I should complete the portrait

I had begun. It gave me a terrible shock, and I kept well out of the way. Bessy and the others eventually managed to persuade the equestrian fury to withdraw.

Loos had also arranged for me to paint Professor Forell in Vevey, where he lived. At that time Forell was already a frail old gentleman. When he was sitting for me he kept on slowly slumping forward and bowing his head, until he awoke to the world once more and sat up straight and awake for a while. It was this semiconscious transitional state that I tried to capture on canvas. He would take his supper with his family while still sitting, and when they saw that I was painting and not listening, they started discussing quite intimate family matters with each other, for example, whether this or that female already had a husband, whether she was going to have children or already had some. I found it very embarrassing as a stranger to listen in on these private discussions, and I made valiant attempts to concentrate more and more on my work, to make it clear to them that I wasn't trying to listen. It was only shortly before I left that I learned by chance that they were talking about families of ants. The sole topic of conversation in the Forell household at the time was events in the life of the ants, as that was Professor Forell's main interest and the subject of a book he was writing.

After some time I couldn't stand it in the hotel any longer and once more wired Loos for help. He immediately appeared, paid my debts and took me back to Vienna with him. Together with my pictures: neither the patients in the sanatorium, nor Professor Forell had shown any interest in purchasing one.

THE FLYING KNIGHT

Vienna, 1908. Absolute authority in the art world was wielded by a certain Dr. Seeligman, a contributor to the *Neue Freie Presse*, the mouthpiece of the semi-educated *nouveaux riches*. He was famous for a weekly column in which he poured out his venom over modern art. The originality of his aggressive attacks on 'modern' art was matched only by the unscrupulous way he, a bungler with the paintbrush, used his position to promote his own miserable daubs and those of his pupils as models to denigrate Munch, Manet, Cézanne, Van Gogh. This had brought him a certain notoriety, well beyond the readership of the above-mentioned stockbrokers' rag. To be perfectly honest, he was the one who had started stirring up animosity against modern art among fashionable society in Vienna, which until then had not bothered with art, its aesthetic interests being completely satisfied with gossip about actors and opera singers.

My first pictures were first shown in the *Kunstschau* exhibition of 1909, a pioneering event in central Europe. From that time on, this Beckmesser of painting had made my works the object of his sadistic persecution, venting on them all his bile and obsessive censoriousness, since I had sinned against the supreme law of portrait painting, namely, 'clothes maketh the man,' by doing what no one in Vienna had dared to do since the days of Waldmüller and showing not tailors' dummies but real people of my time, as had been the norm during the good periods of portrait painting, before the almost one hundred years of decline. The more my name became known abroad, initially in Germany, the more this Dr. Seeligman took it as a personal insult. It was he who, among other catch-phrases, was the first to apply the expression 'degenerate art' to my pictures, even if a certain dictator, who in his dark days as a painter without talent in Vienna probably learned the art section of the *Neue Freie Presse* by heart (as balm to his wounded vanity), later forgot to acknowledge his source. The police removed my posters at the request of the authorities, my first play was banned by the censors. The official bodies with responsibility for cultural life in Vienna consistently made it impossible for me to earn a living at home while keen to do business abroad with modern art, just like the Nazis who, following in their footsteps, 'cleansed' the German, Austrian, and Czech museums of my works, which they then carted round the Reich in exhibitions intended to pillory 'degenerate art,' before sending them abroad to have them auctioned off for hard currency. Much more honest was the archduke who, having seen the offending pictures, was so outraged he ordered the exhibition to be closed down. He did not call me 'a degenerate, appealing to our baser instincts,' but simply gave orders for the bickering among artists to be brought to an end, with the result that until the end of the First World War the only thing that was sold on the exhibition premises was vegetables. It was my turn to realize that an artist has to become an international vagrant. All German painters in history have suffered this fate, ever since Dürer had to go round fairs with a handcart, peddling his wares. Let no one take all the German art historians' romantic gush about classical art seriously! They claim to live with the art of the Greeks, but civilized nations have always lived with their own 'modern' art, the ancient Greeks included.

One night I was crossing St Stephen's Square in Vienna with my friend Reinhold. I was in a state of intense excitement, discussing with him my feelings as a young man who, dragged for the first time into the limelight of public attention, had overnight been branded a danger to public morality. It was after the premiere of my first play, *Murderer Hope of Women*, which had caused a scandal. There was a full moon. My friend, who had played the main role, had a hypnotic stare, as can be seen in my picture of him entitled 'Actor in a Trance' which, until the German Drummer came to power, occupied a place of honor in a German museum. My friend was brightly lit, his eyes hypnotizing me. Without a word he suddenly stopped. Bewildered, I looked down. As far as the eye could see the bumpy cobblestones reflecting the moonlight were framed in neat squares of black shadow, like the meshes of a net over the glistening scales of the fish. My own shadow, on the other hand, had taken on an independent existence, as if the ground beneath me had started to move, and my shadow with it. A moment of suspended consciousness, for which my agitated state of mind was sufficient explanation. The whole thing probably only lasted a fraction of a second, during which I was compelled to make ridiculous, because futile, movements with my legs without being able to get my feet back on the ground, which had left me in the lurch. I was floating, a position which, in water or some other element heavier than air, would have had nothing unnatural about it. I was, however, to suffer from a similar delusion many years later as the result of being shot in the head. In that case the same abnormal reflexes had a natural explanation, since the organ controlling my sense of balance, the 'labyrinth of the left inner ear,' had been destroyed. That night in St. Stephen's Square the reflex had appeared before its physical cause, by which I had contravened a universal law of causality!

Our limited sense of reality has to be satisfied with an equation along the following lines: just as a body does not throw a shadow for someone who has switched off the electric light, so a body does not throw a shadow for someone who has died. That night in St. Stephen's Square my friend Reinhold ran off angrily. It was many years before I forgave him the word 'Liar!' he had shouted at me simply because, in an impossible situation, I had politely requested him to push my body back down onto the ground. It was quite logical! I couldn't stay there floating in the air forever.

The liberal press in Vienna wielded great power and behaved rather like modern dictators in the way it fawned on the public and flattered their baser instincts. After my art had been declared undesirable in Vienna, I tried to make a career as a teacher. But whenever I found a position, the *Neue Freie Presse* would denounce me to the education authorities, who found themselves, willy-nilly, compelled to insist on my dismissal. School of applied art, junior high school, technical school for apprentices, even a private school for girls — at each institution, as soon as I had gained the confidence of the pupils, the principal would come along, pointing in embarrassment at an official *diktat* requiring him to dismiss the 'degenerate' artist. Apropos certain Viennese art historians who fell into line with Nazi ideology but have been converted to my art since it has been publicly recognized in Germany and have belatedly spoken up for it in their university lectures, I would just like to add that, at the time of the campaign against me in the columns of the *Neue Freie Presse,* these professors were of one mind with the journalists and contributed to my eventual decision to turn my back on the Blue Danube. What point was there trying to reform a school where I had to get my education myself, surreptitiously, by the back door?!

I first left the land of my birth, where I was being denied my human rights as an artist, at the same time as they found they had to give way to the general demand for universal suffrage, the right to vote starting at the age which I had just reached. When I was at school Austrian history was not taught as something living, something productive, but as a romantic glorification of the past. One can well understand the reluctance of worthy citizens, for whom patriotism is their pride and joy, to open their minds to the fact that a nation's history resides in the way it responds to cultural obligations. But I maintain that universal suffrage, which European states were granting their citizens, is less a right than mere words as long as the nation is nothing more than a historical curiosity for those citizens. It was my duty as a citizen, then, to take part in choosing a government, to support the state, defend it, die for it when called upon to do so, even though it did not allow me a living. There must be a balance between giving and taking if the law of the jungle is not to replace a binding social contract. Even today there are as many unresolved arguments contained within the problem of society, as there are questions which appear insoluble. In modern Europe the social problem has led to crisis above all because of the impossibility of resolving people's demands for the right to maximum fulfillment.

THE STORY OF OUR DAUGHTER VIRGINIA

MAN DOES NOT LIVE BY BREAD ALONE, as the Church has it; but mere words don't fill the belly either. I learned this the hard way, in my storm-and-stress days in Berlin when I was painting the series of portraits to which no one could apply the saying 'fine feathers make fine birds.' I seldom came to the point of signing these pictures, for in those days I was still shy of selling my work; when the decisive last moment came I always sheered off. I preferred to abandon both picture and paint-box. But then came the problem of how to get more paints. There was no solving the riddle of how to keep going as a free-lance artist without starving. Many a time in winter did I press my nose against the frozen window-panes of the Romanisches Café, in the hope of learning how the celebrities inside there did it.

My first Christmas Eve in Berlin was spent with a friend of mine, an unemployed, now half-blind actor who used to give publicity talks on modern painting at the headquarters of the little Expressionist art periodical, *Der Sturm* ('Storm'), which I had helped to found. Both of us sat wrapped in rugs because we had no coal, warming our benumbed hands over a kettle, on the spirit-stove. The sky was all starry, and from the fourth story of the building one could see down into the backyard, where the icy wind had heaped up high piles of snow, which the caretaker was leaving for the spring thaw to remove. There was a special reason why we had become friends. It wasn't only that we were both alone, on our beam-ends, in the great city and that nobody understood my work and everyone scoffed at his acting — not at all! It was that we both saw things that simply weren't there for other people. Perhaps our blood was thinner from so much fasting. We shared a little fantasy about a daughter whom we agreed to call Virginia. Artists have always been good at going hungry, but no other epoch has ever provided so many technical expressions for the artistic sublimation of hunger: Expressionism, Futurism, Cubism, Dadaism, Surrealism, abstract art, and so forth kept a whole generation of art-critics going until Herr Rosenberg, that authority of aesthetic matters in Hitler's Third Reich, made a clean sweep, declaring it all a degenerate swindle.

One, two, three, four, five I counted on the fingers of my empty hand. What meaning there is in numbers! Raised to the tenth power, cubed, the square root found — only I didn't know how to turn this schoolbook knowledge to account in order to turn the figures into money. It's money, not knowledge, that gives man power on earth! Nobody betting on my chances in life in those days when, together with Herwarth Walden, I was co-owner of the most advanced German art periodical, being copy-writer and draftsman, variety critic, publicity manager and delivery boy, all rolled into one, would have backed me for a place. My wealth consisted of the clothes I got up in, an iron bedstead, a wash-basin, and a towel. My room was provided by the paper. On Sundays I could eat my fill of Aschinger sausages, price limit one mark. Being young and strong, for the rest of the week I got by on bread and tea. The money I had brought with me from Vienna had made its way into the pockets of the barber at the Friedrichstrasse Station straight after my arrival. It was to the exponent of the hairdresser's art that I paid my first apprentice's fee. Because the Establishment wore their hair long, I asked him to shear mine right to the scalp. Meanwhile, with inveigling Berlin chatter, he lured me into laying out my money on brushes and soaps and eau-de-cologne. Having thus escaped from his attentive clutches, I was glad to rid myself of the package in the next doorway.

It was some time before Christmas that my friend and I, sitting together, worked out the destiny of the daughter of our starveling dreams. We decked out that figure, still a toddler there before our mental eye, with all the sparkling tinsel and glory that imagination could provide, lending her so much reality that our life was brightened as by the presence of some familiar, loved visitor, and we no longer felt lonely. However drearily the holidays dragged on, the winter becoming steadily grimmer, the imaginary reality of our Virginia, that bright spirit, enjoyed entirely different conditions in time and space. She grew perceptibly as we watched her, and we took it in turn to tell each other little incidents from her childhood, as though it were already long ago. For instance, how she played with a tortoise and, being still just a little girl, how she could surely have stood on its shell, balancing with outstretched baby arms, like an acrobat on a rolling ball.

Presumably, since it was now winter, the tortoise was hibernating in the cellar. This child of ours was not quite real, and so her parents were also of a somewhat ambiguous nature. Where we ourselves were concerned — the imaginary grown-ups who had to get what warmth we could from the rugs in which we huddled, shivering with cold — the girl had always been the soul of attentiveness, obedience, and affection. But we forgot to reckon with the fact that this being who radiated warmth for us had meanwhile blossomed into a young girl and become the plaything of a great passion. Having become resigned and modest in our demands, we old things could neither understand nor approve of such a love. Virginia loved a young man. So we reproached each other bitterly for having failed to give her this and that piece of good advice while there was still time. It was our fault that Virginia left the straight and narrow path. Perhaps we were out of touch with the new times. Having become egotistical, we simply could not wring from our withered hearts enough feeling to make us be fair to a new generation, a young generation that had different views from those we had in our day. We looked askance at a girlish heart that was stirred by longing and passion to the point of letting itself be lured from its safe home out into the wide world. Should we not have helped the little sapling to grow into a strong tree in the storm? Was this young heart, beating in such agitation, to pine in constriction, all because of our upbringing? Indeed, we would even have stooped to the deception of discreetly warning off some smart young gentleman, letting him know that the maiden wished to be spared further repetitions of his proposals. But in the end he seduced her just the same! Who knows how many sleepless nights her secret cost her, how many bitter tears she wept because now she must face life alone, with all its errors and follies. For all our mature experience, she could manage without us old fogies. Our memory was obviously failing — let's see, how long was it, actually, since she ran away? Let's work it out! The festive table that we decorated, piled high with presents for our absent daughter every Christmas — yes, this was the third time that we lit the candle on the little tree. My friend had come home with a pink candle from a party given by theatrical people who happened to remember his existence. Today she will come, she must come — this very moment!

She must simply feel, deep in her conscience, that we had forgiven her for the wrong she did us. Although the story had been made up only to keep the two of us amused, our feelings could not have been more intense if Virginia had walked in the door, a girl of flesh and blood. My friend kept on bothering me, as the younger and more nimble of the two of us, to go down into the cold cellar and make sure, before Virginia came, that her tortoise was all right. For what would Virginia say! How were we to justify ourselves to her! What wormwood would turn the cup of joy to bitterness if, on her return, it were discovered that something had happened to her pet while she was away. True, there had been no letter from her to say that she was coming. But then she never had written to us — she was too proud to confess her disillusion, Virginia could not play the hypocrite. With broken wings, humbly she stood outside her parents' house, out there in the snow, waiting for the door to open.

I didn't want to go down to the cellar. I had a mournful premonition that the tortoise was no longer really alive. Of course, they do say that tortoises live for centuries, but as bad luck would have it our imaginary gardener had had to get his gun out this very evening and go shooting the crows in the yard. From the empty stubble-fields those black pests flew in swarms into Berlin, in search of fodder. It was that clumsy fellow's fault; the report from the gun killed the tortoise. Tough, indestructible, capable of surviving for ages without food — it's only human beings who are always thinking about meals — these animals are nevertheless known to be of a rare and incomprehensible sensibility. The slightest thing will make them die! It was I who had given Virginia the tortoise for her birthday and I had accompanied the present with some words of wisdom, for anyone responsible for bringing up a child knows the right moment to say these things. Well, so I had explained how even the ancient Chinese had believed in the immortality of the soul and that this was why they took the tortoise as the symbol of immortality. How would the child ever trust me again, with the dead animal giving me the lie, as well as proving I had been incapable of looking after it?

One must only hope that there was no mysterious link — for with increasing age one grows superstitious — between the disaster for which the silly old tortoise was itself to blame, for being so sensitive, and our daughter's own fate! In those novels serialized in newspapers, which we would cut out and clip together in order to read them again with relish, one was always coming across that poor, haggard girl of good family who comes home, spitting blood, dishonored, a nameless child clutched to her bosom, and penitent, broken, lacking even the strength to ring the bell of her parents' front door, collapses in the snow, whereupon her ghost proceeds to haunt her harsh parents night by night. That was why I didn't really think there was any more point in going and looking in the cellar — anyway, we didn't have a cellar. What could we have kept in it? And so in faint tones I confessed to my friend that the tortoise was lying on its back, dead as a doornail.

He opened his eyes very wide — not that he could see anything, for he was almost blind — and he got up and came rushing at me in a fury. I could not deny his power over me, for socially he was the superior. If he hadn't become anything else in life, at least he was older than I. And the younger one is responsible to the elder. Our little room grew icy cold as the cellar — the door had opened. The sudden draft blew the window open, and my friend's rifle, on which the bayonet was always fixed, fell down. The declaimer of futuristic poetry reached out for it. The everlastingly 'resting' actor — once to have become a Prussian officer, but he ran away from the cadet school to go on the stage — engaged in a skirmish with me. Now the gun was being aimed by one of us, now it was being wrested out of his hands by the other and aimed at the first one.... There was a shot. It was the very shot that had scared off the crows a while ago, flying past the window with the snow-clouds. We had become so enraged with each other about the dead tortoise and had insulted each other so gravely that we parted company, unreconciled. Never again was there any talk of Virginia.

JESSICA

I

AS A BOY ONE LOOKS UP TO ADULTS. I was particularly taken with the old men who cleared away the snow that lay many feet deep in the street one severe winter. Often I would give them the two coins that I was given for buying buns in the break between classes. In return they would take me into the tavern with them. There, standing at the bar, they would give me a taste of the schnapps, blow pipe-smoke in my face, and let me listen to their talk. It was all very solemn, and that was the way I liked it. I still remember it clearly — that and another tavern in Paris, where I sometimes used to go before the war. I was on good terms with the *patron*, an Alsatian Jew, who once invited me into the back room and stood me a glass of his own special brand. It was his daughter, of whom I think now, who brought the bottle and the glasses. For her I might as well not have existed. She was engaged to a skinny little red-haired fellow who always wore a thick woolen scarf round his neck and kept his cap on — dashingly cocked sideways over one ear — even when it was so hot in the tavern that the stove-pipe was aglow. He had only a few greenish teeth in his head, and the girl was taller than he. Yet how she looked up to him, how far she was from being haughty — indeed, positively subservient!

But the story I was going to tell is about a young woman in Poland. Her name was Jessica; that I discovered from the cavalry captain. Outside the house where she lived a slate hung on a string, with a piece of chalk. On this slate it said that in this house Herr Isaak Borowitcz functioned in several official capacities. This young person, whose name, as I have said, was Jessica,

was the daughter of this comfortably situated man. He could not
fail to be a personage of high standing in the little town, for he
was the butcher, the distiller, the cantor and the *shames* in the
local synagogue. Let us picture this man of note. He wore a black
fur-lined winter coat, and all the people in the village bowed low
when they met him. That, too, was the reason why he had been
made town clerk. At Easter, before dinner, he was in the habit of
telling his daughter the following story.

A fairly long time ago another town clerk lived in a house
remote from the others. He had a pet lamb that followed him
about just like a dog. In order to test this lamb's devotion, one
day he put a knife in its cloven hoof and commanded it to kill
him, its master, with it. 'O master,' said the obedient lamb, 'I
never learned how to kill, but do you show me and I will do as
you command.' — 'What, you ravening wolf in sheep's clothing,
you mean to say you are capable of killing me? Well then, I will
do to you as you thought of doing to me!' And he commanded
the lamb to come nearer. Totteringly it came and laid its head
between the man's knees. The man slit its throat, let the lamb
bleed to death, roasted it, and, having garnished it with herbs,
served it up, said grace, and dined heartily.

That was Borowitcz's story, he being accustomed always to
reflect on his daily toil before sitting down to dinner with his
daughter. And she was accustomed to say: 'And Father — you
haven't forgotten the poor?' — 'The penny's right there on the
sideboard,' he would say. Nobody could say Borowitcz didn't
know what was right.

His daughter had a lover. But since neither of them had any
money, they could not sleep in one bed like a married couple.
People referred to him simply as Jessica's betrothed. He covered
so much white paper with writing that his sight suffered and he
had to wear spectacles with hollow-ground lenses, which he had
by now worn so long that the steel hooks for the ears had had to
be replaced with strings. His watery blue eyes went well with his
long fair hair, if one saw his eyes, which happened whenever he
took the spectacles off in order to kiss the town clerk's daughter.
He was slightly tuberculous and had been keeping to his bed for

some time. So Jessica was compelled to inform her father, the town clerk, of everything, so that they could marry, making an honest woman of her and giving her child its father's name. The town clerk was not one of those hard-hearted fathers. He did not reproach his daughter but went straight off to see the young man. Now the young man was no longer employed by day at the watchmaker's, since he could no longer sit with his chest bent over the work-bench with all the little wheels. The town clerk came in, took a good look round the room — at the bed, the clothes, the spectacles, which his daughter pointed out to him. The whole lot, together with the paper all scribbled on, was not worth a guilder, and this even if one was on good terms with the merchant, who was a kinsman and would get the paper all scribbled on to turn into paper bags. Schoolchildren are fond of a kind of brown licorice that they sometimes call boot-laces. Then the town clerk's glance fell on the ring on the apprentice-watchmaker's finger. 'Oh, this isn't worth anything, I got it as a present for my time with the watchmaker.' After a fit of coughing he went on: 'And anyway that was only by day, for as long as the sun shines on the just and the unjust. It's at night that the verses flow from my pen as though of their own accord! There's no heart in this world of ours, no heart, that's it! But some day the children in school will be assigned to learn my poems!' He began to laugh softly, but it was not real laughter, more of a giggling. 'Take it for love of your own flesh and blood, take the ring, good sir,' he said, struggling to sit up. And the clerk, who was so good-hearted, examined the ring on the dying man's finger through the magnifying glass that he used for examining the pledges brought to him by such as had got into debt. 'It's worth one guilder and fifty kreutzer,' he said decisively and entered the betrothed couple's names in the marriage register. With one last fond kiss the husband of the town clerk's daughter took leave of her and this world. His right hand, already stiffening, held the fifty copper kreutzers that he had left. The town clerk Borowitcz, who was nothing if not orderly, had already deducted the guilder for the marriage fee. He unbuttoned his fur coat, being warm from the glow in his heart over the two young people's love. As I have already remarked, nobody could say Borowitcz didn't know what was right. He put on his fur cap, and out in the street he began to sing merrily:

> I am the one you only have to call
> For birth or marriage or a funeral:
> There's no festivity without me!

This amused him so much that he himself began to cough from laughing so hard. The young woman standing in the open door did not know whether to scream after her father for grief at the loss of her husband or to put her mouth to the poor corpse's mouth and breathe warm breath into him again. So she inherited the fifty kreutzers from the apprentice-watchmaker's hand and was betrothed, wife, and widow all within one hour.

One day, when spring could already be sniffed in the little town's air in spite of the cesspool, which was open because it was time to empty it out into the fields, some riffraff came to the village. One of these gypsies was called Reuben; he was pock-marked and bore his entire fortune on the green cart that was drawn by a gaunt but spirited nag — an idle wench, fourteen years old, with skin brown as unripe plums, in a red petticoat much too long for her. A charitable woman had given it to this gypsy lass. Reuben thought the girl a moppet and a poppet, for which reason the wanderer did for her sake all that he could think of doing, namely, stealing. Now one day when the girl went begging to the town clerk's house, only the latter's daughter was at home, bending over a photograph. Putting her finger on the picture, the little girl asked her who the young gentleman was. 'Take away your dirty finger! This young gentleman? My bridegroom Reuben!' the widow said, shivering as she always did now. The beggar-maid shook her head contemptuously. 'No, that's not Reuben, Reuben's a gypsy, young and sturdy, a man who steals and is much handsomer than that pale chap.'

That evening the clerk's daughter wrapped her woolen shawl about her shoulders, went to the gendarmerie and denounced the gypsies before they could steal fowl in the night. The sergeant himself, with plumed cap and rifle, was to hide in the elderbush by the garden wall. He felt important, and he had always had a fancy for proud Jessica. For her sake he would have done anything. And it turned out as was to be expected. A sound was heard among the sunflowers growing in front of the hen-house, and then the startled clucking that hens make at night. Out of his ambush leaped the sergeant, with his mustachios, his plumes, and his rifle, and seized the pockmarked gypsy by his shirt. It was a critical moment. The shouting brought even the town clerk rushing out of the house in his fur coat. As he ran he buttoned it up, for he had to be careful not to catch cold in the spring. Without stopping to dress, his daughter ran out of the house, across the moonlit yard, in nothing but her shift, although she was soon to have the child. She arrived just in time to see the gypsy thrust his knife, which he always carried inside his shirt, into his captor's breast. The sergeant dropped from the wall, into the yard, like a sack of flour. The two hens the pock-marked thief had to let go — and feathers everywhere! The widow had seen the sergeant's revolver fall, for it was full moon, and, filled with icy courage, she shot the bold robber dead. 'Well, so that was Reuben, the gypsy,' she said. She did not wonder why the gypsy should remind her of her betrothed, although the latter was very fair and the former as swarthy as gypsies always are. 'Father of mine, do not forget the poor tonight either!' She kissed her father's hand before she went to bed. Her father took Reuben's ring with the stone set in it from the little finger of his own hand and gave it to the fourteen-year-old girl, who fell upon the dead gypsy with a great cry. Doubtless she had been the lookout for the thief. Jessica raised no objection to the little girl's having the ring. And the little girl's love and her misfortune aroused such a glow in the town clerk's heart that he unbuttoned his fur coat again and stood for a while outside the door. Herr Borowitcz had a soft heart, and nobody could say he didn't know what was right.

And that very night Jessica's child was born, a girl, and it was this girl that I later met on the advance into Poland.

II

My face was thin and drawn and the eyes were too big in it, eyes full of the insolence of an alert will, in contrast with the sleepy people all around me. I was beginning to realize what I amounted to. A gentle hand did not shrink from giving me milk as to a stray cat, to a creature that loved the warmth of indoors but refused to become a household pet or, which after every sloughing of its skin became a snake again, cold and smooth. Sometimes my hunger for companionship became so raging that I would go out at night prowling for prey, for people who lived as in birdcages. That way at least I saw them through the brightly illumined windows, from outside. 'You do take an odd pleasure in frightening people who mean well by you — !' 'Awake, sleepers in your kraal!'

I knew this society lady, a young widow. She wore a purple dress of goffered Venetian silk that was so fine that one could have pulled the whole dress through a wedding ring. Her hair gleamed like that of the penitent Magdalenes painted by Venetian masters. She wrote me a letter when I came back to Vienna for a short time: 'You still understand nothing at all of what you have. It's really more as if whenever you succeed you did so by inspiration.'

We went for drives in a carriage with rubber-tired wheels, we sat in her box at the opera, she gave me the key of her house so that I could come and go without being noticed. On summer nights I preferred to climb up the rose-spalier to the balcony leading to her bedroom. Much happened before all that is now mere memory became a reality for me amid the beating of hearts and blushing and tears of delight, until a fairylike being was transformed into one that was tangible and within my reach. There was the awe of the first human sacrifices, from reluctant yielding all the way to complete abandonment, tumult, quarreling, bliss of self-mutilation until one found oneself again. This sacramental condition in the presence of a divine being was something I had never known before, and I would have thought it impossible that at my beck and call the beloved would come, atremble with shameless pleasure. Both of us were adept in concealing this, as a secret vice, our limbs aching with it so that sometimes we could hardly walk upright for exhaustion. How often her maid had to turn visitors away, saying that madam was not yet up and would not be going out today. Day by day I grew bolder, and jealousy is also something that binds one to one's prey. I shut my beloved off from all society, because I scented a rival in every man. What new sufferings could my heart discover? Unimagined joys! I had to press my chest hard against the sharp edge of the doorknob, the daily letter was late, and then at last the postman rang. No one in the world would have understood where such a thing can lead, I thought in those days. One lies clutching the other, shaken by the spasm of desire, limbs inextricably intertwining, and one would gladly kill oneself in this way so that there might be an end to it. We shall go away in spring, in Naples we'll eat the first figs together. To the sea — and then into the mountains! In the seven communes we saw horses, cattle and lambs grazing all solitary, and they came to our call and let us stroke them. It was called the Vale of *Orpheus* — *Valle d'Orfeo.*

Years later, during the First World War, I found myself back in the same region. Through the barbed wire that ran along in front of our own trenches, I crawled forward to the wayside shrine, to take a paper flower as a souvenir. When I had the bright-colored flower in my hand and was turning to crawl back, an Italian grenade blew the little wall sky high. The music of Orpheus's harp, which tamed the wild beasts, was something that had not been heard there for a long time.

When one opens a door there's something on the far side that was not there before. I had a premonition that it would be irrevocable when, from a crate filled with wood-shavings or curly paper, she unpacked the death mask of her late husband. Even when they were drawing up the ground plan of our future house some had thought the choice of site a dubious one, for there was an underground spring there in which the foundations would some day be awash. But with much labor and expense the water was diverted. There was another disagreeable impression I will not pass over. It was like this. When we went to look at the house, which was just being finished — the beribboned tree already set on the rooftop by the master carpenter — there, in the future bathroom, where the spring had been piped and made to provide our water-supply, there was an aquarium such as people use for ornamental fish. It was full of hideous creatures swirling around in clusters. This was the visiting card of someone I loathed, a candidate for the lady's favors, a zoologist who had made a name for himself with experiments in cross-breeding. Presumably he had caught these toads here in order to take them to Vienna and use them for his experiments in the Institute in the Prater. A few days earlier he had committed suicide — this I learned subsequently. So this was his bequest to us. As quickly as I could I emptied the tub full of batrachians into the swampy field that had come into existence all round the house since the previous winter. What I should have liked best would have been to spare her the sight of these fat-bellied creatures, for she was pregnant. Instead she had to watch and see how each of the yellowish, disgusting toads of the larger sort, the females, carried one of the smaller, greenish males to the water on her back. In coupling with the females the males had fastened on to their sides with their sucker-feet. It was early spring.

We were both dismayed by this sexual demonstration on the part of the batrachians — both the slight, pale woman with her swollen body and I with my gaunt frame. What we thought, what each of us sought in the other, was ending, in a new being, a child — in something alien to us. Here was the dread of something that might lead further than one could bear — so she may have wondered. When the crate with the undesirable contents, the mask, destroyed my love that March day, I clenched my fists and screamed into the dead man's face, that is to say, at this yellowish wax mask with the closed eyes: No, I won't have it, you can't be there between us! If the eyes had been open, I suppose their gaze would have brought me to my senses. Does one make a mask in order to exorcise the ghost? It may be that this was why from very ancient times people have modeled the faces of their dead — to keep death away. Perhaps it began with painting the chief's dead face with red ocher, the color of life. Later they covered the skull with gold leaf, which was more resistant to the passage of time. There was the mask of Agamemnon from the tomb at Mycenae. Later still they began to cast such a countenance in metal and to portray it in marble, in effigy. This is how monuments came about. In Egypt such portrait-busts often bear the name of a prince who had his own name put there in place of that of the man portrayed, for his own greater glory. Against the vengeance of those of the underworld cunning is of some help, but the dead are not so easily scared by the living, not easily made to go back below ground.

In the Imperial Vault of the Capuchin Church in Vienna the Empress Maria Theresa had the sculptor Balthasar Mofl portray her life-size, in all her splendor and magnificence, while she was still alive, beside her husband's effigy on the coffin-lid, below which his dead body lay. In Saint-Denis the lecherous Medici, half naked, tries in a last embrace to wring a breath of warmth from the spouse she lost in a tournament held in her honor, when a lance pierced his eye and entered the brain. And let us not forget the Etruscan sarcophagus-lid on which the loving pair is portrayed as though still engaged in private conversation. And then, too, there is the earliest mask-exorcism of a dead man's ghost, in the land of Ur, which happened to be discovered during my journey in Asia Minor. My own impression, contrary to the scholars' view of these finds, is that this is not a priest-king, an Oriental despot who, as death approached, caused his harem to be slaughtered together with servants, slaves, and mules. This misunderstanding arises from the fact that the upper rooms of the palace collapsed into the tomb. It is, on the contrary, certain that the young, newly married prince-consort died of an illness, and that the queen who survived him sent his concubines and his favorite animals to join him in death, in order to keep him there. Instead of following him into death, she gave him a mirror, which the mummy originally held in its hands. The aging queen of the Amazons may often have gazed into this mirror when she visited the dead youth in the chamber below her palace. In this way, reflected in the mirror that the dead hand held, her life extended into the realm of shadows and prevailed upon her beloved, hungering for warmth and the delights of the senses, to stay there, until she, the queen herself, should die and be laid in a tomb above that of her princely husband, in order to be near him. Doubtless with the passing of time the ceiling of the tomb gave way and collapsed, which explains the misunderstanding of the chronology of the burials — a misunderstanding that strikes one in the archaeologists' interpretation.

My union with that lady came to the knowledge of those who are so timorously concerned with reputation. Gossip about town made her uncertain of herself. She could not bring the child into the world without first entering into a legal union with me. How could she do that with a young man who had not earned himself a position and a name in society? Without an income, without property! My happiness was already lying anaesthetized upon the operating table, and I was still full of superfluous fears that in that helpless state she would seem desirable to a doctor — that's how foolish I was! In a moment of ultimate vanity the lovely victim had had her long hair curled, before being taken on the stretcher into the operating room. The minutes of my life that I spent outside that door seemed endless to me at that time. It was an eternity before the unconscious woman was wheeled out again. On the way she began to vomit, and when she opened her eyes she did not recognize me and talked deliriously. There are circumstances that make people strangers to each other, oh indeed, there are many things that I should not care to experience again!

In the following days the newsboys in the streets were shouting their special editions. The world war began. Soon one saw peasant lads with twinkling favors in their caps marching in columns along the Ringstrasse, carrying their little wooden chests, and farm-horses that should still have been yoked to the plow were pulling gun-carriages and ambulances. Horses and riders were thirsty, hungry, white with the dust of the highroad. People talking all the languages of the empire had come to Vienna from all directions. Many of the spectators wept, although the military bands tried to drown the dumb anxiety.

Everyone felt in his own way that this was the beginning of the end. None of the civilians pressing against the police cordons knew when it would be his own turn to be called up and sent to war.

What first makes a human being is, as we all know, the upright gait. All right! But first a human being jumps for fear and runs away, and it is only looking back that he becomes master of himself again, stops, stands still on his two legs, and then walks. But the jump has its abode in the hollow of the knee. In barracks the whole column is drilled in knees — bend! jumping up as though on a single spine — Atten-*shun*! March! On the double! Eyes left! Eyes right! Halt! Fix bayonets! Take aim! Fire!

In war it sometimes happens that such-and-such a number in the army list suddenly throws away his gun and tries to run away. But it won't work. Even if such a number were sponged off the black slate like a wrong sum, he would never again become a human being; no one who has been a soldier ever quite becomes a human being again. One, two, three, four, five, so one learned to count on the fingers of the eager hand. I still had to learn of such a number as this that could shorten one's life, so to speak conjure away one's life out of one's very hand. It was a Russian conscript who showed me how it's done.

That is why even today, long after the end of the war, I avoid walking in front of anyone else. And I always try to get into the middle of the street as soon as the traffic policeman looks the other way. I don't like anyone to stick to my side or to creep along after me, soft footed, like a murderer. In the course of those 'great days' it was not only in my unconscious mind that what was at the bottom was sent floating up to the surface; even doctors lost their bearings and flung themselves into psycho-analysis. Since I have been able to travel again I have been struck by something in the anthropological museums that I never fail to visit in order to gain useful information about other peoples: there are always a fairly large number among the crumbling skulls on display that have a little round hole in the temple, as though made by the skilled hand of a surgeon at a great teaching hospital. The museum catalogues are unanimous in telling one that these prehistoric skulls are those of epileptics, whom people already had the art of trepanning. So that was the time when man began to desire more than merely to pilfer crab-apples from the tree of knowledge. Perhaps in the beginning of social organization the collective concept 'we' — replacing the bald 'I' which was all there had been room for in the human brain — was a particularly painful one, like a delusion. And so they opened the skulls in order to lessen the pressure on the brain. That would mean that the history of human society began with a considerable number of epileptics. But what will our grandchildren say of the era of the two world wars, when the hecatombs of bullet-riddled human skulls are dug out of the earth to make room for planting turnips!

But as to why the prehistorical doctors bored such a nice round hole in their patients' skulls, I have again hit upon an explanation different from that of the ethnological museums. In this way one may even be fairer to the army doctors who examined the Unknown Soldier when he was called up and declared him fit for active service, afterwards treating the wounded man, examining him yet again, declaring him fit, and sending him back to the front again — until he and the like of him, cured of all ills, for ever exempt from military service, were given over to the earth itself. Perhaps the army doctors were under pressure, against their own conscience, being threatened by suspension from service. A man has to live after all! Hasn't he? It was their profession! And so what seemed a sufficiently compelling argument for doctors in the world war does not require any special moral justification in the case of the Stone Age cannibals. Surely they did not collect their slain enemies' skulls merely in order to have a souvenir handy at home, to remind them of glorious deeds of arms. No, they scooped out the enemy's desirable bone marrow, which was rich in vitamins and incidentally increased our forefathers' self-assurance.

There's a saying about not dividing the bearskin before the bear is shot, and there's another about quarreling over the Emperor's beard. In my Viennese days high and low, nobility and lackey, all sported a beard like the Emperor's. In Berlin it was the mustachios of the Emperor Wilhelm the Second, and in Russia it was Little Father Czar's pointed beard. But in France every man who wanted to get on in life had the barber make him into a little Monsieur le President. In the very recent past the States of Europe were all lumped together under one hegemony, and so a certain mustache became the symbol of a way of thought according to which one recognized or distinguished friend or foe. By the Beard of the Prophet! But woe to him who is beardless! The matter is not simple, for in spite of his ready-made coat the average man is really pretty complex. However, I was going to tell the story of the first teddy-bear.

My erratic way of writing will bring me to the point all right. Let us imagine a flash of lightning came down from the sky one night just as a cave-bear was going into a trap. It would be a natural trap, for the savages would not yet have been capable of preparing pitfalls for others.

Perhaps there was some strong smell emanating from the pit, which became noticeable even to the savages gathered around the well. Well, just look! There's a cave-bear! Down where there isn't room for him to move his huge limbs. Waking or sleeping he would have to remain upright, and so the shaggy beast was discovered in the rocks, where he remained for as long as he lived. The cannibals had to await his natural death. According to the proverb that says, 'Where I find my dinner, that's my home', they must then have said to each other: Let us in good time found a society, the first Stone Age settlement.

They dug many passages leading out into the open, similar to the trenches used in modern warfare, a whole net of streets for a town, which thus gradually came into existence around the victualing-depot. Perhaps the hole had been made by some tremendous meteorite when a lunar satellite exploded in an antediluvial catastrophe, and in that hole the first human community was sheltered against inclement weather.

First of all these hairy men must have approached their gigantic, living prey with some reluctance, they being the weaker. How were they to kill Bruin? But the great creature, having no choice but to stare into the light, day in, day out, because there was no room for it to lie down, doubtless grew half-blind in the course of time and almost tame in its intercourse with human beings. They would throw their leavings into the pit to feed the animal as soon as they realized that it afforded them amusement to keep it alive. Now one day a particularly intelligent one of their number called the community together and put it to them about how everlasting panic made human beings antisocial! Up to then it had been the practice to strike down Neighbor Number One from behind, whereupon one suffered the same fate from the club of Goodman Number Two. One against all was the principle in those times, when property was not yet sacred and the good of the community did not override individual interest. Even in sleep the leg was ready to jump. With bow and arrow, club and nephrite knife one was always ready to jump, in those days, at the slightest sign of danger. Uneasy slept the human family. As a matter of fact, in those times there was not yet such a thing as the human family in our sense. Human seed was scattered at random, as blood was. For us nowadays, when everyone knows he has a protective wall behind his bed, police in the street, and armies at the frontiers, it is hard to imagine how it must have been when people were not yet bound together by any higher interest, when foe could not be distinguished from friend, and there was no collective organization to counter anarchy. Still, with all the progress that the armaments industry makes, it remains devilishly difficult to be the most dreaded power on earth. The eldest was certain to be anything but the stupidest of the group; he only played the simpleton. Surely he was the man of most wiles, he who counseled the people to weave a basket to muzzle the monster and thereafter to open the captive animal's skull just a little in order to draw off some of its living brain, which was no aid to it for thinking purposes, instead of some of one's neighbor's brain. The wound, a little round hole, soon healed again, and so when a year had gone round, the next emptying was already a sacred feast, uniting the community on that anniversary. For meanwhile people had learned to count on their fingers, and they had not failed, either, to mark the passage of the stars in their courses. The yearly withdrawal of nervous fluid from the teddy-bear did not cause him to die for a long time, just as the wild fir tree in the forest does not die from being tapped for its resin. A providential flash of lightning had illumined mankind, Providence had put the living roast into their pantry, the veritable Cauldron of Plenty known to us from fairy tale, the Egyptian fleshpot that was never empty. Under the direction of this and of later village elders and magicians, so anthropology has it, *la bombance pour tout le monde* was thus assured and social order arose out of a most primitive beginning of human social grouping. People learned how to domesticate both beast and man, to capture the treasures of the earth and the forces of the cosmos as in a trap, and in so doing those of most wiles usually kept their own skulls safely on their own shoulders. Religions were needed to win cannibals over to humanitarianism; there was also a need for special laws of land and sea warfare, so that wars should be waged fairly and provide adequate moral justification for murder. The idea of penance, the idea of the scapegoat and of the sacrificial lamb! Man's evolution from a cannibal to a paterfamilias is astonishing when one considers that it is all thanks to such a tiny tidbit — *pour une gourmandise aussi modeste!* But the terror has crawled away down into our subconscious. It is in the unconscious realm that we work off our bad conscience, like our pussy-cat decently covering up her excrement in the sand-box provided. However, our appetite for our neighbor's property did not become any the less with the increase in the demands of morality; for our cannibal history did not end with our grabbing only just so much of our neighbor's property as was needed to fill us. For that greater self, our country, we thought up values of a higher currency as a substitute for the cannibals' tidbits of yore. It was above all the unshakable faith in our God, Who is of course on our side, that united men and strengthened them in the struggle against the archenemy. Yet the progress made has been most strikingly noticeable since people ceased to gobble up at least those in their own immediate family circle, and it is a mark of our delicate breeding nowadays that we all know it to be a mere figure of speech if someone indicates his affection for wife or child by saying he could just eat them up.

After a certain amount of time had passed I volunteered, no longer believing in the prophecies made by the armchair strategists, namely that the war would be over by Christmas, a walkover for us. I had never previously done any military service. After six months of it I was sufficiently licked into shape to be able to volunteer for a unit going off to the front, and in this way I avoided being clapped into irons on account of a violation of discipline. On my horse's back I swam the wide Russian rivers without myself being able to swim. I was lucky. Some of the best horsemen in my regiment were swept away by the current and so perished. Together with people I did not know, men previously as much strangers to me as my enemies on the farther bank, I daily discovered a little more about how to get used to the thought of imminent death.

We came to the marshes. The first dead that I encountered were young comrades-in-arms of my own, men with whom, only a few nights earlier, I had been sitting round the campfire in those Ukrainian forests, playing cards and joking. Not much more than boys they were, squatting there on the moss in their bright-colored trousers, a group of them round a tree trunk. From a branch a few paces further on a cap dangled, and on the next tree a dragoon's fur-lined blue cloak. He who had once worn these things himself hung naked, head downward, from a third tree. The horses lay with their hooves in air, swollen-bellied, swarming with flies there in the forest. At the sight of this huge dunghill my own horse reared, so that I had to dismount in order to quiet him. My patrol had been sent out to relieve these friends, who now sat there together as peacefully as if they were picnicking. Only now they would never speak again, and when I thrust my hand into the hair of the youngest among them, it came off in my hand and his scalp slipped sideways.

The next moment I was ambushed for the first time in the forest. My patrol had gone riding ahead. As in an old oleograph there was a flash of sulphur-yellow from the Russians' rifles. My horse reared and whirled round, and I could not help mentally comparing myself with the equestrian monument to that victorious general, King Victor Emanuel, which I had seen not so very long ago in Naples. Like him I flashed out my brand-new sword. What did not seem to belong to this picture at all was a wicker chair by a tree, on which the Russians had fixed up their field-telephone. I had no chance to get a closer look at this, for my Hungarian remount, Minneloh by name, which means 'All horses,' was already settling into a gallop, and he kept the lead in that race, leaving the little Russian horses simply nowhere. When I looked round and saw with relief that the distance between us was rapidly increasing, I expected to see the Cossacks at their equestrian acrobatics as in the circus. I was not yet ripe for war, though to be sure I was already miserably lousy.

Our advance ceased long before those famous communiqués from headquarters ceased to reassure those at home. The armies had already dug themselves in, and to a large extent all troops had already been put into the field-gray uniforms in which the Russians had made themselves invisible from the beginning. It was on that account, too, that we had sneered at them for cowardice. A thing that surprised me about the Russians over there, whose dead were lying in front of our trenches, was that they looked so fat. They had been out there for several days. The contents of their pockets were investigated by experts, with a view to establishing the strength and tactics of the enemy division opposite. On the whole the dead Russians looked rather amiable, like peasants. On the earth lay crumpled photographs of their wives and children, which were of no military interest; but obscene postcards were handed around among us. Even our cavalry regiments were now partially equipped with spades, by way of experiment; but once again it appeared that the Russians had more experience with the spade. Later not even gas attacks could establish definitely where a whole army had dug itself in, with mole-burrows and stinking underground passages in all that burned, bombed filth, like the insects in a bug-ridden house. If it had not been for the barbed wire one might have thought there were armies of rats dug in there. For the first time I heard heavy artillery fire. We learned to distinguish the explosions of shrapnel, the cloud of pink smoke from the enemy's side from the gray of our own. There was a weak point where my cavalry regiment was moved up. The cavalry, being used to being in the van, considered it anything but heroic to be led through the rain at night, in Indian file, up to the trenches. We had to go on tiptoe in order not to make a noise, for the clatter of spades or carbines would have betrayed our presence to the enemy. It was said that a murderous battle had taken place nearby. The previous day we had passed the newly made mass graves of the Tyrolean rifles. So it was no empty rumor that those mountain troops bad held the Ukrainian marshlands and forests to the last drop of their blood, never having yielded an inch.

Then we advanced upon a Russian town that the Germans had already taken but had had to relinquish again. Up to now the Austrian cavalry regiments had always been in the van, and I myself enjoyed the cheers with which my regimental commander — riding, strictly contrary to regulations, at the head of his regiment — was received in Lemberg, Warsaw, and Cracow. However, on the far side of the blue and white Russian frontier barriers not only the peasants but the townspeople too had fled at our approach. Some were hanged as suspected spies, as an example to the rest. And the more the front was shortened, the more of the population hung on the gallows. Only the indispensable Jews were there again. Since the days of their forefather Joseph, these strange people from the ghetto, who also have their uses as a scapegoat whenever a government has to massacre somebody in order to divert public attention from domestic difficulties, have regarded war as a typical Christian amusement — *goyim naches*. But since the days of the Pharaohs they have also maintained their special talent for dealing in grain.

Many who survived the world war and returned home might not have found their parents, wives, and children still there had it not been for the cunning of the Jews organizing food supplies behind the lines. Not merely in the two last winters of the war, but from the very beginning everyone would have starved while the men were playing at soldiers instead of working and the women were not only keeping house, bearing and looking after children, but working in armament factories. The army itself went to the Jews. In quiet sectors, however, they would be rounded up from the villages and forced to dig graves, which they did not like. They hid like fieldmice in subterranean storage places where they had stocks of corn, hay, bonds and other valuables.

Once our squadron was relieved from its turn in the trenches, and we went back to the horses, which were with the reserve in a little Jewish township on the River Bug, which is very wide. The sergeant handed out billet-slips for the officers, who were quartered in houses, whereas the men slept in barns. I too slept in a bed again for a change, in a room strewn with feathers, for a former occupant had gone to bed with his spurs on. There was still a mahogany chair in the room — a miracle that the legs had not been used for firewood. All that had happened to a glass case in one corner was that the glass was smashed; it still contained two coffee cups with painted hearts and initials on them. It was wonderful to sleep in a real bed again! Over this bed there was a framed picture, ingeniously done with hair. It must have been a souvenir of peaceful days: a pair of sweethearts, the girl with dark eyes and the young man in spectacles, with a white cravat made of paper, pasted on. Barbers also have their artistic urges.

My Swedish captain, a mercenary who had joined our army out of a taste for adventure and who now commanded my squadron, was up and about at dawn, searching the house for something to drink, while I was still tucked in bed. Reveille was not till six, according to daily orders. I heard a woman shrieking and the captain laughing, and I got up, looking forward to having a shave, for it was a long time since I had been anywhere near hot water. In the yard I found the Jewess and asked her for some water. She merely looked me up and down. Scarcely opening her mouth, she made a contemptuous gesture and said: 'Fetch it yourself from the river.' I followed her slowly and watched her walking down to the river in her tattered dressing-gown, with a scarf wound turbanwise round her head. There was a ford. She waded in and, paying not the slightest attention to me, lifted her clothing above her waist and patiently washed her body as clean as she could. In spite of everything, I liked her, for it was a long time since I had seen a woman. I thought to myself. What these females can pick up in the war can't be washed off even with all the water in this river. What a jolly change the war had made even to life in this little township — how right the armchair strategists were at home, talking of a bath of steel! It was some time before our squadron moved on. With my first pips on my collar, I did not have to groom horses anymore, only to make the rounds of the stables morning and evening. So I had time to go round here and there and find out a little about my landlady, while my comrades-in-arms were playing cards on up-ended buckets meant for collecting the horse-droppings. Her name was Jessica.

A bugle sounded — fall in! The horses were out in the street, all saddled, and the stable smell had caused me to drift off into a dream. One of the military police was marching off a group of tousled-looking peasants. Among them was a dramatically pallid, fat Jew with a big black beard, wearing a fur-lined winter coat, one Herr Isaak Borowitcz, who had been black marketing in grain and had not wanted to turn it all over merely in exchange for a scrap of paper with a rubber stamp on it.

To horse! The bugle gave the signal. Out again, to war! The dashing cavalry — to war! First of all we attended Mass, which was celebrated at a field-altar, and when the salute was fired the horses became restive, swords flashed from their scabbards like a single flash of lightning. Officers — to the front! Silence — as of iron. My horse stood two paces ahead of my troop, dead straight in line with the other cadets. I was lucky — my horse stood as quiet as if he were a statue, man and mount cast in bronze. The regiment ceased to breathe. The Prussian Field Marshal von Mackensen, the chin-strap of his shako, the shako of the Death's-Head Hussars, martially pushed up on his chin, his dolman bordered with leopard skin — decoratively flung back over one shoulder, and mounted on his high-bred Arab dapple-gray — came riding along our lines there on parade, his entourage following him. Mackensen himself gave me an order, and I, lost in admiration of the splendid spectacle which reminded me of my boyish enthusiasm for Napoleon and his generals, did not hear it properly and promptly forgot it. They said he always had a French chef with him, for be liked to give magnificent dinners in his temporary headquarters, which was also the headquarters of our own troops since we had suffered that great strategic setback. Beside the Imperial German helmets, eagle-crowned, gold and silver braid, glittering orders and stars, the Imperial-Royal Austro-Hungarian Generals held their own with the gleaming blue plumes in their cocked hats. On either side the staff officers could be recognized by the red stripes on their trousers. I had to take a message to the staff mess, where the table seemed, so far as I could see, to be plentifully provided and where, modestly separate from that of the loftier warlords, there was also a table for the chaplains. The latter all wore black, most of them with a large cross bobbing on their breast. The war of religion between the seven confessions represented in our army, the Gospels' message of love for one's neighbor, seemed to be settled over the wine and the not entirely dry bread for the shepherds of souls — which set my mind at rest. An equal, a peer among his peers, there was the rabbi among them too, doubtless with his own personal reasons for rejoicing. The German Supreme Command had sent a special call to Jewry to make common cause with the Germans. 'To my beloved Israelites!' Ah, the darling man, General Ludendorff! A heart of gold! What goodness came gushing forth from the source of German strength and joy!

Then it was war again. The cavalry was to cover the flank of the retreating army. Each of us tried to work out his own way of how to correct the strategic disaster of which we could speak only in whispers. If it came off, there was the order of Knighthood of Maria Theresa, if it didn't — court-martial for insubordination. Passing through abandoned villages, we saw swarms of bees in tree trunks, not in proper hives, as at home. In a clearing in the forest we saw a pig that had lost its way. Before the words 'Catch it!' had passed from man to man, the pig had breathed its last sigh and was chopped into as many slices as the troop had horsemen. Every trooper found room in his saddle-bag for his allotted portion. We were thirsty for fame, but we were hungry as well; all we got our fill of was rum. Once our field-kitchen ventured as far out as the forward patrols and even had an independent skirmish with the enemy.

In one of the hutments in the forest, in tumble-down thatched cottages, our cholera patients were housed, and most of them died there too. We were pretty used to sleeping dreamlessly on the same straw palliasses from which we had just seen the dead being carted off. We were tired, that's the truth of it. One night in an abandoned village, which I had ridden to over felled tree trunks instead of along a track — the place was so swampy — I was wakened by a sound. An old peasant with a long beard and the staring eyes of a madman was bending over me. The sound was a faint one, like that of a knife being whetted. His bleached hair was like a thatched roof over his wrinkled forehead. The dirty coarse linen shirt he wore hung down over his trousers. 'You shan't slit my throat like a pig's!' I yelled, making a jump at him as he disappeared into the darkness, nimble and soundless on his bast-soled shoes. All I managed to do was to knock over the spinning-wheel, which looked like an old man in the light of the dying fire. Perhaps I'd been mistaken? Was it my own heart beating so loudly? After that I couldn't go to sleep again, so I looked round among the old world domestic utensils by the light of a resin torch. Everything was made of wood, as in one of those villages built on stilts, except that there was an icon hanging under an oleograph of the Czar in one corner of the room.

There was something stirring at the edge of the forest. Dismount! Lead horses! Our line was joined by volunteers, and we beat forward into the bushes as if we were going out to shoot pheasant. The enemy was withdrawing deeper into the forest, firing only sporadically. So we had to mount again, which was always the worst part, for since conscription had been introduced the requisitioned horses were as gun-shy as the reservists who had been called up were wretched horsemen. After all, most of them were used to having a seat only on an office chair. In the forest suddenly we were met by a hail of bullets so near and so thick that one seemed to see each bullet flitting past; it was like a startled swarm of wasps. Charge! Now the great day had come, the day for which I too had been longing. I still had enough presence of mind to urge my mount forward and to one side, out of the throng of other horses that had now gone wild, as if chased by ghosts, the congestion being made worse by more coming up from the rear and galloping over the fallen, men and beasts. I wanted to settle this thing on my own and to look the enemy straight in the face. A hero's death — fair enough! But I had no wish to be trampled to death like a worm. The Russians had lured us into a trap. I had actually set eyes on the Russian machine-gun before I felt a dull blow on my temple.

The sun and the moon were both shining at once and my head ached like mad. What on earth was I to do with this scent of flowers? Some flower — I couldn't remember its name however I racked my brain. And all that yelling all round me and the moaning of the wounded, which seemed to fill the whole forest — that must have been what brought me round. Good lord, they must be in agony! Then I became absorbed in the fact that I couldn't control the cavalry boot with the leg in it, which was moving about too far away, although it belonged to me. I recognized the boot by the spur: contrary to regulations, my spurs had no sharp rowels. Over there on the grass there were two captains in Russian uniform dancing a ballet, running up and kissing each other on the cheeks like two young girls. That would have been against regulations in our army. I had a tiny little round hole in my head. My horse, which was lying on top of me, had lashed out one last time before dying, and that had brought me to my senses. I tried to say something, but my mouth was stiff with blood, which was beginning to congeal. The shadows all round me were growing huger and huger all the time, and I wanted to ask how it was that the sun and moon were both shining at the same time, I wanted to point at the sky, but my arm wouldn't move. Perhaps I lay there unconscious for several days.

I returned to consciousness only when enemy stretcher bearers tipped me off their field-stretcher as a useless burden, beside a Russian with his belly torn open and an incredible mass of intestines oozing out of it. The stench was so frightful that I vomited, after which I regained full consciousness. Hadn't I promised my mother to be home by a certain date? Can't remember what date it is at all! I kept on trying to work it out — yes, well, it must be about the time. One, two, three, four, five I counted on my fingers, and there was that little round hole in my head. Was I actually still alive? Oh, definitely. After all, when I said goodbye to my mother I gave her a necklace of red glass beads to keep which a certain lady had given me. Only I could know that. But what horrified me most was that I couldn't scream, I couldn't utter any sound at all, and that was far worse than suddenly seeing a man standing over me. I opened my eyes wide, which hurt, because they were all sticky, but I had to see what he was going to do to me. Actually all I could see of him was his head and shoulders, but that was enough: he was in Russian uniform, and hence my enemy. I watched him so long that I thought I should have to wait all eternity while he stood in the moonlight setting his glittering bayonet at my breast. In my right hand, the one that wasn't paralyzed, I could feel my revolver, strapped to my wrist. The revolver was aimed straight at the man's breast. The man couldn't see that, because as he bent over me he was in his own shadow. My finger pressed the cock. I managed to do it lightly, and only I heard it, but the sound went right through me. There was a bullet in the chamber, in the regulation way. Then his bayonet pierced my jacket and I began sweating with pain, I thought I wouldn't be able to stand the pain, telling myself that it was only fear, while the bayonet came sliding through the stuff of the jacket. A slight pressure of my finger, just such as you, dear readers, exert in order to flick a little flame out of your cigarette-lighter, would have sufficed to bring me back alive to Vienna, home to mother. After all it's our mothers that bring us into the world and not our fatherland. Now the point was beginning to pierce the skin, was searing into the flesh. My ribs were resisting, expanding, I couldn't breathe. My capacity for endurance was failing. It was unbearable. And still I went on telling myself, as I grew weaker and weaker: 'Just a second more! This ordinary Russian is only carrying out orders!' Then suddenly I felt quite light and a wave of happiness

— never since then in all my life have I felt it so physically — a sense of well-being positively flung me upward, I was buoyed up on the hot stream of blood that was coming out of my mouth and nostrils and eyes and ears. I was floating in mid-air. So this was all there was to dying? I couldn't help laughing in the man's face before I breathed my last. And the ordeal was over. All I took with me to the other side was the sight of his astonished eyes. The enemy ran away, leaving his weapon sticking in my body. It fell out under its own weight.

What happened to me then I do not know. There are gaps in my memory. Death has lost its terrors for me, like a rusty key that has been broken in the lock. it seems that one, two, or more days later they lifted me into a railway car, and there was a Russian conscript who had lost both his feet who kept trying to push a withered apple into my mouth — but even a surgeon couldn't have opened it, my face was so swollen. Then they lifted me out, and Russian guards officers saluted, presumably mistaking the yellow cotton threads on my collar, the cadet's badge, for real gold. Yes, it was the scent of mimosa pollen, that was what I hadn't been able to think of before. It was mimosa that I used to send to my lady love in Nice every evening by express train from Vienna, so that she should have the scent of it before she encountered it in the flower markets there. And then I was required to write out my 'particulars' before I died — so one of these friendly people kept on insisting in broken German. He even guided my hand as I wrote, but the sheet of paper had not enough space for my name. Several times we poised the pencil, and I wrote right off the edge of the paper, as if into the sky. So I might almost have ended as the Unknown Soldier of the World War. Thanks to this medical orderly and another one who also came along, I was able to study the white shrapnel clouds mingling with the pink ones over the railway station, during the hours that the train stood there. On my promising to protect them, they stealthily lifted me out of the cattle-car and stayed by me that night, while the train traveled eastward. They were both Balts. I would have promised anything only to get that rumbling to stop, the wheels going round in my head! As often as fur caps came bursting in, asking in menacing tones if there wasn't some damned German or Austrian there, I answered only with a smile, whereupon they too remained. After the thunder of the guns there was now rifle-fire to be heard. It was our troops coming closer. There was a bugle signal! Then, in my own native language, an order to attack the station. The Russian orderlies lifted me up so that I could be seen in the window, which was scorched, with no more glass in it. They held my arm so that I could salute the lieutenant, saying: 'Cadet XY, reporting back for duty with eighteen prisoners.' For this my colonel pinned a medal to my breast, in front of the whole regiment. And there was a rose that someone had laid on the stretcher. Heaven alone knows where it had been picked.

It took six months to get back home from the field-hospital. In Vienna the young countesses lionized me; I was a lieutenant now, bemedalled, and before the year was out I was getting around on crutches. Yet this time, too, the fun was spoiled for me by a dashing general still in the prime of life, whose nickname was 'the hyena of the homeland hospitals.' Three times a month he came on a visit. He would play a few rippling arpeggi on the piano and then ask one: 'Well, lieutenant, are you feeling nearly ready to get back to the front?' I wasn't in a hurry, I still had to sleep sitting up, and when I walked I went round in circles like a hen with beriberi. That was from my head wound; which had destroyed the membranous labyrinth, which, as everyone knows, is what gives us our sense of balance. The first time I went to see my mother, in my clumsiness I knocked over a flower-pot, which had only some dry earth in it. There the shards lay on the floor. My poor mother, whose three children were serving the fatherland on three different fronts, had grown discouraged in these years of shortage and anxiety. Out of the dried-up earth that had been in the flower-pot she pulled out the red beads and held them up quite close to my face, like a child proudly showing a grown-up how clever it is. To that my first words had been to ask about this bauble and not why her brown hair had all turned white!

So it was because of the spring in the hollow of the knees, where the reflex no longer functioned properly, that I was declared unfit for active service. I was given sick leave. A fellow who runs round in circles is no soldier. The fact that my thoughts also went round in circles didn't make much impression on the medical officer examining me, for otherwise half the army would have had to be sent home. Yet my case was clear. The little round hole in my skull was a fact. I thought I couldn't waste my time in a world war, and I was more concerned about getting my mental balance back. Meanwhile I managed to get to the front just once more, with wangled orders from the Army press office. I hid among some sturdy Honveds, elite Hungarian troops, who didn't know me and who were homesick. They kept a gypsy in their trench with them. However, in spring gypsies get the wanderlust, and so they strapped him to a post by his legs, leaving his hands free to play his fiddle. Connoisseurs said he played particularly well, just as blinded nightingales sing with the most melodious sadness. But I wasn't a hundred-percent unfit for active service until after a shrapnel-burst on the Isonzo front.

III

What did I care any more about the woman I blamed for my having volunteered for the army, where everyone had ended up by then, as in a trap! Now peace had come, much disconcerting those who had not done too badly out of the war. I was again living in Berlin, in my old room in a cheap lodging-house. It was during the revolution. The rifle that had belonged to my friend the actor, once a cadet at the Prussian officers' training college, had come into the possession of a girl from Poland who was, however, making her living on the streets in Berlin. When business was bad, she slept in a room on the same floor as I. This rather slow, good-tempered creature, who looked as common as her accent sounded, was called Jessica. That was why I had noticed her! Berlin was turned upside down, full of new people the like of whom had never been seen here before. People behaved differently now, just as the things that happened were quite different. Homosexual sailors sniffed cocaine, promenading the pavements arm-in-arm with lesbians in broad daylight.

Officers tore off their badges of rank with their own hands, lest someone else should do it for them. But respectable citizens kept out of sight, for their order of things had ceased to exist. The street-woman had a half-grown boy living in her room, a boy that nobody ever saw. This tall, clumsy girl was able to live with her strange love undisturbed so long as there were cannon ready for action in the streets and barbed wire preventing traffic from circulating. People went out only when they absolutely had to, for passes provided by the parties fighting for possession of the street were no safeguard against being arrested by one side or the other, or perhaps still worse.

When neighbors pointed out to the girl what she was letting herself in for after the restoration of civil order, through the fact that her strange infatuation might well be interpreted as an offence against a minor, or even kidnapping, her indolent, common voice grew harsh and threatening and a dangerous light flickered in her dull eyes. She kept the boy hidden in her room, hidden even from the men she picked up for a living; for she had an alcove curtained off, with a bed behind it. If anyone tried to look behind the curtain, she would reach out for the rifle. A minor is under the protection of the law. In the event that parents cannot be traced, officialdom provides the guardianship of official orphanages. At the moment law did not prevail. However, people in the know had got wind of a reorganization of the police, which would be sure to put an end to anarchy in a few days. The boy would be taken away from the girl, even if she protected him with her own body, like a lioness! Since everyone had been cut off from the streets, the metropolis had decomposed, dissolving into separate elements, into cells. Even in our sordid little backstreet hotel, in an outlying district, there arose a spontaneous, primitive form of a human community of interests, in which nobody either needed or wanted to know anything of his neighbor's past or future. We helped each other from door to door, as best we could, never quite letting go of the door handle. Nobody had much thought to spare for the girl's male visitors, nor for her passion for the boy. Who was concerned with respectability in the days of the revolution?

The next day a truckload of heavily armed, uniformed men descended outside our lodging-house. I heard soldiers at the Polish girl's door. I was sorry for Jessica, who would now have to pay the price of the silly affair. Prison! Poor Jessica! Then the truck, bristling with machine-guns, drove off down the street. Only when everything was perfectly quiet did I risk going to the window. Down in the street a little old woman here and there crept out of her door, setting off with a handbag for whatever basic necessities she could contrive to get for her brood on the black market. Just a bit of something to eat! What nonsense, all this shooting! People just going crazy with the lust for power, people who ought to be allowed to handle a gun! There was no other reason for it that anyone could see, for there was no enemy in the streets. As soon as the truck had gone there was peace and quiet — if that uncanny stillness could be called peace and quiet. A street-sweeper came round the corner with his familiar cart, supplied by the city council and came along sweeping the street and gathering up the rubbish with his shovel. From my window I had already seen that heap of horse-droppings in the street, which was usually so clean, not a soul far and wide, and I had also seen the horse-cab, which had somehow strayed into this district, getting in the way of the military truck. The gray-bearded cabby, in his threadbare blue top-coat and tall felt hat, had cracked his whip sharply. The poor old nag probably hadn't picked up his feet so fast since he was a foal in Poland, where he had become a prisoner of war and been sent off to Berlin. With the luck of the meek, both the horse and his driver, some demobilized peasant, passed unscathed through the hail of bullets. Only this little heap of horse-apples remained on the battlefield, the victor's trophy, until that too was removed and Berlin was once more that model orderly city as it will always be known.

Since everything remained quiet, I went and opened the door of my room, to see what the neighbors were doing. What a sight! The door of Jessica's room was wide open, the curtain had been torn down from the alcove, and the tumbled bed could be seen. The room was empty. Later a great deal was heard about that simple daughter of the people, that common girl. People claimed to have seen her all over Berlin, in many different places at the same time, with a fiery red cap on her head like an avenging angel — wherever anyone set fire to a building. Her harsh voice inspired the fighters wherever they grew faint-hearted because their barricades did not hold against quick-firing guns, which had now been brought up at all salient points. But her crazy laughter also disheartened many of those on the other side, in those times when there was suddenly a common people that for a few days wrested the streets from the forces of law and order. This was a common people that no one had known before, and since there came to be more and more shooting from the roofs into the windows of houses opposite, one might have thought that war had now corroded the very bowels of human society. The big city was one huge trap! These mountain ranges of brick, concrete, and artificial light, and more than all else the basement dwellings and filthy backyards of the slums! One huge trap, and into it the healthy people were sucked, as into a vacuum, from their fields and meadows. It is a trap in which man perishes, for there he is tapped for the marrow in his bones, like the bear in the pit. Children and old people, the sick and the healthy, workers, parasites, and criminals vegetate together, huddled together in the construction of the great city. The people soon had no more heart to go on trying to shake off their chains by violence, and of their own free will went back into their cage of stone. Now there were newspapers again, and the wireless conveyed official announcements about the daily progress in the restoring of order. Someone lodging in our hotel came across a paragraph in those law-court reports that are printed in smaller type, which brought to light what the police had discovered about one Jessica Borowitcz, found guilty of kidnapping a minor. Having been got out of the Moabit prison by party comrades, she had, apparently, been killed in some street-fighting. At the instigation of this Jessica Borowitcz the boy had run away from his father, the headmaster of a Polish-German boys' grammar school. The girl had been in service there for a time. The days of the revolution made many things possible that might well seem more alluring than the paternal household to a half-grown boy with a longing to see the world. Furthermore, the headmaster himself admitted that his boy had perhaps been brought up on principles somewhat too severe. But it was plain to see that father and son were not birds of one feather, for in the reformatory, where he was put, the boy committed suicide after being told that the person he kept on vainly asking for had been shot while trying to escape. It was his mother.

THE FIRST LETTER FROM THE TRAVELER

Stockholm, Winter 1917

I should be very grateful to you if you would revive your former custom, so pleasant to me, and from time to time increase my scanty delight in living by sending me a sign of life. How well I remember the way you helped me to regain a taste for being alive, the way— when I had a craving for the open air — you took me out of Count P.'s Hospital to your parents' beautiful estate with its great shady park, and how we then went for drives in the Lainzer Tiergarten and were gay together, with the obstinate little donkeys trying to lie down in the road in front of the donkey-cart! And how you found a way of talking me out of my dread of forests, which I had had since the time I was ambushed in the forest in Poland and almost lost my life These things are among the better of my war memories. And I still have the rose that you twined into the hilt of my sword when I said good-bye, leaving for the Isonzo front. You mustn't forget me, dear Countess! For then how would, for instance, that large painting ever be finished, the one I began, where you are sitting on a tree-trunk with your little brothers and sisters, in the depths of the virgin forest? Your brother Alexander will have told you about his visit to me in Stockholm and how I rejoiced to see him again and to hear news of my old friends. Later I was in Falun, at Frau Lagerlöf's, doing some drawings, when I heard of the bad luck that befell your mother, the dear Princess, and how she was forced to travel back to Stockholm. If it had not been for that and if I could have got there in time, I would tremendously have liked to pay my respects to her again personally and to have asked her to be so kind as to convey my most affectionate greetings to yourself, my dear Countess. Actually I had soon found it unsuitable to go on living in Stockholm There is the intense cold of autumn and the same thing in the hearts of the people — even though the Stockholmers make an effort to be warmer towards strangers and foreigners, for their eagerness to get into history, as in our own country people are eager to get into the newspapers, makes them ready to do anything they can for anyone they suspect, even in the most innocent sense of the word, of knowing something about how that is done. And so I was resolved to return to Dresden with all speed. Despite all the talk of peace conferences in Stockholm I realized even in the first few days that none would take place there, where the warmth of the heart decreases with the increase in distance from the part of Europe that is tearing itself to pieces. The Stockholmers are too far off in the North and have achieved something like historical detachment, which deprives them of the temperament to inter-vene in any way, sympathetically and actively, in order to hasten the coming of peace.

This struck me in connection with a little incident that came to my knowledge when I, as much a stranger as they, saw the Three Kings from the East standing frozen and helpless in the streets of Stockholm which made me very curious about them as they were holding each other by the hand, as though they were afraid of losing each other, and how in spite of their turbans and immense woolen cloaks they looked yellow and ill, so far as one could see their faces at all under all that bright-colored guise. Some days later I saw the three pagans again, on a visit to the anarchist Burgomaster of Stockholm, Herr Lindhagen, whose name you may have come across in the newspapers, as the leader of the ... Party. So far as I was able to get to know and form an opinion of the politicians then in Stockholm he was the only idealist among them.

These three were sitting there at table, looking very depressed and recounting the following, each confirming what the other said, and rolling their eyes, their teeth chattering the while.

The first had come from India. His younger brothers had been fetched away from their buffaloes to the barracks, where rifles were pressed into their hands, so that they should shoot at their mortal enemies, the inhabitants of some incredibly distant country, where these enemies were hiding, cowardly and cunning as they were, disturbing other people's peace and trying by violence to stop the progress of civilization.

The second was an Egyptian. His date-palm grove had been felled, the site being the only suitable one for an urgently needed airfield for training pilots. He had been forced to sell his camels, receiving in exchange a rubber-stamped and signed assurance that once the war was brought to a successful conclusion steps would be taken to settle the matter satisfactorily. Meanwhile, since nothing is more beneficial than exercise when one is sorrowful, they had ordered him to fall in and start marching, pressing a rifle into his hand so that he could shoot at his mortal enemies, the inhabitants etc....

The third, a Negro from Ethiopia, had had a still worse time. One could tell by looking at him that he must have been a cheerful, sturdy fellow: under his woolly mop, as curly as a poodle's, he still kept trying to curve his pale lips into an amiably roguish smile. Frau Lindhagen, a pretty young lady who held forbidden wine under his nose and regarded all politicians as ungallant — 'she knew from experience with her husband that being so busy with the welfare of the community left a man no time to think of his wife's welfare, to say nothing of his own' — had won his heart. This black man must have been a very idle fellow who wanted nothing better than just to lie about in the African sun and let it burn him a still deeper black, when they had caught him lounging around and had pressed a rifle into his hand, so that he could shoot at his mortal enemies, etc....

Now one day when they were very weary of their life, these three pagan creatures had seen a star with a long tail on it. That is to say, they had heard that away up there to the North of Europe, in Stockholm, philanthropists had banded together to reconcile all the enemies to each other, and they were going to distribute beautiful presents among all the nations that were poor, so that they should forget their misery. Presents of the following kind: autonomy, equality in the comity of nations, etc.

— a whole list of things, properly drawn up in clauses and points.

That was why the three holy Kings from the East had resolved, each in his own heart, to follow the star with the wonderful tail, pursuing it however far it might lead until they came to the kind gentlemen in Stockholm, who would tell them why their enemies hated the poor Negroes so bitterly that they deprived them of peace and quiet. And what could be done to reconcile them. For this purpose they had brought presents with them, such as would, they knew, be very pleasing to those enemies. American chewing gum, French eau-de-cologne, scented soap, and English safety razors with which one didn't cut one's throat! And they couldn't help wondering if they wouldn't also find something, among the lovely things displayed in the Stockholm shop windows, to rejoice their own hearts and to take home for their families, who were so anxiously waiting for their return.

And on the long, long journey they had made, through many countries of which they couldn't even remember the names and where they had marveled how anyone could learn and understand the languages spoken there, though they had sometimes had a good laugh at the customs and behavior of the inhabitants, they had met as though by appointment, all three having the same purpose and following the same star, which was still shining ahead of them. And so it was natural that they should keep together, if only so as not to get lost in the wide world! So after many months, days, and nights, they had come to Stockholm where, bowing deeply, they asked the people in the street to point out the building where the Stockholm peace conference was being held at the moment. But the people they asked about it did not seem to know anything of such things, shook their heads, and went about their business. One went to an armaments factory, the next to his newspaper office, and the third to a cinema where, according to the posters outside, one could see the latest photographs of an attack — photographs taken during military operations, right there on the battlefield, and so thrillingly true to life that they were quite different from those made far behind the front lines or in Berlin or Paris or New York, which would by no means have satisfied the fastidious public in Sturegatan.

They also heard the people remarking that they were dreamers or something yet worse and to move along, the street being meant for traffic, and the like. Then the three travelers began to fear they had taken too long on the road, for all that they had traveled as fast as their feet would carry them. They were hungry, but all the money they had left was one Maria-Theresa thaler, which they wanted to save for the journey home.

And so they were standing outside the windows of the Stockholm *Social-Democrat*, discussing what to do, when they were struck by a notice in large lettering. 'Leading newspapers in friendly foreign countries are in agreement that our editor, Herr Hjalmar Branting, is Sweden's dominant personality, and we may well congratulate ourselves on being able to provide the cause of world peace with such a champion.' There and then my three friends turned round and hurried off to Branting, who had just become a Minister, with the title 'His Excellency,' and who was in his office from morn to night, wearing a frock coat, with a star on his breast. It was true he had a very big head (so he might have a big brain), and his mustache and his tuft were perhaps even bigger and fiercer, but when they saw the star on his breast they rejoiced and waited patiently until it was their turn, whereupon they presented their case to him in careful detail. Unfortunately Herr Branting happened to be extremely short of time, for he was due at the British Embassy in a few minutes. But since he was good-heartedly simple and direct with simple people he took leave of them kindly, impressing it upon them to be sure, the next time they were in Europe, not to forget to leave their cards with him, and he would bear their case in mind. Well, that was some comfort anyway, for now they knew they had been on the right track, and they were moved to think of the tremendous amount of work he had to cope with besides the endeavors in the cause of peace — all those letters and newspaper-clippings scattered and piled up all over his office, in the wastepaper-basket, on the polar bearskin on the floor and even behind the marble bust of himself — they would never have thought it possible that one single man could get so many letters from the post office, to say nothing of reading them. But now — having grown still hungrier as a result of waiting in the antechamber and listening to Herr Branting's good intentions — they decided to hurry along to Herr Huysmans, to find out some more details about the peace conference before they went home again. Herr Camille Huysmans was yet more simple and direct and said straight out that they had certainly come to the right place, and he showed them the words painted on his door: *Comiti provisoire pour la Paix*, rubbed his hands, and then buried his high forehead in them. Besides, he didn't wear a morning coat and was not yet His Excellency, two points that had, frankly, made them a little shy of Herr Branting. And so they presented their case to Herr Camille Huysmans a good deal more boldly, asking where they could find out who their enemies were and how they could secure the rights that those enemies were trying to deprive them of. And they even thought of asking if they could have a little bit of that autonomy and so forth to take along with them now, so that they could bring it home to their wives and children: for everyone is pleased to have a present brought from abroad, and none more than women whose husbands have been far, far away in Europe — especially if it was something that the other women didn't have! A woman takes pride in her husband of course, only he must do something to deserve it.

But Herr Huysmans shook his head for a long time, and then he did the same thing once more. After that he reached out for a big map mounted on cardboard, all done in very pretty red and green and blue and other colors, and, pointing with his long, thin index finger, showed them that the conference, about which they had heard so many and varied things told in their own countries, would probably be held here, right at the table where they were now standing. And these heathens rejoiced again and suppressed the rumbling in their bellies, lest anyone should think they did not appreciate the seriousness of the matter. But, Herr Huysmans observed, the date when the conference would begin was not yet fixed, he could only say, with a good conscience, without being too much of an optimist, that it would be some time in the near

future. Certain difficulties — although of a minor nature — had
arisen, and there was also the fact that because of the war (the
very subject under discussion) the express trains coming from
France and England were meeting with various obstacles that had
hitherto prevented their arrival, but — he said, giving them a
grave, almost stern glance through his horn-rimmed spectacles —
'C'est la guerre!' And he might as well tell them at once, what
they would doubtless find a little disappointing, that, as one
could see from the map (the very same map done in all those gay,
bright colors), there was no more room on it to paste on still
more peoples, those of Egypt, India, the Indies East and West, the
Sudan, and all the various colonies here and there, since there was
barely enough room for the white race, including the smaller and
more inconsiderable members of it — such as the Albanians,
Georgians, Croats, Slovaks, Estonians, Lithuanians, and the like.

Even supposing that something could be done about that,
there still remained the problem that at the first preparatory
meetings preliminary to the conference it had not been possible
to reach agreement whether the language henceforth to be
regarded as the chief world language, by means of which they
were subsequently to be helped to achieve their rights, should be
French, English, or American. But now they could go home with
easy minds, knowing that they would be sure to be informed in
advance whenever the time was actually approaching.

Well, now my friends lost heart completely, and they were
nearer to tears than to the conference. They could not even bring
themselves to ask whether they might at least be given a few of
the presents that they had heard about, for they did not want to
make things still more difficult for Herr Huysmans. And by now
it was evening and there they were out in the street, with nothing
to eat and no ration-cards either. So they were found by Herr
Lindhagen, who had just lost his mandate at the elections and
who, in his usual way, was quietly whistling to show he didn't
care. He was still Burgomaster, and the Stockholmers refused to
let him go. Herr Carl Lindhagen smiled a bitter smile when he
heard the purpose of their journey and their endeavors and what
they had led to, which they were by now able to recount as if

they had learned it by heart, and then he proposed that to make a start they should come and dine with him. After a hearty meal in a heated room — and from the look of them it was obvious they could do with both — he could see about considering how to settle matters without putting the cart before the horse. And they accepted very, very gladly, and that, then, was where I met them and heard the whole story!

Some days later I asked about them, for the thing had stuck in my mind, and I discovered that Herr Lindhagen had himself got permission from the police — for the Stockholm police are very strict, just like the police in Berlin and Vienna, and they did not permit any more public meetings about peace, because the previous ones had led to disturbances — for the three holy Kings from the East to speak in his own house, to people specially invited — provided there were no children or members of the armed forces present (Note: I am not absolutely certain about the latter point but will make sure) — about their adventures on their travels in all the countries they had passed through, Sweden excepted. But there was to be no talk about peace, mind! the commissioner of police had said with severity. Otherwise there would be difficulties with Herr Branting, who was concerned with the subject very seriously. (Note: I am prejudiced against the police in every country, because they are very brusque when asked questions, especially if asked twice. That is why I won't guarantee the accuracy of remarks made and conclusions drawn on this subject — and besides, as you know, my dear Countess, in the war I got a bullet in my ear and am now rather hard of hearing.)

And now, my dear friend, I wish you a happy New Year, bringing you all that you would wish yourself, and looking forward to a letter from you,

I am, yours sincerely,

Oskar Kokoschka

THE SECOND LETTER FROM THE TRAVELER

Dresden, Spring 1919

The war was over, and I was again passing through Berlin. Foreign bankers, whose governments had speculated on a German victory and who had therefore been severely disappointed, were sitting right there on the doorstep of this revolutionized country. In the country of the defeated one noticed sooner than in the victorious countries that the middle classes had not merely lost their former prosperity — they had lost everything. What surprised me was that after the armistice foreign financiers pressed gold on the German revolutionary government and on the banks, as if they were begging for a favor. With every day that passed the class of people that lived on dividends were becoming worse off in the West. It is a practical necessity to keep money circulating; money must work at any price. So it was necessary that the German people should get to work again, and work even harder than before the war, now that they were no longer lolling about idly in the trenches. Peace-loans would bear interest all the sooner. True, in the world outside the German frontiers great things had been heard of the industry, efficiency, and honesty of the German citizen, who was supposed to be quite a special brand of human being, comparable only to the Japanese, who simply work, without having any personal needs whatsoever. Did any State ever repay foreign loans? No doubt, then, the whole loan business was simply a matter of commissions for the intermediaries. Yet the French are supposed to have a peculiar insistence on investing their money in such loans, even though clear thinking is said to be a national characteristic of theirs. The banker's business strikes me as very like that of the conjuror, who pulls a rabbit out of your hat and spirits the gold watch from your waistcoat pocket. I drew the conclusion that all that was required to make the money market look steady was not a profound knowledge of economic conditions but merely some special flair. After all, the marble edifices of bank buildings were positively shooting up like mushrooms out of the sandy soil of Berlin in those days. People began to gamble on the stock-market, risking whatever was left to them of what they had owned before the war. Everyone went in for speculations, the result of which depended on mere chance. Nobody could follow the rising and falling of stock any more, and even children were already learning to reckon in those dizzily high figures that came with inflation. If you went to the baker for a loaf of bread, which consisted of precious little flour and a very large proportion of all sorts of *ersatz*, you had to be prepared for the price to change hourly and for it to be something, like the stock-exchange rates, that ran into a great many figures. And how did things stand with 'property,' which it is, as we all know, the function of the State to protect? Financiers rushed away from the stock exchange to borrow money, in order to cover their losses and continue gambling. Nobody could ever be sure whether he was a creditor or a debtor. When I went to the bank to pick up my salary from the Dresden Academy, I had to take an attaché-case with me. How many pines and firs must have been felled in the German forests to make the paper to print all that money on! After long queuing up in order to arrive at the counter where I was to receive the packets of dirty banknotes — a deathly weary teller worked it all out with a calculating-machine — I was supposed to count it all, flipping through the notes with a moistened finger-tip. Then I was overcome by such disgust that a painful sore suddenly formed on my lip. Leaving the rest of the money lying there on the counter, I cleared out. The next day my lip was all right again. Autosuggestion?

This got me into a disagreeable situation. I knew that both at the Academy and in my apartment, in the Pavilion in the Grosse Garten, there were fretful creditors waiting for their money. Any delay might have the most serious consequence. There I sat on a seat in the gardens, as it were at a crossroads, undecided whether to go on or to turn back. Then I saw a loaded cart coming along the path, drawn by white cows. This somewhat distracted me. With all the dignity of sacred Indian cows they were hauling a city garbage cart. How tranquilly and surely they set one foot before the other, with no trace of haste! The wheels grated in the sand. How reposeful, I thought — what a contrast to human hustle and bustle! There's a lesson in that, I thought to myself. It was not unusual to see cows pulling a city garbage cart here in the capital of a province, for the horses had gone in the war and had not yet been replaced. No sooner had the cart passed out of sight than a second came along, and after it a third. The fever of speculation, which had infected everyone by then, suggested the idea of betting with myself. If as many as seven garbage carts should go by, then my financial troubles would somehow settle themselves. The word 'somehow' had become fashionable during the war and was still the quintessence of wisdom, in politics as well as in everything else. Tensely I waited. After the fourth cart there came the fifth, then yet another, and finally — sure enough — the seventh came too, like a lucky number turning up in the lottery. But now there mustn't be any more of them if I was to go on believing my seven an auspicious omen. *Cherchez la femme pour corriger la fortune!*

Two feminine hands were laid over my eyes from behind me. A youthful feminine voice said I was to guess who it was. 'Fortuna!' I exclaimed. I was made to promise not to look round, and as a reward she would come to luncheon with me. I heard her unhitch the reins and jump into the saddle, and when the sound of hooves could no longer be heard on the riding path, I stood up. First I went to the flower shop that I patronized, where I had credit, and ordered orchids for the luncheon table. I was no longer worried about my creditors. Hadn't Fortune herself set the wheel spinning? No sooner had I opened the door of my apartment when I saw that almighty art dealer from Berlin, Paul Cassirer, waiting in my living room. He had come to offer me a big contract, the only one I ever signed. All my signature pledged

me to was to paint better than my contemporaries. Now I had no
more worries. But I did ask him first to satisfy the creditors
waiting outside in the hall. I had become a gambler, and evidently
I was able to make everything I wished come true. My life was
the stake and work was the currency, since money had lost its
value.

I had a large circle of female admirers whom I once asked to
the Opera, all of them at the same time, without any one of them
knowing anything of the others. I was the only person who
knew where each of the fair creatures sat, directing a yearning
gaze at me where I sat in my box. It was *Don Giovanni* they were
doing that evening, my favorite Mozart opera. Thanks to
Mozart's genius the world of the passions — of the sublimest and
of the basest — became as transparent for me as the world of the
stars. *Don Giovanni* is all Nature, due to the dematerialization of
the instincts. For a long time afterwards those harmonies echoed
in my mind like the sound of a miniature harp that I bought in
an antique shop and tucked into the décolleté of a lady who was
in love with me, so that the exquisite notes should be audible
only to me. For what I sought from the beating hearts of women
was the answer to the fire blazing in me, like a child laying its ear
against its mother's heart.

> One, again one, when I count the beats,
> My heart slips into the beat of yours.
> One, two! Sweet Orpheus sighs his life away!

At this time I was writing a play, 'Orpheus,' which I had
thought out in the Russian military hospital in memory of the
woman to whom I used to send mimosa every day when she was
in Nice. All that still linked me with that woman was the
necklace of red glass beads. This evening the necklace was
glimmering round the neck of another woman in the darkened
auditorium. As for what she whispered to me then and what I
asked her — let Orpheus and Euridice, up there on the stage
reveal it to everyone! Word for word I committed it to paper
from memory, in those days in Dresden. 'O crudele . . .' This is

the greatest artistic audacity of all, an anticipation of the euphoria that tore Mozart's heart to shreds when he had a hemorrhage! During this staccato aria I had to ask my fair neighbor, whose face was all this time concealed behind a mask, to lend me her lace handkerchief. Her eyes glittered like stones! In the previous interval I had heard her rather childish voice, like a python's, trying to coo like a turtle-dove! It would have been almost ridiculous if it had not been so exciting — this marble form, this Juno in the black velvet dress with the deep décolleté, whose voice was suddenly shrill as that of a young girl awakening. Was her voice too high-pitched? Was she covering up a speech defect? She was irresolutely fingering a little figurine of polished bone, a fossil that I had pressed into her hand as a keepsake. At that time I liked giving little presents as souvenirs to people who were nice to me. It was the time when I was still afraid of people. She let me keep her handkerchief, for it was red with my blood. I even had to leave the opera house, because I could not suppress the attack of coughing. True, the lance-wound in my lung was healed up now, but Mozart's aria had been too much for me. The lady had some time to spare, saw me home, because I was unsteady on my feet, and stayed for a little while. So I tried to capture her features with my pencil, after she had removed her mask. Her name was Gela. 'What have you been making of me there?' she sighed faintly, after looking at the drawing. 'This is the very image of my daughter, whose existence I have hitherto concealed from you. Here is a confession I will make to you. I scarcely know you — but it's a real relief to me to be able to speak out frankly and admit that today I cut off the girl's long hair with a pair of scissors, because I was jealous. Suddenly it horrified me to see my own flesh and blood, this child of mine, almost a woman already. My daughter is precocious, whereas my own nature was slow to awaken.' Whatever the incomprehensible thing about this woman was, there it was again when she closed her lips, and it seemed instantly to make her unlike the drawing. No! I hadn't gone wrong with the likeness! It was what she was like when she was talking. The lady had a certain charm! I would even go so far as to say there was something faintly hypnotic emanating from her, which I don't really think she was aware of. There was always some mystery about her, and no less so when, the next day, together we looked at her sculpture — outsize fragments of ovoid or conical symbols, monotonously repetitive. The chilly garage where she took me was stacked with them. Nature sometimes goes in for such instances of abnormal productivity, and Frau Gela told me how she had been overcome by the sculptor's urge positively overnight. Like dreaming one has been kicked by a nightmare.

This could not be the whole of her story. But I couldn't work out for myself what exactly it could be, although I had now known her for some time. As if one got anywhere by saying that this person or that looks like this or like that, as though a human being were no more than a stage-figure! People change right in front of one's eye as soon as one has any intimate relationship with them. So long as one has the Mozartian order ringing in one's ears one can also understand what is meant by saying that mathematics is frozen music, with numbers standing for vibrations. Emotions, passions, breathed into mathematically calculable vibrations, human worlds in the darkened theater where the touch of the conductor's baton causes them to ring out and become a language that everyone understands as if it were his own, whereas in ordinary life nobody really knows what anybody else is talking about. Don Giovanni, Donna Anna, Don Ottavio, Donna Elvira, Leporello, Zerlina, the Commendatore and Masetto — bright glass spheres moving about, in and out between each other, worlds resounding in infinite space, worlds great and small, each a star in its ordained orbit. By knowing how to set them vibrating the magus Mozart could make them here attract each other, simply and sweetly, there tragically repel each other, all in their courses forming one great unison that becomes life itself, Nature itself. Who can ever adequately thank that purest of all artists for the fact that so long as his work echoes in our ears it cannot but seem to us the interpretation of some more sublime happening?

Outside it was still intensely cold. Surely spring must come some day, perhaps suddenly overnight?

The next time I met Frau Gela the snow was melting on the trees, and towards noon a warm shower from the green buds sprinkled down on the delighted pedestrians. Then they hurried into church and I continued on my way, along the avenue of steaming trees leading to the Academy. It was Sunday. I was all alone in the big, gloomy building, because this State-run Academy was closed on Sundays and holidays. I thought I heard someone whistle, but there was no one to be seen on the Brühl Terrace. The broad river, the Elbe, swept thunderingly under the arches of the Augustus Bridge. And anyway how could anyone have heard a sound through the closed windows! In the distance, on the farther bank, there were two people now approaching the bridge. One — a man, as I could now see — stopped and then walked off. The other was a woman — Frau Gela! I recognized her only when she had climbed the many steps and stood outside the main door. I opened the window and leaned out. She set down the withy basket she was carrying, with a cloth over it, which must have become too heavy for her. With her free hand she waved to me when she saw me at the window. She whistled. I should always know her by that special whistle of hers. Now I could hear it distinctly, and I was amazed at how a little while earlier I had imagined I heard the very same sound, when she was still on the other side of the river! I threw the key down to her.

'What put it into your head to come and whistle under my window, when you would surely expect to find no one here on a Sunday?' I asked when she entered my room. She began to stammer again in embarrassment. 'I suppose I'd better go away again?' But instead of going away she told me a rambling, disjointed story about having torn her fingernail and how she could not find the scissors with which she had cut off her daughter's hair. 'You know, I always use those scissors for marking the eyes of my clay figures — it's the last touch I give them, and that's why I always look forward to it! But yesterday I couldn't find the scissors anywhere. By the time I had ransacked the whole house it was dark, and I was quite frantic from having been hunting so long. I was frozen, too, because the fire had gone out in the meantime. As a matter of fact there were still some logs on the floor, I hurt my foot on them, but I was simply too tired to pick them up and put them in the stove. And I didn't touch the supper waiting on the table for me. When I was undressing I just sat down on the edge of the bed and cried, I was so tired — I simply ached. And do you know what I suddenly noticed? There on the edge of the table was the little Maya figurine that you gave me at the opera, glinting at me spitefully, looking at me almost as if it were human, as if it meant to jump right in my face. It's a grasshopper, isn't it? I took the little bone thing and clutched it tenderly under the bedclothes, and I couldn't go to sleep for a long time, I was so looking forward to this Sunday morning, because now nothing more — no searching high and low, no excuse of any kind — would keep me from seeing you. But what I haven't told you is that the scissors with which I cut off my daughter's hair have been at the bottom of the Elbe for days. I threw them in the water. Actually that was all I came for — to tell you that.'

She had flushed again as she talked, and she reached out for the basket as though for some pretext. I wondered what was hidden in that basket. She raised the cover, and at once I began to feel uneasy. How else can I put it except that this is what pythons are like to the touch — desires beginning to stir and suddenly driving one crazy, like something pushing from inside one, like stagnant water being stirred, all scum and decomposing matter. What she took out of the basket and unwrapped — it had been wrapped in wet rags — was an abortion in clay that I'd have liked to fling straight out of the window, into the river. It was a sort of idol. It even had some human hair — perhaps some of Frau Gela's daughter's hair? — glued to its forehead. 'Keep that thing away from me! It looks like an embryo!' I screamed. Her eyebrows, which were actually too regularly modeled, were unpleasantly near to me, so that I seemed to be seeing each individual hair growing out of the human skin. On the other hand, her eyes seemed to be so far away from me that I could not decide what color they were. Her mouth was shut, but her nostrils were flaring so that it seemed to me I could watch the red corpuscles circulating and I was strongly aware of the smell of blood. Her arms and neck, and her body, wherever it was bare, swelled up as though from a tourniquet. I felt a hunter's temptation, but I had no knife in my hand, so just let her keep on talking, or else something'll happen! Only she mustn't slip off the chair in front of me and grab at me and pull me down to the floor with her! I resisted as obstinately as a mule that the mule driver uses the last ounce of his strength to pull by the reins across a dangerous place against the beast's will. But this woman would go together with the animal, rolling down into a bottomless abyss! Frau Gela was still talking in that excessively high voice of hers.

'. . . and in that same sleepless night, which didn't leave me tired — on the contrary, it put new life into me because the weather suddenly turned warmer — I got another attack of my "nerves". Hugging my bed like that, very wide awake and all alone, while the whole town is asleep, I feel I could give life to a whole generation of new beings. When it was dawn — and I'm telling you this now because this is just the way it happened to me, although really I ought to be ashamed. . .' She wore no gloves and now she slapped the doll with her bare fingers. In the end she packed it up in the basket again, as though someone she had been trying to sell it to had scorned it. And once again she began cooing like a dove: 'Are you listening to me? As I was combing my hair I saw to my horror that it was full of lice! What I would have liked best would have been to cut it all off — my own this time! After a while I was free of them and a few days later I dared to go out again, but this involuntary isolation explains why I didn't come to see you before, although I kept on thinking of you all the time. The surprise in the basket I made specially for you. I simply had to combine some of the feeling of gestation that I had within myself with the earth, and that's how I made you a child of clay. Don't you like it? But this is what a baby looks like when it's just come into the world. Exactly like this, no different at all.'

'I don't like babies!' I shouted. I was extremely irritated and trying to escape from this insinuation, which was slowly tightening around my guts like a vice. 'Do you often become a mother in this way?' I asked sneeringly. She reflected. 'I must admit, some years ago friends invited me to stay at their place in the country, and in the morning the ground was covered with plump quails together with their young, so that the servants were able to catch them with their bare hands, and nobody knew what to do with so many, it was as if they'd come down in showers from the stars!' 'Let's go out into the open air!' I gasped. We went out into the street. I asked her point blank: 'Frau Gela, are you trying to make me believe the quails in the fields were as much the result of your fertility as the lice in your hair?"... just like the child of clay,' the woman said decisively, at the same time pointing to the steps of the Brühl Terrace, where there were always a lot of children playing when it was sunny. But today, oddly enough, they were all girls, lots of girls, heaven knows how many girls on those endless steps. They were all playing with dolls or babbling to babies that they cradled in their arms or were rocking in prams. By now it had become very hot, the first hot day of spring. The electricity in the air had such a stimulating effect even on the trees that those that were in bud burst into leaf as though something invisible were passing by, touching them with green fingers, tree after tree. Frau Gela took me by the hand as though she must guide me, and as we walked she kept pointing to benches where young women, all of whom seemed to be pregnant, were exposing their swollen bellies to the blaze of the sun — seemingly in a rather absentminded way, as though their consciousness were not entirely with them, but to some extent already in the unborn creatures stirring within them. My disgust revived. 'All men need some time to get used to being fathers' my companion remarked in a matter-of-fact tone. 'You have brought a child into the world, haven't you?' I did not hear what she answered. Exhausted, I leaned against the wall of a brick building where all the windows were barred right up to the top story. I wouldn't have minded being inside in the dark coolness, I was so tormented by the brilliant rays of sunlight reflecting from everything. When she whispered in my ear: 'There's yet another thing you may as well learn from me, although you won't like it. Just think about the fact that a being who is pregnant with another must always remain somehow unknown to a man. Abstruse, perhaps? Weren't you secretly amused about my lice and quails and the day baby, as well as about my sculpture in the garage? But don't your logical conclusions strike you as equally abstruse? Being a man, you claim to have made life spiritual; just try bringing a child into the world with your mind! Look up at that window: up there in the fourth story a prisoner used to be housed, whom I met only once, the way servant girls become pregnant by some soldier on leave, with whom they perhaps spend only one night on a park bench. Before that I was in correspondence with him. Friends of us both had asked me to intervene on his behalf with a certain personage in a high position. One single time I obtained permission to visit 'my protégé in his cell, without anyone else present. That time I gave myself to him. I couldn't do anything else for Him, for my intervention turned out to be useless. That's all I know about it. Perhaps he was a spy. Nor did I ever discover exactly when he was executed. But he is the father of my daughter. You remind me of that prisoner.'

Oh, I'll kill this woman if she dares to get closer to me! . . so it's that well-known law of Nature! The eternal cycle of life and death. Is that supposed to make me fall flat on my face?' I said in the most off-hand tone, although I was feeling very far from comfortable. She simply laughed at me.

'Gela, you're so entirely filled with the lusts of the flesh that I can't help regarding you as simply an out-and-out egoist. Look, a father's relation to his child is much more moral than your idea of motherhood. A charming goddess of destiny, I must say, who produces lice, quails, and sexual symbols. Ha ha ha! Oh, it's flying in the face of all logic and tradition to think of playing with us men as with dolls!'

But what is it that makes you dread me all the time as if I were your destiny? You must dare to turn the cards up, to look a woman in the eye!'

I urged her to walk on. It would be the last straw if through my doing this creature, too, were to get a swollen belly, like the servant girls on the park benches, shoving the crumbs of their meals into their mouths, scooping it up out of the bowls they had brought with them or bolting whatever they had there wrapped in newspaper, while nausea seized them as they swallowed, so that they vomited it all up again. Away from all this greenery! Perhaps there is more shadow there among the houses, there by the church of St. Elias, where now a string of carriages was drawing up. Descending from the first carriage were white-clad girls with lilies in their hands. Perhaps there was a service going on? First Communion? As a child I too used to go to church. . . Gela! When I was small I used to sing in the church choir! Once, during the Canon of the Mass, I got stuck in a solo, for the Assumption of the Virgin Mary painted on the ceiling suddenly seemed to be real and actually happening. My voice was just breaking.'

Gela smiled like a little girl. 'Didn't you make that up just to distract you from your instincts? Even that's a sin in thought, else it would be much too natural for a man to think it. It gives men a brainstorm. That's just as easy to suffer from as sunstroke or snake-bite. Isn't there something in St. Mark's Gospel about "taking up serpents?"' In her eagerness to convert me she was dancing on her toes, which looked comical, and yet at the same time it fascinated me. She clenched her teeth and made a hissing sound, not like her usual whistling. What was the use of trying to argue rationally against the evil spirit that seemed to have taken possession of this woman? I preferred to watch what was going on outside St. Elias's.

Here was another carriage, from which soldiers in field-gray came hopping out, carrying music-stands and musical instruments, and there was even a Turkish jingle too. They took up positions in a circle, set up their handy little music-stands, the uniformed conductor raised his baton, and someone tore open the door of the last carriage to arrive. A bride and bridegroom got out and walked up the steps, the bride white as a swan, her train carried by bridesmaids, and the bridegroom removed his glittering eagled helmet. The aged parents were already waiting outside the church door and joined the couple's hands. Before the band had finished playing the wedding march from *Lohengrin* I too began to go crazy, for everything was spinning like a top before my eyes. 'I'm fainting! I must cool my head, else my brain will congeal!' The sun flashed from the crest of the helmet, the cuirassier stabbed my eyes like a horsefly. I could no longer see where I was going.

'There is a garden gate open in front of you. Inside there's a cool marble bench,' Frau Gela said maternally. She almost carried me into the garden. No, I won't enter a strange house — not at any price!' Nevertheless I was greedily drawing into my lungs the balmy coolness of some strong scent of flowers. 'At last you are giving way to a natural instinct,' she said softly. I opened my eyes, at first unable to see anything but a mass of white stars, fluttering in hundreds of neatly pruned whorls. Bloom upon bloom they hung there, waiting for the moment when the air would stir, making them tremble and fertilize each other. All these flowers opening themselves to the wind, to the bees that would carry pollen into their calices! I had sunstroke! Enough of this woman Gela! Was she trying to make a fool of me now with these fairy tales about the glass forest? My head bored into the darkest corner of the marble niche, but I could no longer find any way out of the maze into which this woman had lured me. Pull yourself together, for God's sake!

This house is not strange to you at all, and the garden so full of pear trees was, as you ought to know, laid out in the eighteenth century by a French emigrant, an amateur gardener. Apparently you have never looked at your own garden properly! just as you don't look at me either! Am I not seductively beautiful? just a little while longer and you will take your pleasure with me, you will call me Angelica, your angel. It will happen soon, indeed today, now, for tomorrow I am leaving for America. I am going to marry a merchant. Darling, come with me!'

The wall I was leaning my head against now yielded: all this time I had not known it was the door of my apartment. I should never have thought that this would happen where I lived. As I lay on the carpet with her, her impenetrable mask fell away. Was it to this end that I had struggled through the story of my life, enduring hardship, surviving error, only in order to be stabbed in the back with a hunting-knife? Now I was nothing more than a lay-figure set in motion by the sexual urge, a wounded animal, without a will of my own! The male of the praying mantis, just waiting to celebrate marriage with her in her inexorable arms.

Afterwards Frau Gela rose, pulled up her black stockings, looked vaguely for a record to put on the gramophone, and said casually: 'It is written in the cards that you dare not turn up. The cards say that tomorrow a rival in your own field will cross your path.' 'A merchant, a rival? That's a bit much!' I murmured, too exhausted to move, yet feeling more secure here in my own apartment, where I could hide as in the jungle. Wounded, yes, but not wounded as is a hunted animal. The gramophone was whining: 'The girl I left behind me . . .' and Frau Gela said: 'What ideas you have! Tomorrow I shall say to him: "Put on your smartest clothes and assign your name to me, my husband! Henceforth your wife belongs to you alone. To make up for it, she wishes to be kept in comfort."'

THE THIRD LETTER FROM THE TRAVELER

Dresden, 1920

I shall now return to a subject that probably can't be of much interest to anyone else. For me, in those days, in Germany just after the First World War, it was a matter of to be or not to be. Anyone who likes can skip these pages, and we'll still be good friends. I certainly couldn't have coped with it on my own, without Reserl. Since more time has passed, it strikes me as pretty absurd, come to think of it, that in Saxony and Prussia there should have been a regulation that anyone who took employment under the Government automatically became a German citizen. At least one thing is certain: that I was born in the old Austro-Hungarian Empire, even if it has meanwhile vanished from the map. The idea that just because of some government regulation I should have to become something that I wasn't struck me as just as impossible as jumping out of my Oman skin. Afterwards one learned to see such things in their proper perspective.

Perhaps I can talk the Deputy Minister into making an exception? It's the exception that proves the rule: which says all one needs to know about rules. Equality for all was just on the way in Germany at that time; nobody was supposed to take it seriously. I needed adequate grounds. But just as I was about to seize hold of an idea looming at the back of my mind, Reserl came tiptoeing in. Patience! Just patience! Haven't I just said I was waiting for Reserl? One glance at me told her — although I was lying on the sofa with my eyes shut — that I was by no means satisfied with the world as it was, indeed, that it seemed to me in urgent need of reform. What she said was that if one started the day by not liking the world the way God created it and saw that it was good, where *was* one to begin? One would have to go back and back — if this were not so, if that were different, then the white swan wouldn't have grown dirty either! 'Enough of all this theorizing!' I exclaimed. The world looks rotten, I have my reasons, which annoy me, and I'm not going to have anyone arguing me out of them. But I shall here spare the reader an account of them. One of the reasons was certainly this: Reserl was late. Fortunately she will never know what it means to wait for someone. It was too bad, I had had to wait so long that I had forgotten what I was going to ask her, and now there was no time left. I had to rush! Hat! Stick! By force of habit more than anything else, I lingered for a while, watching her flicking round with the feather duster, although even with a magnifying-glass one couldn't have found so much as a grain of dust on, for instance, the Bohemian glass paperweight; it was one of those in which a snowstorm softly rose and descended again if one turned the sphere in one's hand. In her subconscious (the very word makes me quite frantic) — all right then, in her heart, I say (another word, though frankly a little too poetical for the dreariness of everyday use), there must always be something important going on, something that I was wholesomely shy of. This too was why, as soon as Reserl was anywhere about, everything seemed to move to a different rhythm for me, in a livelier way, and I forgot about time, which creeps into life like a thief. In my ivory tower there was no such thing as time. I never discovered how Reserl brought this about, although for a whole year I had the opportunity of studying her ways. Taking me by the hand, she led me out of the labyrinth of the world, out of time and space, back to myself.

But the girl couldn't be taken hold of the way one grasps something that substantially stands for what it wants to be taken for: a thing, an affair, a human being. I pulled my watch out. I ought to have left long ago. But everything was upside down out there. There was a general strike, there were no trams running, and there was some shooting too. There were beggars all over the place, and in general people were more pushing, in fact rude and dangerous. Here I was in safety, for Reserl was accustomed to get rid of unwanted visitors by saying: 'The Captain's in bed, thinking.' She said it so demurely, and the violet eyes of this scarcely eighteen-year-old girl shone with just the sort of clear conscience one would like to have oneself, waking up early in the morning.

Suddenly I remembered this tiresome business with the Deputy Minister. Before going out I must expound it to Reserl, who had a clear brain. Actually Reserl's name was Hulda, and she was a Saxon, a maid in the household of the director of the gallery — I lodged with him in the pavilion in the Grosse Garten in Dresden. How well that frilly cap looked on her corn-yellow hair! And the little batiste apron, so fresh and trim, also came from the black market. I needed a little comfort, the illusion of peace! Was this really peacetime? The war was over, that was all. These things, and the black silk stockings from Paris, she wore only when waiting on me. In Germany at that time there was a shortage of the barest necessities. When I bought these things from the ex-soldier at the corner of the street, I did not ask where they came from, whether Venus had been indulgent or Mars had been harsh. Silver shuts the mouth, iron opens it, they say.

The matter I had to see the Deputy Minister about no longer seemed urgent. It would settle itself 'somehow' to the advantage or disadvantage of the German State, a citizen of which I did not wish to be. After all, the State is there to protect people. Order must prevail. What's the use of an umbrella if you, we, left it behind and it begins to rain?

'As I was going to say, they'll make an exception in my case, it's simply the very least one can expect of the German State, which is obviously coming unglued, isn't it?' I said to Reserl, who agreed with me entirely and went still further. For, as she said, if there hadn't been a policeman to be seen in the street for days, didn't that prove that the State was already as dead as a doornail? A State without police! She couldn't help laughing. But she did not waste any more words on the matter, for she was obviously bursting to tell me a story of the kind she always had a store of after she'd been shopping.

I capitulated, laid aside hat and stick, and lay down on the sofa. 'Well?' I said encouragingly. There was no sense in pursuing the boring business any further, after all, and I was eager to discover whither Reserl would lead me, with dancing steps light as a feather. It was only for a little while, for she never had much time, but for as long as it lasted I was spirited away out of the melancholy world of everyday. It was a time when everything was going wrong, an interregnum, with rioting and disorder everywhere, and — in the bargain — the pathetic misery on all sides, which was continually spreading. Is there any sense in racking one's brains when things are wrong instead of right? In her little head the chambermaid had the means of putting it all right in an instant. The lever that also sets in motion the games that children and primitive peoples play was waiting for the touch to release it. Reserl began her story.

The marketplace in Dresden, where no peasant had dared to bring a fully loaded cart for months past, was suddenly over-flowing with all the good things that one couldn't even remember anymore. At first I couldn't quite get the hang of it when, as with a wave of a magician's wand, that celebrated thinker and philosopher Rabindranath Tagore took on fairy-tale form, becoming a figure akin to Ali Baba and his Forty Thieves. 'Who? What?' I asked, amazed. Irreverence, which at that time one ought to have been used to, is something that always gives me a feeling rather like that of suddenly stepping barefoot on a pin. 'Surely you don't mean the Indian sage that everyone raves about as the Great Master?' She put her hand on her heart, as though she herself could not have imagined such an alarming development in the situation, but then she repeated gravely: 'The gendarmerie took the Indian sage away from the market.' 'How distressing for him and the world!' I said, but even at that moment I was thinking rather maliciously that the final outcome of the situation conjured up by Reserl, which was still in the balance, depended solely on her. How would she manage to liberate the great man from this calamitous situation, having put him at the mercy of destiny like a helpless infant in its cradle pushed out on the ocean! Of course, she had picked up his name from Count Keyserling's book, which had been gathering dust in a bookshop window since people had no more time for boring themselves with such long travel books.

I asked her how she had recognized the philosopher, tactfully passing over the fact that she herself had said there was no longer a single policeman to be seen in the streets of Dresden. Whenever Reserl chose, they were there, and there indeed they were when the fisticuffs among the market people approached its climax. 'How did I know it was him? Go on, there's nobody else who never goes and gets a haircut when he needs it!' I myself hated going to the barber when I needed to.

It seemed that I needed to do so now: her searching gaze told me as much. Even in the swirl of people in the market it was easy to recognize the philosopher by his long, silvery-white hair hanging down to his shoulders, even without his nightshirt, which was white, even if no longer quite clean. Only an Indian goes about Dresden like that in broad daylight, as if in a kindergarten. I had myself seen such a photograph of the venerable Sage in the store window, and Reserl's sharp eyes didn't miss much. 'But what made the police intervene? They're never around when they're wanted.' 'He was trying to get away with a bagful of fresh onions.' 'Go on — fresh onions?' Anyone who was there at the time and knows what it was like vainly scouring the market even for old potatoes will stop reading at this point, for even old potatoes were obtainable only on showing one's ration-card. 'What else does a vegetarian live on but vegetables? Before the war there used to be vegetarians in Dresden, too, they lived out in Hellerau and slept in the open air, and, as if that wasn't enough for them, they went in for nudism as well! An Indian won't think of touching old potatoes. They say the peasants have plenty of new potatoes hidden behind their baskets, only we never get any of them. Naming no names — some of us know a thing or two about the market-women.' 'There's some truth in every rumor,' I said, 'although for my own part I shall save your face by assuring everyone that all you've told me exists only in your own little head.' At this she let her little head droop, because I couldn't help laughing. 'You mean the old man didn't pay?' It was a pleasure to put the little creature's ready wit to the test. 'How could he, without any valuta?' 'Valuta?' 'How do you think we're going to build up our national economy again without valuta from the foreigners who come and cart away our stuff?' To an economist this may sound surprising, but then the layman can never follow a specialist's thought processes either. Reserl did not continue this line of thought. She was already describing the shouting among the peasants, who were left with only the snake-man's nightshirt in their hands.' 'Watch this!' he exclaimed, slid down into his shirt and then out of it and out of the silly peasants' grasp, only to run — with his silvery hair waving in the wind, his long beard like that of God the Father, and for the rest practically naked — into the hands of the law, which came up on the double from the far side of the park. The police arrested him because all he had on under his shirt was — not pants only a loin-cloth. You can't have that sort of thing going on in a Christian country! 'The man is causing a breach of the peace,' the superintendent said. I cast a speaking glance at the crucifix on the wall, and Reserl glanced at it briefly. 'Foreigners aren't Christians!' Without trying to make myself out any better than I am, I must insist that for me logic is logic. 'What happened to him then at the police station?' I asked. 'He took such a fancy to it there that he wanted to tell the superintendent's fortune from the cards. Don't you think that was bold of him, seeing he'd never tried it before on anyone, least of all on the superintendent?' the girl went on. 'Being asked whether anything he had prophesied had come true yet, he thought for a moment. Then he said he could remember many things that had come about the way he had foretold. But one thing he would never forget was this trip to Dresden. Every time he sees a ticket collector he's reminded of it. Thanks to his clair-voyant gift, he escaped the fate of becoming the victim of a crash when a train ran off the rails. They objected that no train had gone off the rails recently. Just so, he said, because it stopped when he pulled the emergency cord, which he did when he saw the ticket collector coming. Then everyone congratulated him on having prevented a great disaster and perhaps having saved many people's lives. He was too modest to accept their congratulations. But even an empty train that stays all in one piece is better than one that's smashed up. So the market people had to remind the superintendent about the onions. Oh yes, the onions! The very thought of it made the Indian's heart grow heavy, so heavy that he was almost in tears. All he could say was that he wished he were at home, he was so homesick for far-off India, whenever anyone mentioned onions. In India everyone could conjure them, and anything else they wished for, out of the air, if they only concentrated hard enough. "How is it done?" the peasants asked. "Sit you all down, my friends, and be still. I will give you a demonstration of how it is done, so that each of you can repeat it from the beginning to the end." And he asked for a sheet of paper and a bottle of ink, which he poured out on the paper. Then he made the people search him, to be sure he had no secret pockets on him, for — he said — he did not work by trickery. Then he raised his hands like a hypnotist and looked at them all hard, out of his black eyes. "These are onions, as no one can fail to see who understands anything about art. Only a most unedu-cated person can see on this paper nothing but an ink blot!" Because no one wanted to put himself in the wrong, all the peasants looked at the paper and saw onions on it and wagged their heads. Then they divided the sheet of paper among them, tearing it into as many little pieces as were needed to go round, and they let the Indian go.' I said gravely to Reserl: 'My dear child, this is a problem with which humanity has been occupied from the earliest times: how to turn water into wine and stones into bread. What a good thing that our Indian is no ecclesiastic. Else this story of yours about the onions would have gotten him into hot water.' Reserl looked penitent and said in a low voice: 'What can be done about it now?' 'That's all right! We won't let the story go any further. After all, it's no way to treat a great man by going around saying he pinched a bag of onions. A great man — it's not an expression I use often, and if I do, then where it's appropriate, but if I say it, I mean it.' I gave her a kiss, an entirely brotherly one, but all the same she blushed up to her little ears, and I looked at the clock. 'Anyway, there are no thieves where there's nothing to steal.' I turned away, preparing to go out, while she looked woefully at the cold fireplace and up at the sky whence the hero of antiquity had brought stolen fire for mankind. There was neither coal nor wood in the house for the rest of the winter, and I was supposed to go and put in a word with the merchant. What with my interview at the Ministry, I forgot all about it.

On the main staircase, after my interview with the Deputy Minister, I heard a raucous yelling from the street. Two charwomen were looking out of a window, and I went and joined them. They at once asked me for the stub of my cigarette, which was something more valuable than money. The official had given me the cigarette. I asked the women if it was unsafe to go out now, with the unrest in the street. 'A riot?' Automatically they repeated 'Riot?', as though they hadn't heard rightly. One put her hand to her ear, because everyone expects a foreigner, who speaks in such an incomprehensible way, to shout as if one were deaf 'You are a foreigner, sir? A financier, I dare say? Waiting for the Government like the rest of them, eh? She was making fun of me, so I said sternly that the State must be set on its feet again first, something of which there was absolutely no sign. That was neither a charwoman's business nor mine, but the business of those who were marching along the street down there, said the younger of the two hags. I was cross with the blue sky because it lured people into the streets, to move in excited groups towards the Elbe bridge that I too had to cross if I was to get home. Did the charwomen know any more about what was going on? At that they seemed to shrink to a still smaller size, and instead of answering my question, they pretended to be entirely occupied with their pails and brooms. I had to repeat the question. Their mocking answer was: 'Want to know what's going on, do you? It's a revolution, of course! Being as you're a foreigner, sir, can you tell us if it's long till twelve o'clock? Since they melted down the bells, nobody knows what hour has struck.' 'Twelve fifteen, by the railway station clock, my good woman.' 'Quarter past twelve, did you say?' they both squeaked resentfully and would have spilled their pails at my feet if I hadn't been quick to jump back. 'Now the Deputy Minister will resign too, so there's no sense waiting to see if any of these foreigners'll throw away a cigarette butt. Eh, what a life! Nothing but toiling and trouble!' Without paying any more attention to me, the two women went on their way, not without spelling out the announcement on the door, which had not been affixed there when I came in. What it said was: 'Unless order is instantly restored in Germany there will be no foreign loans.'

Incidentally, the Deputy Minister had not made the impression of being about to run for it, for he still had a lot of engagements ahead of him, as I could see from his notepad, and in the Ministry there were back-stairs, and there's plenty that goes on there that the public never hears about. This official was one of the old school in whose hands government still lay, provisionally, because there was no State. In confidence he had hinted to me that they were now being compelled to put out feelers towards the professional revolutionaries. These latter had their own sources of supply as regards foodstuffs, which is the sort of thing that gives a professional revolutionary a start over other people. The official sighed, but consoled himself by saying that once order was restored foreign loans would simply come pouring in, floods of them.

Whether I liked it or not, I had to cross the Augustus Bridge, and I walked the lighter of foot in order to be the quicker past whatever I could not help seeing there. Human beings must always suffer or watch others suffering. It's a scandal: afterwards one goes about one's daily business as if nothing had happened. One washes one's hands like Pilate. So I too yielded to curiosity and peered like the other people and was able to say that I too had been there. On both sides of the Elbe there were crowds of former front-line soldiers, who had nothing better to do with their rifles, now that the war was lost, than to shoot at a man whom they had first thrown into the water from the Augustus Bridge. At other times there were swans swimming there. He is said to have been a Minister. Whenever he came near to one bank or the other, a salvo stopped him from climbing out of the water. This got the people worked up, and no one any longer gave a thought to the question of what political party the victim belonged to. What wouldn't I now have given for a tram, for something was rising up within me. I wanted to get home. At that time any humane appeal not to play cat-and-mouse with a man who was drowning anyway would have been futile; one had to take care not to attract any attention to oneself. I have no recollection of how I got home, threw myself fully dressed on my bed, and somehow got over the disgusting episode. For a long time I kept seeing the water closing over the swimmer's head.

A drop of fresh blood stained the breast of the girl bending over me. Reserl had there incised my initials, O.K.! Highly irritated, I demanded an explanation. She had done it for fun, she said, with a red-hot needle, because I didn't come home. Among all the notions she had had this was one that I did not like, and now least of all. I tried to send her away, but she stayed. She seemed to be listening to something, and now I thought I could hear it too. It was like a tap dripping when it hasn't been turned off properly: drip, drop. With a splintering crash something made of glass fell to the floor. Instantly I glanced up at the big Venetian glass chandelier. That was still hanging from the ceiling, safe and sound! Was something wrong? The violet eyes of a second Käthchen of Heilbronn, disguised as a chambermaid, staunchly following the knight on all his adventures, were gazing at me bravely. All I had meant to say remained unsaid. Who can explain what was going on there! I could not turn my eyes away, I was inclined to disbelieve what I saw before me. But this didn't get me any nearer to the truth. It was a fact, there were little pools forming on the floor, as though the waters of a subterranean spring were rising through the boards. Our shoes were becoming wet, and the water went on rising. We climbed on to chairs. The force of the flood was now threatening to overturn us, and there were cracks appearing in the walls. How long does such a moment last? In a state of panic one loses all sense of time. Through the cracks I could see far out into stormy waves wildly whipped by the wind, a tide racing down on me. White horses, with St. Elmo's fire flickering on their manes, the electricity flashing out of them in sheaves. But one can't drown like this! What's this uncanny trick being played on me, flying in the face of reason? Had anybody asked me if I wanted to join in the game? There was no understanding what was going on all round me and extending away out into infinity. It was a phosphorescent sea, foaming and writhing! This is the way a surgeon must see the exposed brain of a patient lying on the operating table as he operates on the open skull. I was assailed by an unendurable thought: with these electric currents jumping this way and that from my own nerves on to this ramified, tremulous mass, the gelatinous infinity could not be anything other than my own naked brain. It was an infinite projection of my own brain, convolution after convolution of it unfurling into something that no human eye had ever before beheld! I struck my head hard against the floor. I don't know how long I lay in profound unconsciousness, from which I was aroused only by the rumbling thunder of the approaching storm. Here at last was the spring thunderstorm! For a whole month the sky had been always of the same ice-cold blue, pitilessly dear. Again I heard the voice of the girl bending over me. She was asking if she might close the shutters, because there was a storm coming up. No! I told her to open the windows wide! The upheaval of the elements! I wished that the whole sky might empty itself upon the springtide earth, drowning the park and the tall trees under sheaves of water. A tremendous flash of lightning struck. A globe of fire rolled into the room and ricocheted like a billiard ball from one end of the room to the other. There was a smell: something had been set on fire. No! There was no burning, no burning! What I was smelling — like the air pouring back into the lungs of someone whose life has been despaired of — was like ozone from the oxygen bomb. That was it! Oxygen, as it is generated by the splitting of the air! An ear-splitting detonation made the whole house rock. Lightning had struck! The long white curtain that hung from above the window right to the floor was hurled towards the ceiling, swirling like a great sail, flung this way and that by the storm, until it struck the glass chandelier. A single glass drop loosened. I watched it falling and heard it hit the floor and splinter into particles. That was the sound I had heard before.

I said it's a mysterious lever that sets simple people's imagination working, one such as made Hulda, whenever she was being the chambermaid Reserl at my place, live as in a daydream, yet with both feet firmly on the ground. A miracle may awaken the dead to life. Not that I want to go so far, for at that time I was only half dead. Even if someone were to set about cunningly and methodically tracing the threads in the magic tapestry of a life such as a daydreamer leads, he could never discover the secret that lodges in a heart like that girl's heart. There was nothing of the erotic about her state of mind, none of that feeling that wreaks its foolish havoc in the veins of one who is in love. It was something very rare, different from the love of the sexes. *Caritas* was the gift that Reserl had, the greatest of the three theological virtues, above Faith and Hope. *Caritas* meant going fearlessly, without hesitation, into the purgatorial fire, scorching one's wings, in order to save some poor soul. Eros has grown too pallid, whatever science may think out in order to bedizen love with new enchantment after it had lost its wonder and become a mere physical act of procreation, for the continuation of the species. It is no longer love. Would love ever have shrunk from embracing death in the bridal night? *Caritas* goes round in the circle of eternity, and should eternity itself come to an end, then *Caritas* too will have spent itself and surrendered entirely.

Why is it that today, when we modern people are bound by the law of cause and effect, so that everything stands and falls with it, nobody is surprised that causality should cancel out the existence of a magical world? Has causality not been thought out to a logical conclusion? Is it not rather that the law of cause and effect has lifted the things of this life out of their isolated existence as mere objects — which is the way they necessarily appear to us from the material point of view — in order to arrange them once more in a clear and distinct pattern, in a continuum of relationship between past and future? Logically, then, the law of cause and effect works in two directions: forwards and backwards. Whatever happens on one side remains dependent on something on 'the other side'. We are too much accustomed to regard the cause of all phenomena as lying only in the past. Who would dare to draw from effects any inference as to their future causes? Telepathy might, of course, offer some information here, yet for fear of siren voices we stop up our ears like the mariner drifting in waters that are not marked on any map. We do not believe in ghosts, because we do not know that we ourselves are ghosts on our journey into nothingness. This is most clearly manifest in our view of the world as something material and objective, as a sum of inanimate objects, a world of *things*. I should never have thought that one could exist most of the time in a state of catalepsy, without noticing it. One rushes along, entirely absorbed in one's pettifogging daily affairs, full to the brim of trivialities, always surrounded by too many people who dare not be what they would like to be and do not say what they mean. Suddenly the heart is plucked at by the wire that works the puppet, one is in the pantomime of everyday. We are so hypnotized by the negation of the spiritual in the whole realm of matter that the notion of a disembodied spirit means no more to us than a ridiculous poltergeist throwing stones, shifting the furniture, rocketing about and being a downright nuisance. But isn't a body without a spirit the worst monstrosity of all? Isn't such a man a cataleptic, one of the living dead, the man without conscience?

To serve was as natural to Hulda, as inborn, as it is to a lizard to flit busily to and fro, to a brook to lisp in gentle ripples, to a fire to blush in the night. Apart from this, however, she had the rare gift of leading another life besides that of a servant girl in the household next door: a life in the realm of fantasy, as lady's maid to my doll, which was an invention of mine. Only Reserl could guess how near I was at that time to the end where even playing ceases. For the gateway into reality, into the everyday world outside, was something I neither could nor would open any more. Let it remain shut, for my nerves could not endure the screaming and wailing of an inferno!

When this girl, who came from the country, entered my service, it was her own wish that I should call her by a name that came more trippingly to my tongue. So I called her Reserl, which is the common abbreviation, where I come from, of the name Theresa. A woman of this name lived in Spain in the sixteenth century. When the intoxication with gold that came about after the discovery of America led to an unparalleled bestial corruption of morals, the cause of the social decay from which we are still suffering today, she took pity on the spiritual wretchedness of the world. She could no longer lift up her heart to God, because the others took His name in vain, swearing false oaths by it and blaspheming, robbing and slaughtering, and because the Holy Inquisition was roasting the Agnus Dei alive. She was so bowed under the burden of love, like a mother carrying her child in her body, she felt: God is invisible in Heaven because He dwells within my heart. God is love. This is not the place to describe the way in which a loving woman's vision within a very short time became known even in the most distant lands and how this woman actually founded the science of the heart that psychology and related disciplines are nowadays exploiting without knowing anything of the mystery of *Caritas*. *Caritas* is a gift that comes to one suddenly, like a call to bear the soured wine of love up into the rarefied air of the heights, where it regains its true sweetness.

I was disenchanted with all I had ever believed in, nauseated by the ignoble events of the time, and sickened with life. How did this simple girl from the country know what made me suffer when I came home half demented? And how elementary the machine was that brought about the transformation, elementary as the gilding, the painted marble and incense of a country church, as the curtain of a confessional! All I had to do was to speak into the vacuum cleaner that the girl imagined for me, saying the things that had soiled my soul in the course of the day, and she cleared away, as it were emptying a bagful of dust out of the window.

I had been on the downgrade for some time past, finding it daily more insufferable to associate with human beings. While others were able to go on talking about how they had emptied machine-guns at advancing masses of human flesh, hurled hand-grenades against living bodies, and finished 'them' off with the bayonet, not omitting the description of the compulsory visit to bawdy houses where they had coupled like animals with the compulsorily recruited women there, I too was beginning to let myself be dominated by aberration. My *idée fixe* was that I must own a lifesize female doll. Subsequently a correspondence about this doll was published, which at one time was the cause of considerable scandal. I actually enjoyed this. People regarded this, too, as a symptom of the slyness with which a madman sets about his handiwork. It was a long time before, finally, a spinster in Stuttgart was found who was prepared to take on the commission. It would never have done for me to make the doll myself, for even the surrealist takes good care that the link between himself and reality shall not quite snap! It is far from being my purpose, in these lines, to present myself as a hero of a romance of our time. I am merely trying to sketch in the background so that the idea of the mechanical may stand out the more clearly: the idea of the great puppet-show. Progress hangs on wires, and it is only in the future that the hand that controls them, the cause, will be recognized.

What resembled intellectual unrest behind the tense faces of the youth of those revolutionary years was aimless, undirected energy, which endowed them with a phantom quality. They mistook even their own fantasies for something real! So it was with their utopian politics too. Undernourishment, illness, and war wounds may have contributed something. After all, it was no more than a year ago since one had been a hopeless bundle of nerves, daily, even hourly, prepared to become a mangled corpse like one's innumerable brothers-in-arms. Carrion for the crows. True, 'those glorious days' were over, but nobody knew why it should be precisely he who had been spared, or for what. Life seemed to us like an unexpected leave from the trenches, and as a consequence the revolution was a mere farce that everyone pretended to himself he believed in, a dream-life from which one was afraid of waking up, to find oneself back in the trenches again. 'Somehow' one tried to fill the emptiness. Not that people were outwardly so very different from the generation that had known what peace was: not that people were now born with thicker skins. It was more as when the force of gravity ceases to be exerted on a body. Life was like looking forward to a première that never took place. In the darkness one wept and was not ashamed of one's sentimentality. If the light was turned on, one laughed at one's own glycerine tears. Love was bedizened, no longer distinguishable from vice. Nor did one suffer from life itself, like the Romantics — one just suffered from claustrophobia. Just as traffic is regulated by changing lights, one reacted automatically to signals, slogans, clichés.

What was it really that so scandalized people about my doll, whose arrival I was so feverishly looking forward to? I admit that there is something indecent in keeping a lifesize female doll as a companion. Towards the end of the First World War, however, the Buddhists in Japan had introduced a special religious cult as part of an educational reform in schools, in order to placate the spirits of broken dolls. And the Japanese, after all, are the people who have become the masters of those whose pupils they were in matters of mechanical progress. Nevertheless, they can imagine things to be animate when the things have done human beings good service! How different such a conception of things is if one compares it with the farce that is enacted annually at the Tomb of the Unknown Soldier, who was after all nothing more than strategic material in the war.

That the housemaid Hulda should, as Reserl, act as lady's maid to my doll had originally been meant only as a joke of my landlord's. Thereby the pretty skivvy from next door was provided with a stage on which, being really quite a moppet, she could play her role to the full. I intended making a great to-do with my doll, taking her out daily in the carriage that I had hired especially for that purpose, and to a box at the Opera so that I could hold her hand the moment the lights went down. After all, every other hand that was held out to me seemed to be stained with blood.

First of all Hulda, the housemaid, had to do her apprenticeship, in order to learn the art of illusion as the lady's maid Reserl. Shoeless, only in her black silk stockings, there she stands in the doorway. I must pretend to be asleep and am supposed to wake up at the slightest sound, which is why for a brief eternity she does not dare to open the door but stands holding the handle. She is captive for as long as I please. If I stir she pulls the door softly to again and also lets go of the handle. At last I seem to be sound asleep, and she can escape from the trap. Reserl was particularly fond of playing with a situation that seemed to offer no possibility of escape. People will say: What is so special about someone's having whims? If we knew more about the reservoir within us that feeds such whims, perhaps we should find that they are manifestations of a constitution with which we are born. Yet here the case was different. We were all in a situation from which there was no escape, and hopelessness weighed upon the human race like original sin. Perhaps the demiurge himself had had the whim of blocking a whole generation's escape. I watch the cat at play. Or rather, she is the little mouse that is trying to outwit the cat and, with a glance at me for reassurance, she pushes a chair to the cupboard. The little mouse's mind is relieved: the cat is fast asleep. She climbs on to the chair and observes me critically once more as she looks for the tidbits in the cupboard.

Well, the tidbits aren't where I generally keep them, in the cupboard with the door that creaks when you open it. What will she do now, in this situation in which she might be found out? It is too late to abandon her intention. Away with all qualms, to the devil with decency, when she discovers the dish high up in the cupboard, just within her reach. Just one last glance at me, an intense one this time and merely to assure me that it is all a game, as it was agreed in advance between the two of us. After all, I'm still the patient whose temperature soars dangerously whenever the least thing goes wrong. Now she's getting the dish down. Sure enough, she turns quite pink, she can't resist the temptation any longer, and in ecstasy she puts to her lips the brown stuff that has only the name in common with chocolate. Then she has to drop the key, which startles me out of sleep. Now, relations between us were not the usual ones between young people. Furthermore, she had a high regard for good behavior, just as one is proud of getting ten for industry and good behavior at school. Tears rise to her eyes. in accordance with the truth I have to confess that she has been caught in the trap that I set. For at the same moment she loses her balance on the upholstered chair and in the next she is lying in my arms. Now it was no longer Reserl who fell from the chair, but Hulda, the maid who is ashamed because the master has caught her being as greedy as Eve. Yet whatever my intentions were when I caught this pretty girl in my arms, it would be too much to expect that Reserl now prove in every way complaisant. No, our abandonment did not go so far, and the curtain was not allowed to fall upon this scene just yet. 'Wasn't it nice, Reserl?' I had to ask, almost pleadingly, several times. 'Nice enough to give me a bad conscience,' she said bashfully. This had become the great moment, perhaps the greatest between us, because now it was not the lady's maid or the servant girl who stood before me, but 'the unknown human being.' Both of us were embarrassed, and this did us good. The girl had laid one finger against her forehead as though she had some remark to make about this. Both of us burst out laughing. This too did us good, for, candidly, it is awkward to feel as embarrassed as a schoolboy who, when a girl speaks to him for the first time, doesn't dare to confess to himself that there is nothing he has yearned for more than that she should take him home with her. So far as I was concerned, any girl could lie in my arms at that time as soon as chance caused her to cross my path. Forbidden fruit, that was it! Was anything at all forbidden in those days? Simply nothing at all! If there had been anything unsuitable of that kind about it, this girl would have proved as complaisant as every other, seeing that the times were bad and the number of young men had been so much reduced by the war! That is what some sly persons will think when they read this, and they will insist that I had simply turned the girl's head. This all the more certainly because I now intend confessing, into the bargain, that, like children who shiver with delicious terror at the thought of all sorts of adventures in a dark forest, Reserl said to me: 'I am at your service body and soul — dispose of me as you like, sir!' From that time on this was her salutation to me every morning. I was naturally delighted at this; it was expressed in precise terms, and Reserl had the hang of the part, which demanded that the stage should never become reality. How much may one poor soul know of another in purgatory? No more, or not much more, than what one knows of things, of objects: A bicycle is a machine that one mounts in order to go out for a picnic, or caviar is something one eats before a meal because it whets the appetite, and tomorrow is something of which one knows little, perhaps that one will hang oneself from a stout piece of rope that will take one's weight. The word 'love' would have offended the delicacy of anyone who said it to another person: one had a distaste for it as for some bodily defilement. What the official loudspeaker meant by it was the production of human material for the fatherland: cannon-fodder, that was all. Love for one's country, yes! But one ought not to talk about that to a girl seeking self-renewal in a delirium of the heart, at the very fount and origin of pleasure. Would she not unfailingly retort to the young man: Why are you still hanging about here? You want to elevate me to the heavens: but for that you must first lie in the grave. Sixteen-year-old lads were sent to the front. Each of the crosses planted on their graves — two flimsy wooden laths over a mouldering body — was a reminder: Words are a waste of time! And the hopes of hundreds of thousands of foolish virgins who had hidden their light under a bushel had also been mangled, mutilated, done to death, and all they could do was await their bridegroom in Heaven, which was why they had such transparent skin and sleepless eyes.

'Wasn't it nice?' 'Nice enough to give one a bad conscience!' the maid had said. Even if these words were no more than a faint beam of light from a candle, they penetrated the indifference that is like a mist working its way through one's pores into the very soul. That was what I had to learn again. Shame was like a physical blessing — strong current of warmth, at one stroke blowing all the fuses that had given me such a sense of security! The unknown human being in my arms, feeling shame! For that was something that didn't exist any more, out there in the streets, which were full of armless cripples, men without legs, and the heedless man pushing his way ahead, thrusting the helpless aside, stepping over those who had been flung on to the streets. That was the thoughtless way I lived then, with something like a film over my eyes that prevented my seeing properly, and even I couldn't understand what was happening to me. As unsuspectingly as the rest of them I had mistaken my marching orders for a passport that promised the adventurous man all the wonders of the world. Just as Columbus did not suspect that he was about to land on an unknown continent when the sailor in the crow's nest called out: 'Land ho!' how should I guess that, being a soldier, one would be at such a remove from the world of human emotions? When I was ashamed, I thought I could look down as from a great height and watch myself sinking deeper and deeper into apathy, where the everyday blunting of the sensibility was becoming more noticeable from day to day.

I confessed to the girl that one positively ought to be frightened if there were really nothing any more that was still illicit for the like of us. It is as in a bad dream, when one falls and falls. I was suddenly seized by nostalgia for the lost Garden of Eden that childhood knows,' with the forbidden apple from the tree. Reserl also grew solemn. Yet, like a child drawing a deep breath after it has had a fright, she smiled and was stretching out her pretty legs in the black silk stockings, when unluckily the stern housekeeper called her from next door. 'Now I must leave you to yourself. Try to sleep a little, and I hope you won't dream of plunging into the depths. When you come over for dinner be careful on the stairs, for there's no light.'

The scent of flowers coming in the window reminded me of the flowers dropping from a funeral wreath. Its sweetness had none of the tang of incense, nor was it the refreshing scent of lilies-of-the-valley and violets, nor like the hot breath of carnations or roses — nor was it like jasmine, acacia, and lime flowers casting their fragrance exquisitely far upon the high air. There was something oppressive about the scent in my room, so that I got up and shut the window. It was like mould, as though emanating from those bunches of flowers laid at the feet of the painted statues of St. John Nepomuk along the country roads from Belgrade to Vienna, from Eisenstadt to Prague, and northward as far as Dresden and Cracow, and which had fallen to dust when I passed that way in the war. The saint had been thrown into the water from the bridge over the Moldau in Prague, by the Bohemian king Wenceslas, because he sturdily refused to violate the secrecy of the confessional and repeat what the queen had told. Oh for a conscience like that, since it is conscience, as legend has it, with which we are rooted in Paradise! What does the modern science of psychology know of the conscience, which Saint Theresa, who was in love with God, worked at with hoe, shovel, rake, pruning-knife, bast, and watering-can, until what came about was a Baroque park full of illusions! Now our hearts have the look of a rubbish beap, strewn with the old-fashioned, withered flowers from the altars of our childhood. just as the species that are bred in plant nurseries now are roses, tulips, and hyacinths only in name.

In some such way a poor sinner, having lost consciousness under the Inquisition's torture, may have dreamed that for love of the Lamb of God he was being taken from the rack.

With open eyes I yet went on dreaming and seemed to be seeing something feathery light: Reserl on skates, pirouetting as on a skating rink, with the precision of the balance in my watch. Was she trying to dust my Bohemian glass paperweight with her feather duster? I'm mistaken; the little doll was not the maid and was carrying no feather mop, but a lighted candle. Who it was, it was impossible to tell. It was like the poor soul of one unborn in Dante's Inferno, one who will never have a shape, a voice, and the color of life, because it is not saved. I awoke with a start of fear, drenched in sweat for aren't we living in the age of *Neue Sachlichkeit*? Who was it? It was myself.

Perhaps it was that noise outside the door of the house that wakened me. The crate containing the fairylike creature had arrived and it was being unloaded outside the house. The doll! Beside myself with eagerness, I tried to see to a hundred things, all at once. It was already dusk, but the old manservant had followed my instructions and had polished the chandelier and got out the silver, and all the glass and the covers were glittering in the way I wished for this occasion, a particularly festive one. Wearing his best suit, a survival from the good old days, he was to light the way up the steps for the guests as soon as their carriages arrived. I was waiting in person for a Venetian courtesan, in the park, under the magnolias, which were just beginning to open. The lady's beauty was celebrated all over town. She had been invited as a special surprise for the ladies and gentlemen who were already waiting in the drawing room, unable to control their curiosity and chatting about the meaning of this doll about which so much mystery had been made. Those who were in the know presumed to draw the inference that there had been an original who had played the fatal role in my life. Everyone expected a great deal — and yet more, for instance that after dinner the doll would sing an aria, Donna Anna's staccato aria, by means of a musical box built into her body. There was the sound of wheels on the gravel, and I ran to the carriage and opened the door, then carried the courtesan up the stairs myself, in my arms. She was robed in a panther skin, her bare arms loaded with heavy gold bangles. She felt quite assured of her victory in the beauty competition with a lifeless doll, and this promised to win her new laurels. Yet even she could not conceal some slight embarrassment from me, for it was one thing to bear away the palm from the Three Graces, who were flesh and blood, and another to compete with a ghost. Wine flowed freely. After all had risen from dinner, a little while passed, because the robing of the doll was planned to be the climax of the festive occasion. She was to appear before us in all her adornment, as in antique Athens the goddess was drawn up to the citadel from the sea by the virgins, robed in her new peplum all embroidered with flowers.

When the doll was lifted out of the heaps of stuff in which she had been packed, what stared back at me was not the realization of a presumptuous wish-dream, not the seductive creature of dream that had so feverishly obsessed me, but a phantom. What I saw had dead eyes and revealed an indecent nakedness to the gaze of all, in the merciless light from hundreds of candles in the glass chandelier. No illusion was possible. Here in my arms lay — not the warmth of the heart, the breathing skin of a seductively feminine creature — but a botched thing, a lay figure. It was a fearful blow, and words are inadequate to express my disappointment. Of course my expectations had been pitched too high, which is understandable, since I had promised myself the realization of something that must remain mere fantasy. The Venetian courtesan tried to offer me consolation, which I had not asked for. It was obvious to me that she, like all the rest of those around the table, was scarcely concealing a certain malicious enjoyment of my situation. I resented the fact that no one refrained from expressing his sympathy for me. What a disastrous disappointment, they whispered to each other and went out into the open air, where, on my instructions, a quartet had set up their music-stands in the great pool, among Kändler's nymphs and satyrs. In the moonlight every drop from the fountains glistened on them like thousands upon thousands of diamonds. We drank until we were all drunk, and the party degenerated into a wild orgy.

Early in the morning we were awakened by a patrol of the gendarmerie. The corpse of a woman, lying in her blood, in a flower-bed in the park? Passers-by had seen the corpse through the park railings and reported the matter. Neither I nor my landlord could recall the circumstances clearly. Sleepily we followed the arm of the law. 'A doll? That isn't blood — the body's been drenched in red wine!' 'The thing must be cleared away, it's a scandal! There's no excuse for this sort of thing!' Muddy and pathetic, there in a field of flowers the lay figure sprawled. My last impulse was to fling myself upon it like a lover. To hell with the people standing around! 'Get up and come along with us! You have caused a public nuisance and committed an offense against morality and decency. You are liable to prosecution!' Thus the policeman barked at me and took down my name and address and so forth. He gave orders that the thing, the object, should be taken away on the garbage cart.

But my manservant had also taken offense. I should never before have thought of hiring someone to wait on me. Ridiculous! Only invalids and children needed to be waited on. I had taken him on for the sake of the doll, but mostly because he was recommended as out of a job. The times were bad, especially for old people. Unfortunately this man had an unconquerable aversion to the female sex, in general and in particular. When he would be serving the usual cabbage soup at luncheon, he would try to convert me by means of pietistic sermons, while I tensely watched his thumb, in the threadbare white glove, dipping distressingly further and further into the only dish that rationing permitted. The old man worried a great deal about things that did not concern him. He was possessed, besides, of a morbid jealousy, and often played extremely disagreeable tricks on me. After the episode with the doll I specially sent the girl to his room to see why he had not put in an appearance that morning. She found him lying fully dressed on his bed and was afraid he was dying. When she bent over him, to undo his collar so that he could get some air, he must have seen my initials on her breast, for he had an apoplectic fit. His eyes were open. I had to go and talk to him kindly for a long time before he came to his senses again. In a broken voice he then gave notice, once and for all, because of the girl Hulda, to say nothing at all of the doll! Glad as I was when he awoke from his cataleptic state, I had to let him go, and I bought him a place in an old people's home. When his hour struck, in spite of all I found it somewhat painful, saying good-bye to the jealous old boy. There he was, with his little suitcase in one hand and in the other the feather duster, which he had recently appropriated, dusting the banisters for the last time as he went down the stairs.

This man reminded me of a canary I had had before the war, when, as a result of my great disappointment, I myself was prejudiced against the entire female sex. The canary was very teachable, and I could have sworn that he understood every word I spoke to him. During the time we were together the horizon of this bird's brain seemed to expand daily. What a lot he learned! I tied a string across the room, and he would run along it with the nimbleness of a tightrope-walker, and whenever I called him back he would instantly stop and return. The cherry that I held to his beak as a reward he would take with a worried expression, as though his whole existence depended on my being satisfied with his little accomplishment. And he would have said so, too, had he been able to talk. However, after awhile he began to make ever greater demands on my attention. He simply would not let me out of his sight. Now a bird's eyes are so placed that it can see on both sides at once, so I could not escape his gaze. The waxen eyelids, characteristic of a bird's eye, which my canary would close in enjoyment when I stroked him, were something that my manservant also had. And he too had been as jealous as the little harpy. When I began to consort with human beings again, the bird did everything he could to maintain his exclusive rights over me. He would cling to my face with his thin, cold claws, angrily pecking at my lips the moment I dared to speak to other living creatures. At night, when I tried to sleep, he even began pecking at my closed eyes. The bird had become a torment, and when I went away on active service I gave him to my mother to look after. On my return from the war I saw that he had again become a perfectly ordinary canary, with ruffled yellow feathers, hopping about his cage taking an interest only in his food and his drinking-bowl or splashing in his bath. He did not recognize me.

By a lucky chance I got hold of some champagne: I had been able to buy up a whole crate of it in an outlying tavern where nobody suspected its existence. This was something special for me during my convalescence — I would never have regained my strength merely on what one got to eat in those days. At this same time my landlord had a decoration bestowed upon him, and to celebrate this he got out his best cut glass and we drank to a happy future. While Reserl — who was called Hulda when waiting tables — was removing the usual turnip pie (all the variations of which we were all too deadly familiar with), my friend recalled the suppers there had been at the balls that his Hussar regiment used to give in peacetime for young society ladies. He went into raptures, remembering those delights, and we were both excited by the champagne, which we were not used to. Generally we ate together only on Sundays, and after the table was cleared I used to make coarse, sensual drawings in an album that the director had had bound in leather especially for this purpose — he used to assert in the most positive fashion that the leather was from the charming posterior of somebody's mistress at the Court of the Elector of Saxony in the eighteenth century.

This delicate human skin had been tanned expressly for this purpose. And with the same disrespectfulness, appropriate to the eighteenth century, my drawings mocked the hypocrisy of our own times. In this album I painted the most indecent love scenes, and my jolly boon-companion was permitted to enhance them at various points with silver and gold. The thought that his puritanical housekeeper or posterity might poke their noses into our album caused us a delicious *frisson*.

That evening was not meant to end with the same gaiety. The director's housekeeper came in, and we scarcely had time to slam the album shut and hide the brushes and paints in the drawer of the table. She was stuttering with agitation about what she had to tell. The General, the director's father, who lived on the top floor of the pavilion, had been found dead in his bed. In the afternoon he had complained only of not feeling very well, for which reason he had refused to eat any supper, but he had insisted that his son and I were not to be disturbed. The director became yet thinner and stiffer than usual, but his face did not change expression — it was a face somewhat like that of a stork, and he heightened the resemblance by wearing incredibly high stiff collars. He remained master of his feelings. But the ornamental tie pin that I always used to tease him about seemed to have lost some of its brilliance, as though that had been rubbed off. Together we went upstairs. The old soldier had died in bed, which seemed to be the only irregularity in a life of strict devotion to duty and a sense of German orderliness. His uniform was neatly folded over the back of a chair, his sword on the wall, and the oil lamp was not smoking. The dead man lay in bed with his hands already clasped, as though ready to be put into his coffin. He looked as if he were asleep; his eyes were shut. I was glad about that. I had never before noticed that my friend the landlord was already turning gray at the temples. I became aware of it when he took the lampshade off while be was binding up the dead man's chin with his handkerchief. Somewhere in the room a fly was buzzing. Certainly the director had himself well in hand, yet now he looked at me, and his spectacles were moist. How distressing social forms can be! Who was to catch the fly?

I laid my hand on the place where the soldierly heart had ceased to beat. I thought to myself — A sad end for a general, dying in bed like this. But to my friend I said: 'He passed away peacefully.' I resolved to make a drawing of the face that very evening as a memento for my friend. Not with the sort of motive that people have in ordering a death-mask as a token of remembrance, or the way one erects a monument to someone's memory which time and a few tears then wash off the slate of eternity. I did the drawing with the tranquillity of a naturalist studying a species that is dying out and who happens to come across vestiges of a world that has ceased to exist. With a gaze at once shy and burning I touched those frontiers beyond which there lay the past — security, a country, firm ground — and I expected no ghostly apparitions from that other side. A drawing records what photography cannot do even in a series of photographs of ourselves at various ages, in which one still finds oneself as one would like to be. Whereas confronted with a drawing, the beholder becomes confused, like a conjuror whose double-fined sleeves and secret pockets have slyly been emptied of the apparatus that he needs in order to perform his tricks. The drawing contains the spirit of the person, of the time; but one is afraid of spirits. The best way to overcome fear is to give permanence to the last form in which that spirit manifested itself to us. I had finished my drawing. The impression of the dead man that I had received in this last minute was at the same time that of the face of a whole generation that had said good-bye forever without uttering a single cry. A vanquished generation had died out.

Its time was over, that was all. Those were men the like of whom is not seen today. The case did not concern me further, I argued to myself as I went, alone, down the dark staircase, a spiral one such as one finds in old houses. Everything passes, even the fear of being alone. Then I suddenly realized that I was not alone. There was a warm body brushing past me. Reserl! We both held our breath, for we did not dare to be heard together on the stairs because of the stern housekeeper. So we went right down to the cellar, hand in hand. Actually it was our bathroom, to which use the empty cellar had now been put. But the bathtub had been requisitioned by the army — perhaps melted down to make guns. Nowadays we bathed in a big barrel. It was filled to the top with water, and because the night was hot we both cooled our hands in it. It was not quite pitch dark in the cellar, for light slanted in through a small grating whenever the moon was not obscured by cloud. When the surface of the water was again still, we both saw ourselves as a two-fold being, inseparable there in the universe. I did not mention the dead man, who was lying in bed alone in the topmost story. Reserl was too easily influenced. I was amazed at her gaiety and abandon, for now she wanted to have a bath, right in front of my eyes, she whom no man had ever seen naked. 'Because of the dead man upstairs, so that he won't come back in your dreams.' She had already pulled off her nightdress and was standing up to neck in water. I must confess to being surprised, even I who thought I knew her so well. What talent enabled this simple country girl to read me like an open book? Darkness prevented my seeing more of her. Actually I could only hear her naked body splashing in the water. This too she did on purpose — a fairy in this ridiculous grotto where damp dripped from the walls and the cheap war-time paint was already peeling from the bricks. What distinguished her from Melusine, I wondered, and so I asked her if she too was cold to the touch. That made her laugh, while she was already getting dressed again. What difference did it make that in the next few days one would be burying a dead general? The war was over.

The candle at the foot of my bed burned like the Tabernacle lamp in church. Now I shall sleep soundly, I murmured, my eyes shut. Reserl was already standing beside me, disguised as a lady's maid, one knee, in its black stocking, close to my eyes, her head supported on her hand like the Thinker. Or perhaps she was the nun at the Black Mass, wedded to the young priest. Drunk with sleep I opened my eyes once more and saw her. It was no dream. She had waked up in the night, afraid that she was really cold to the touch, like Melusine, although I had only said that for a joke. So she came to my room, to make sure that she was really a girl and alive. 'I am at your service body and soul — dispose of me, sir,' she said in my ear. 'At my service body and soul,' I mur-

mured as I fell asleep. But supposing the stern housekeeper had
caught us then!

Postscript

Some years later, when I happened to be in Dresden again after
I had found a number of things in the world different from what
I expected, I could not help stopping by the garden fence and
looking at the house and garden where I had spent the winter at
the end of the war as though in an ivory tower. Snow had fallen
upon the war's pools of blood, and grass had grown over them,
and there was no Hulda there, only some girl or other that the
housekeeper had brought from the country, shoveling manure in
the garden. A big city tends to turn a girl's head.

THE FOURTH LETTER FROM THE TRAVELER

Aigues-Mortes, Summer 1924

There are brave people who don't mind admitting they have been wrong. And perhaps anthropologists will discover discrepancies in the account of what I experienced; so if I have gone wrong, I shall gladly let myself be corrected. My friend, Dr. Posse, the director of the gallery, had a tapestry in the dining room where we used to lunch together on Sundays. It showed St. Louis's arrival at Ascalon at the head of his crusading army, and this picture became more familiar to me every time I set eyes on it. I asserted that it was with the Crusaders that the gypsies first came to Europe, which is proved by the numerous representations of jugglers, minstrels and dancers that suddenly crop up in the Books of Hours of that period and in the grotesque figures on Romanesque churches. The Jews had already used the great migrations as a springboard to Europe. At that time I read that the celebrated Anglo-German Sanskrit scholar, Max Müller, had so far modified his well-known theory about the Aryans that it amounted to a complete retraction. Presumably he was horrified by the intellectual devastation that it wrought in many addled brains even before Hitler's time, as was exemplified by Count Gobineau or the English philosopher Houston Stewart Chamberlain. What there was still evidence for, at least so far as I recall, was that the only dyed-in-the-wool Aryans in Europe are the gypsies. I share with the gypsies a taste for roving, which is why I got on the next train for Aigues-Mortes in Southern France, where the French Crusader had embarked together with his knights. Since that time the sea had receded, and today Aigues-Mortes is surrounded by marshes. Of all the Crusaders the only one that appeals to me is Richard the Lionhearted, because he was unable to do what most heroes of the Crusades did and plunder the countries he passed through and set fire to Byzantium in order to earn himself a halo and a reputation in the school-books. The Viennese took him prisoner and kept him in Burg Dürnstein on the Danube. On a school outing we were shown the little barred window in the castle wall under which his faithful servant Blondel, the only person to stay with the king, sweetened the dreary days of his long captivity by playing the harp for him. On thinking this over, however, I find I am not sure whether this happened before the journey to the Holy Land or only on the way back.

I arrived in Aigues-Mortes just in time to see the gypsies from all over Europe praying to the Madonna for a general absolution. According to legend, she is the black madonna that was wafted on a red cloud of sand from the Orient to Saintes Maries-de-la-Mer in a house, or a shrine, or a stone coffin together with the other two Maries — hence the name of the place. Presumably this legend is an allusion to a matriarchy that once prevailed there, which was destroyed by the moral Romans, who would not tolerate any rule by women. The memory of it survives only in the legend among these pariahs. But according to another apocryphal legend, the Mother of God is supposed to have died at Ephesus in Anatolia, where the most ancient sanctuary of the Earth Mother is known to have been; this seems to be more than coincidence. There is still a little chapel there to this day, built over a modest dwelling house that is said to date from the first century A.D. and which is locally known as the house of 'the Holy of Holies.' Now, the legend says that the coffin was found empty. In one of her visions Katherina Emmerich, the ecstatic, gave the most precise and detailed description of this place of the Virgin Mary's death, although she was never outside Bavaria. I should like to believe that the two other Maries — who also survive in Byzantine iconography and that of the Russian church, which derives from it, and who, although they are not mentioned in the Bible, also occur in a late Coptic version of the Gospels — are the midwives. They also aided the mother of Prince Gautama when her hour came, when, standing under the tree of life, she brought the gentle Buddha into the world — who, like another Indian, Gandhi, wanted to put an end to violence in the world. The gypsies originally come from India.

On that day the swarthy gypsies in their caravans came pouring from all directions to the meeting. The next day I saw them leaving the little town by the chalky roads, their wagons drawn by young horses and shaggy donkeys. I watched them for a long time from the town ramparts, where one can stroll for hours. Four towers facing the four points of the compass are still well preserved. One tower is historically important to the custodian, who in return for a tip will tell the tourist that Simon de Montfort starved hundreds of Cathars to death there, while other obstinate persons, during that great religious war, were thrown into the sea by means of ingenious machinery in ships with specially constructed bottoms that could be lowered. One striking feature of the landscape is an aqueduct with immense arches, a testimony to Roman engineering prowess. Even today the poor people's little white-washed cottages are veritable museums of antique art, because fragments of Greek marble were used with the mortar for the walls, just as the swallow carries off anything that it can find to build its nest. Aigues-Mortes was a Greek colony.

I knew of a woman, a seller of fish, who had a lovely daughter. The mother, a buxom woman, was fond of wearing blouses with a more generous décolleté than was necessary. She had scorching black eyes, which conveyed their meaning eloquently. But the daughter, called Cora, like the antique goddess, had not inherited her mother's coarse features. Recently they had taken on a young lad who came with the gypsies but certainly was not one of them. Gypsies do not take employment with strangers; they remain in the clan according to the matriarchal system that they have not yet abandoned. It was part of his job to fetch the fish from the harbor and then take it to market, for the little house was not in the town itself. The mother spent the early morning weighing the fish and the late evening counting money. In the interval she swatted flies, and at night she yawned, for she slept badly. Her heart was heavy. The lad spoke the local dialect badly; he wore a wide-brimmed straw hat with coins sewed on it, in the manner of the gypsies who come like grasshoppers and vanish overnight. And as soon as the lad had received his wages, he too vanished overnight. The next day he returned without his hat. On being asked where he had been, he only grinned and muttered something about '*seiches*' — sepias, fat, round, smooth cuttlefish with white arms. And the hat? That was hanging on the tip of the Aigues-Mortes, the rocks nearby. He asked the fish-woman for an advance, and then he fetched his hat back.

When he was away, the girl was absentminded, snappish and cross, naturally, because she herself had to do the boy's work until he returned. Her mother, on the other hand, left the flies to buzz in peace and merely looked dejected. She could not look out of the window, for as in the East there were no windows overlooking the street. Another thing I should like to mention is that there was an antique stone serving as keystone of the single opening in the wall; on it there was distinctly to be seen the strange smile on the mouth of the goddess Cora, while the chalk with which the houses had been whitewashed countless times so completely hid the shoulders and the naked breast of the archaic goddess that by now the fragment could scarcely be distinguished from the wall itself.

One day the lad again did not come home, and the girl Cora herself rode down to the harbor on their only donkey, to do the bargaining with the fishermen. The boats had not yet come in, so she stopped half-way, where the arches of the Roman aqueduct come nearly down to the seashore. The heat was overwhelming; it was tempting to bathe. She tied up the donkey and undressed. If I had not happened to be standing on top of the arch, from where there was a good view as far as the hills whence the water was once brought to the town, I should not have noticed the lad, who was down below, sleeping the sleep of the just. Although it was still early in the morning, the only cool place was in the shadow of the arch. The girl frolicked at her ease in the clear water, which only the cuttlefish darken if someone tries to catch them. Then all at once the donkey began to bray most heart-rendingly: Cora had forgotten to throw it any hay. The lad woke up and came around the corner; his gaze traveled from the donkey to the clothes that were lying in the sand, thence to the water and to the naked fish romping there, which surely felt the skies darkening when it realized it was caught. Cora slowly came out of the water, outfacing the lad's impudent gaze: but her mouth wore a stony smile, like the mouth of the goddess of fertility on the wall outside the house where she lived.

It was still very hot that evening, and the scent of thyme and mint was very strong. No breeze sprang up. No coolness came from the sea. This sort of stillness always heralds the mistral. Cora's mother had been sitting there all day without moving, not even touching the sweetened orange drink opposite her. Finally, and contrary to all custom, the lad came riding home on the donkey together with her daughter, fish in the baskets to right and to left of them. Now the mother sprang to life, had no more need of sleep, and even went down into the cellar to make sure that the lad was washing the baskets. She weighed out the fish, counting the naked creatures, lending him a hand with his job, and even giving him an encouraging poke in the ribs. Yes, she went running up the stairs and down again, actually bringing a big bottle of red wine and two glasses back with her. To begin with they sat together on an upturned basket. That was a sin and a shame on the Lord's Holy Day, treating the taciturn fellow — whose only language was boozing — to the good wine. Still, he was only a heathen, after all, and the first Christian commandment is to love thy neighbor as thyself — or isn't it?

That night Cora did not sleep either, and the next morning she was tired and fretful, whereas her mother came up from the cellar much refreshed. But the next time Cora paid the lad his weekly wage she would not let go of his coin-embroidered hat, which she held in her hand. He could leave the hat as a pledge here in the house just as easily, instead of on the crags of the Aigues-Mortes, in the event that the cuttlefish should make him thirsty again, as is their wont.

O.K.

THE FIFTH LETTER FROM THE TRAVELER

Jericho, 1929

In a glass case in a museum in Dublin, years before my journey to the Holy Land, I saw a bronze wind instrument, many yards of beautifully convoluted tubing. The director of the museum, a fellow-countryman of mine, and obliging as all the Viennese are, at once accepted my suggestion of seeing whether notes could still be drawn from this ancient tuba. After the instrument had been cleansed of the petrified matter adhering to it — it had been excavated from one of the tumuli, the grave of a Celtic chieftain — we were very disappointed because, for all his strong lungs, not even the horn player in the city orchestra, who had been brought in as a specialist, could manage to get more than some squeaks out of it. Then it struck me that all fundamentals have harmonics. So how about trying the harmonic? But for this we needed to be on a hill. True, harmonics have meanwhile been forbidden by Herr Rosenberg, the *arbiter artis* on the theory of 'racial purity' in Germany, in a book of his; for after all, twelve-tone music which makes use of harmonics was originated by Arnold Schoenberg, a Jew. Anyone who has ever been present at one of those Swiss competitions when the mountain-dwellers skilled in the art of Alpine horn-blowing vie with each other across the valleys — anyone who has heard that must admit that the *ranz des vaches* must always have been sounded in that manner in the Alps. So, too, the language of drums is traditional among the Africans, who can use it for sending signals and news over vast distances, whereas we nowadays use the telephone for that purpose. Hadn't I heard something, in physics lessons at school, about sounds simply not perceptible to human hearing, which has a range limited to only a given number of wavelengths, and not everyone has even all of that. This was already clear to the contemporaries of the deaf Beethoven, who rejected him as a musical innovator, preferring Rossini, for all that their ears were not diseased. 'Music' is a term with many connotations. Young Siegfried understood the language of birds. The Americans make use of the psychological effect of music while milking cows, which give more milk when they are played to. Progressive managements install radios in the factories to stimulate the workers, and conveyor-belt production increases. Good society loves good music, and likes to eat well surrounded by pleasant din, at the same time engaging in lively conversation. In Scotland I was once present at one of those sheep-dog trials where the dogs are expected to know as many as forty tunes if they are to pass their examination. An old sheep-dog like that is more musical than one might think! Just watch him driving a flock of wethers this way and that, chasing them for miles and bringing them back again, tricking them, and making those sheep of the hills dance to the shepherd's tune, the shepherd himself remaining out of sight, blowing on his pipe heaven knows where — ah, that's a sight worth seeing!

What were the Jews of old but shepherds? Doubtless their tubas did not look very different from the bronze horn that I saw in the glass case in Dublin.

That was why I resolved that, although I am merely a layman and no musicologist, I would investigate right on the spot the passage in the Bible about how the walls of the ancient Moabite city fell down as though by a miracle as soon as the old Jews blew their trumpets. I went to Palestine. In Ascalon I disembarked. On the shore lay half of a gigantic swordfish, not making the air any sweeter. The harbor was no longer where it once must have been, the coast has grown swampy, and the sea has receded. Ascalon was full of malaria-bearing mosquitoes, so I proceeded further, to Jerusalem, the Holy City, which each of the various confessions claims for itself alone. There I admired the phlegm of the English Tommy preserving order among the native Arabs and the Orthodox Jews who came from Eastern Europe on pilgrimage to the Wailing Wall and stood in long queues before it. I visited the mosque that is one of the three chief holy places of Islam and which shares a feature with St. Peter's in Rome: both are built over a rocky cavern in which an antique priestess once prophesied. Then I continued my journey, traveling through the desert as far as the Dead Sea on a bus as full of natives as a basket is full of chicks, so that each time the vehicle swerved one or other of the Bedouins fell off. At the Dead Sea one is at the most low-lying point on earth, and there had been nothing but salt there since Sodom and Gomorrah were transformed into a desert because of Lot's sins.

There I spent a long time watching the old city walls of Jericho being excavated from the sands. To this day an Arab town wall is made of no more than clay bricks baked in the sun, just as in ancient times. When one builds a city wall, it naturally means that the space left for the human beehive is circumscribed, and that was why the old Moabites built upwards. The same effect is caused by real-estate speculation in New York and other large modern cities. However, in order to give the Arab skyscrapers more stability, even today palm-trunks are built into the walls at regular intervals, so that if one goes to pay a visit one climbs from story to story on these palms as up a chicken ladder to an attic. Goats have an easier time of it, being born climbers. Today there are no oases around Jericho. Yet many of the fossilized palm-trunks that have been dug out of the sands prove how accurately historical conditions are described in the Bible. How many palms must have waved in the wind, that the oases produced so plentifully as to provide the lovely Queen of Sheba with more than enough to cover her own expenditures on cosmetics, salves, and blue eye-shadow and thus provide her with legendary wealth: for in the ancient world the beauty industry that she organized acquired a reputation only equaled today by Elizabeth Arden's beauty parlors. Perhaps that was why King Solomon wished to woo her when he decided on that famous visit. He was not only one for the ladies, but also a good accountant, as appears from the Song of Songs, however it may be interpreted, in which his fair one's charms are listed as in an inventory: two breasts, two thighs, two eyes, one mouth, one lap, etc.

And so then these walls fell because the old Jews blew their trumpets! Yet the desire to see this fact as a miracle demonstrating the Almighty's partiality for the Chosen People may perhaps be due to the abominable way the Bible has been translated into our various languages. All I have before me is the German Bible translation. Not that Luther was by any means devoid of musical sense, and many a good bawdy-house ballad tune is sung by the congregation to words of puritanical piety, without any Protestant's having knowledge of the musical background of those hymns. But physics was something of which Luther knew nothing, so far as anyone was aware. He drank too much heavy beer, which turned him into a nationalist, as is proved by his fight against Rome and for the German church. Music, like alcohol, has a stimulating effect on nationalistically inclined emotions. One only has to hear a march of Sousa's, preceded by fanfares, during a presidential election in God's Own Country. However, this won't make a wall fall down in Jericho, first of all because clay has no emotions, but secondly and above all because there are laws of physics that explain the miracle in a way perfectly satisfactory to the rational mind. If a note is sounded sufficiently loudly, what is heard at a certain distance is no longer the fundamental note but the harmonics, their wavelength being in relation to the distance from the center. The best place for the center is a height, whence the sound-waves spread out spherically in all directions. The army of those fighting for their religion against the Baal-worshipers descended on Jericho from the hills. Undoubtedly the vibration caused the smallest clay particles in the wall to vibrate in their own harmonic as soon as a certain relation was established between the wavelength of the harmonic peculiar to the particles and the distance to the chorus of trumpeters. Let us remember the strange sound patterns that arise on a glass plate strewn with colophony as soon as this is touched with a bow. Similar transformation takes place in the electromagnetic field on the membrane of a telephone. An old clay wall that the sun had been drying up long enough tottered and crumbled into dust. just imagine what a revolution Albert Einstein would have brought about in the world of sound-waves if he had gone in for composing instead of playing the violin...! We cannot quite ignore the possibility that even in antiquity musical innovators knew more about the laws of physics than we think, which, according to my theory, would have brought about the Chosen People's victory without any bother to Jehovah. In wartime everyone does his duty as best he can: let us think of Archimedes and his magnifying glass, with which he set the enemy fleet on fire outside Alexandria, and of Greek fire. Every invention that is made has to serve to strengthen the nation: it has always been so in history, from fire-making by means of two sticks rubbed together in the Stone Age right down to the atom bomb.

Just think that here, in this heap of ruins, Asiatic merchants from China, India and Persia once drove their caravans ahead of them and laid out their cargo in the bazaars — the glory of costly brocades, silks, gold filigree work and enameled jewelry, scented salves, attar of roses, and fragrant resin! How that must have piqued the vanity of the ladies of the harem! And now even a cheap little pocket-mirror, which I had bought in a shop in London and happened to drop, had its effect too. The sun was burning straight down on the sand now covering the trade-route that once seethed with new life at every sunrise. At that time East and West were woven together, like the warp and woof of a single carpet, to form one Paradise. Of all that colorful world nothing remained but the sun that sent out the same beams year in, year out. My imagination conjured up a *fata inorgatia*, silvery threads of rivers alive with strangely formed boats made of precious wood, or bulrushes or earthenware pitchers and distended goats' bladders, the colored gateway of the town through which the caravans entered, swaying under their burden, and the solitary walkers, all streaming into the many narrow streets and the buzzing bazaars. No less vividly did imagination paint all this for me as soon as I shut my eyes. It was very hot. I could still picture the obese town clerk, clearing the way ahead of him with a long stick as he rode on his donkey, his slippers trailing in the dust, and he deep in somber thought. What might the Babylonian's worries be? Perhaps he was a bookkeeper in the export business belonging to the Queen of Sheba, and each oil vessel was sealed with his own seal. It cannot have been easy, in those days, comparing bills made out in Babylonian cuneiform with Egyptian receipts, which were written in hieroglyphics. And then, into the bargain, there were those cunning Phoenicians from North Africa, who introduced their innovation, the decimal system, which they had deduced from the number of fingers on their greedy hands. How soon will the time come when, with the aid of an abacus, on which the beads are pushed this way and that, a mere child can deprive the clerk of his job, in which he has grown gray! No doubt that was what he was saying to himself. Half asleep, I dreamed of the caravans, now weary, halting in the shade of the city wall, the camels lying down in rows, opposite them little pyramids of cakes, made, as they are to this day, of date stone and dung. The camels swallow these cakes before they go to sleep and dream of lush meadows. Chewing the cud in their sleep, they bring this gift up again, out of the stomach into the crop, belching all the while. Not everyone among the people who feed these animals has all his ten fingers still on his hands. The camel driver thrusts the cake down the animal's throat with his naked arm, reaching in right up to his elbow. The camel is a treacherous beast, and sometimes at the last moment it bites off a finger.

All this passed the time away for me until I fell asleep, for the excavations had not yet progressed so far that there was anything more to be seen than old, crumbled clay bricks.

I woke up to see a yellow cat racing over the sand, its tail held high to keep it away from the hot, sharp grains of sand. It is wrong to throw stones at animals, and sleeping cats should not be teased with pieces of broken glass, which was just what a sluttish young person had been engaged in doing. Finally the cat had sneezed, because its ink nose was being tickled by a sharp beam of light from the little looking-glass, which the beggar-girl had found. Clearly since the time of her birth she had never heard of the invention of soap. The girl had her head full of foolishness.

For a long time the cat lay with closed eyes, putting up with the nuisance, merely blinking, having no inclination to look at the dish of goat's milk that this nomad girl had set out in the sand in front of the hole in the wall. The animal was not thirsty. All it wanted was peace and quiet! As an over-excited child clutches at its mother, so did the cat remain close to the house in the noon hours when the sun poured red-hot like molten metal, into the dried-up basin of clay. Or rather: close to the hovel, which was the remains of some tumble-down heap of a Sumerian, Babylonian, or Assyrian ruler's palace or of a caravanserai or of a Roman legionaries' camp in the Jewish War described by Josephus Flavius. Who can read the history written in stones? Who has not heard of that great strife between brothers which once divided the world of Islam into two hostile camps? The Bedouins here are followers of the Prophet Ali, of the tribe of Kahenna, which was persecuted in Medina. The nomad girl knew nothing of that story, and all the cat knew was that there are often scorpions hiding behind stones, especially the brown ones that flick their tails over their heads quick as lightning, before one knows what is happening. These scorpions sting like poisonous vipers and mean death even to a cat, which has, as everyone knows, nine lives. Was there not something brown stirring there among the thistles, or whatever it was growing by the wall where the cat was lying? The cat held its breath and stretched its paws out. True enough — something was moving! The five black toes of a human foot reared into the air. There's my naked beggar-girl sitting in the opening in the wall! Did anyone ever see such coquetry? In one hand she held a looking-glass, and with her fingertip, which she had moistened on her protruding lower lip, she was smoothing her eyebrows, first right and then left, then the tousle of hair over her brow and the black fringes at her temples, as though that were all that washing amounted to for her. And this was no profane action; on the contrary, it was a matter of Rule handed down from ages of ages, and from Granny Witch herself. Apart from the bits of broken glass there was nothing much to the girl, just as there was nothing much on her person. Such vanity made the cat yawn, and then it began to lick its own paws and then to wash its face too. Thus the two feminine creatures surveyed each other from a respectful distance, each following her own thoughts. From where I was watching them they looked like two brush-strokes in the bright sand, like a yellow and a blue character on the china dish with the goat's milk in it.

I approached and stopped in front of them both, drawing circles and spirals in the sand with my walking-stick, as though I were making a plan for the restoration of the Tower of Babel, as the moon worshipers once did in the Land Between the Two Rivers. What an interested audience I had! One was born an animal without a soul, the other a human being without a mind — the yellow cat and the plum-blue savage-girl. What does the little mirror say? Are white men thirsty? Both the cat and the girl knew that every year the learned men came to the Holy Land to dig about in the sand, and came with much to-do and with cooks and waiters and with flags all the colors of the rainbow. Why is the stranger looking at us? they both wondered. 'The foreign gentleman does not drink out of my dish?' the one said. I assumed that the girl was asking for baksheesh. With a tinkle the little coin fell in the sand. I was attracted by the dark hole, by the little woman sitting in it, feeling herself rejected, timid and shy. She turned her little bowl this way and that and then upside down. The cat was able to lick up some of the goat's milk before the sand could swallow it all. A wasted droplet ran over the thin hand of this young woman, who was playing with a knuckle-duster that was suddenly — and I have no idea where it came from — on her hand. I creep into the hole in the wall, after the little girl, and try to grasp her hand, which scratches. 'Give me cigarettes, then you can have me.' I gave and took. Afterwards the young thing puffed her smoke-rings into the empty air. Why did I stay instead of going after the deal had been completed? In order to say one thing more. 'Did not the Prophet forbid your people to smoke?' I flung at her. 'Allah gave no commandments to us women. Allah is great. May Allah drive the unclean ones out of the land,' the nomad girl answered angrily. 'And a moment ago you were kissing me? Truly, Allah gave you women no

soul!' 'The works of Allah are great and wonderful,' the beauty
asserted. 'To you white devils he gave no brains — you were
about to go, so why don't you? Every day you go running about
here in the noon-day heat, as though you had lost something!
Can't you sit still like a decent person?' I stroked her gently, but
I could have screamed. You are mine! The nomad girl now had
a dejected look. 'Why is your heart full of lies? When the True
Believers sit together, they tell stories, sing the old songs about
the heroes to the sound of the fiddle, or they smoke hashish and
are in Paradise with the houris.' I'm a jealous fool, I thought.
Why did I really not go?

What barbarians those crusaders must have been, leaving
their ladies at home with a padlock round their bodies, the key
of which those knights took with them to the Holy Land. Many
of them drowned on the voyage, many fell under the scimitar,
and many simply mislaid the key. How we white men always
have to regard whatever we love as our property! Aloud I said:
'And when your lord thrusts you away and summons your
younger sister to him, do you then suffer?' 'If I stayed in his tent,
what good would it do him? And me?' I asked her where the rest
of the women of her tribe were — out with the grazing herds?
'We do not sit at the table with our men like the wife of the
American yonder, who keeps our men from us to shovel sand. In
return, we know nothing of bitterness, just as under the earth no
one knows that in the upper world it is all over for him. Women
are like quails, in a good year there are many of them, plump in
the hand, in a bad year few and old and tough.'

Indolently she spat out the date-stone. She had a handful of
dates, all that she needed for a meal. Toying significantly with the
brass knuckles, she pulled away from me. 'Not every date-stone
that falls to the ground grows into a palm. Find yourself another
girl!' 'Put away the weapon! That knuckle-duster is no plaything
for you.' I insisted. 'Our women all bear arms. Aysha was the
mother of our tribe — she was already twelve years old and yet
she did not take the Prophet in her arms until he had recanted,
but he did not keep his word. Aysha led her daughters into the
field, which reddened with the blood of the men who had

treacherously slain her son in the night, the beloved Ali, Ali the Beautiful.' 'What is your name?' I asked. Aysha, like the mother of all the tribe of Kahenna.' She went. I would have followed her. 'Away from me! Unclean ones, keep your quarrels among yourselves, fighting like dogs in the dust of the earth that you divide among yourselves.'

Outside the sun was no longer shooting its arrows vertically onto the sand in which history blows away as the light turns to shadow. Across the amber-yellow desert the nomad girl was walking into the distance. I rubbed my eyes as though I had found what the archaeologists have not seen in the sand. Did the Queen of Sheba once upon a time test Solomon with just such riddles, when, to woo her, he left Jerusalem especially to come down into the Valley of Jericho? The cave was as empty as a temple without a divinity. Only the woman's odor still hung upon the air like incense.

THE SIXTH LETTER FROM THE TRAVELER

Djerba, 1929

In Jerusalem I heard praise of the beauty of the Jewish girls on the island of Djerba, which is, according to legend, the island where Odysseus dwelt with the nymph Calypso. The island of Djerba belongs to Tunisia. In the little capital of the island, which is Houmt-Souk, I engaged a deaf and dumb Negro chauffeur to drive me around the countryside. It is the orchard of North Africa, with palm-grove oases scattered like jewels. Apricots, figs, and almonds flourish in a climate that is never too hot or too cold. Old Greek fishing villages along the coast . . . the women wearing pointed straw hats like those of Tanagra terracotta figurines of antiquity. They dress in very full, white, fluttering robes that keep them cool in summer and warm in winter. The population is mixed: Berbers, Arabs, Greeks, and Negroes live in harmony with each other. On Djerba there are Jewish communities, the oldest of which, Hara-Srira, was founded by the Jews even before the Babylonian captivity. These are not ghettoes, as in Tunis, Algiers, or Morocco. While in North Africa plumpness is the ideal of beauty in the female sex, these Jewish girls were said still to be the equal in grace of their Biblical ancestresses.

I was surprised when I set eyes on the whitewashed, barrel-shaped roofs of the houses, for these buildings might just as well have stood in ancient Crete. So too the pottery, the weaving, the dyeing from the juice of seaweed, and the jewelers' work remind one of Minoan art. At one spot the mainland is so near that in Roman times a stone bridge led across to Zarsis; whereas the Nomads now embarked their camels in little sailing boats. The foundation stones of the Roman bridge, sunk into the sea, can still be clearly seen at the bottom on windless days.

I had a personal introduction from the resident-general in Tunis, which made such a good impression on the authorities in Houmt-Souk that I was provided with an interpreter for the purpose of explaining to the venerable Caid of the communities what it was I had come to the island for. It was not easy to convince this personage of the purity of my intentions and that I had come from so far away in order to choose the Beauty queen of Djerba, as was now the rage in Paris. At least this was the way that the interpreter represented it, he having recently visited France for the first time — actually only Paris, and there only to go to several hundred cabarets and see their dancing girls. All of these had, after all, also begun as beauty queens, or at least so they claimed.

Nor did my interpreter fail to play his trump card, which was: what an honor and what a gain it would be for the seven Jewish communities if in Paris Rothschild should become curious about the beauty queen and insist on seeing her face to face. Rothschild, the Croesus of money, reverently let his name be uttered together with those of the heroes of antiquity, of whom, as everyone knows, three are Jews: Joshua, David, and Judas Maccabaeus, and the other three unbelievers: Hector, Alexander, and Caesar. Negotiations were prolonged in elaborate oriental style. I empowered the official to go into the material aspect of the question with the mayor entirely according to his own judgment. Thus I had on the very first day deplored the dilapidated conditions of the synagogue, he told him, which was why I meant to go to some expense getting cedar wood especially from Mount Carmel for the restoration of the building. I knew, after all, that among the many Orthodox from the ghettoes of Morocco as far as the Persian Gulf this synagogue ranked as the most venerable, because it had existed on Djerba even before the destruction of the Temple at Jerusalem. The Caid saw that the affair was to his advantage; it was a clear case. Furthermore, all this offered him some welcome distraction, which is something for which an Oriental is always ready. And finally, it enhanced his standing with the authorities if for once they had to ask the community for something instead of sending a demand. The Caid let himself be persuaded to get into my car and from there to address the crowd that had gathered around the well in the marketplace. To the women, who wore loose, brightly colored, Oriental trousers, as well as to the men in their colorful caftans and round skullcaps, the dignified old man now with great eloquence presented this strange request. I could not understand what he was saying, but from his lively gestures I concluded that there seemed to be a prospect of good results. Our tour of inspection through the Jewish communities was arranged to take place in the following days, the interpreter assured me. I would be permitted to set eyes on all the girls that came into question, that is to say, those of marriageable age. And there was more than one of these in each household. I also thought I could regard the waving of hands and the merry flashing of eyes from the crowd of women as a good omen. I was looking forward to making the selection. And my fat Negro was positively beaming with pleasure, showing all his white teeth, waggling his hips like a dancing girl holding her bobbing breasts with her hands. For this was how he imagined the beauty queen that I would choose. After all, he knew no better!

I was not particularly disappointed when I failed to get an interview with the Caid either the next day or on the days following. He had simply vanished. Yet in a place where the sun shines all day long one isn't ever in a hurry about things. However, after a week had passed I decided that I had been kept waiting long enough. The longer the sun went on blazing in indifference upon my useless existence, the more hotly was I consumed by impatience to see the beauty. Let her soon appear before me as my own sun! I went back to the capital again to question the interpreter. Fortunately he was able to arrange things so that in spite of his urgent business he was able to make the trip back to the community with me the very next day; and this time that Caid was at home. And so loudly did the interpreter shout and threaten that the Caid became very small indeed: for although the interpreter was only an Arab, he was talking to the old man in the name of the government. The whole case had to be presented to him once again in complete detail, for in his old age the elder of the community had grown forgetful and was hard of hearing. Only when the interpreter dwelt on the easy-going attitude that the high-and-mighty government had hitherto taken towards dilatory taxpayers, an attitude that the community was now obviously acknowledging only with ingratitude, did the head of the community suddenly begin to hear tolerably well, and he likewise became capable of remembering everything. Probably he himself had a bad conscience about taxes; so Jacob ben Jacob ben Israel had his donkey led out. From both sides we helped him into the saddle; with a long staff the rider pushed himself off the ground, as a heavily laden barge is pushed off the shore with an oar. We followed him in the car and did not lose sight of him. Our car bumped through the little twisting streets between whitewashed walls where over the doorways, as on Arab houses, the symbols of good fortune, the fish and the tree of life, were painted in blue. The party stopped outside every house, the wooden bolts on the doors were pushed back, and the doors were opened at the orders of the resident-general in Tunis. There is only one God, whether Moses or Mahomet be his prophet, and only one supreme power, namely, in Paris. In the name of that power we knocked at every door. Each time shouts arose from among the wild-looking, black-haired men sitting around a cauldron of sharply spiced fish soup in the courtyard. The gaunt, brown, beringed hands dropped the slices of bread into the gravy and were raised on high. The women uttered piercing screams. Before our very eyes the naked, pot-bellied children relieved themselves out of sheer excitement there in the courtyard. But the unmarried girls, who were the ones I was after, curious to see what was going on, pushed up the spindle-lattice wooden windows and, when their names were recited from a long list, came out of the house, the Rachels, the Myriams, the Annas, and paraded hesitantly before my eyes. The interpreter put a little star opposite each name on the list whenever, in my opinion, a girl deserved to be short-listed.

The decisive day had dawned, when I was to meet my happiness. I think I ought to mention, as an afterthought, that I wanted to paint the most beautiful Jewish girl. With nods and becks and wreathed smiles I did my best to make myself understood by the many women old and young. Where was this going to lead? The Caïd's reception-room was already full, and there were still over-excited women pushing their way in, many with their infants at their breast. Angrily this one nagged me, and shyly that one tugged at my sleeve, but my choice had not yet been made. The interpreter had whispered to me that the most beautiful girl in all the Jewish communities had hitherto been kept hidden from me. She was the foster-daughter of the mayor himself. Despite all the old man's denials, pleadings, and tears I remained inexorable, insisting on my rights. The old man had the door shut against the crowd pushing its way in after me, and finally declared himself prepared to bring the girl into my presence. The curtain is still drawn across the alcove, the old man claps his hands, the curtain rises, and sitting there, supported by her mother and other female relatives, is a strange, lovely being that I thought I had seen the day before, only for an instant, fleetingly, carrying a water-pitcher on her head at the well in the marketplace, in the rays of the setting sun. So the sly fox had let me inspect all the girls in all the communities, yet had hitherto concealed from me the treasure in his own house. And without my Negro I should not have seen that fleeting white cloud drifting past, when she went to fetch water. He went on nudging me until I turned round and just caught a glimpse of the shy gazelle's movements. And so it was the mayor's foster-daughter on whom my choice fell, and none of the old man's refusals, objections, and pleadings availed anything — the girl was more than betrothed, indeed as good as married to the son of a merchant in Tunis, the bridal money had been paid, the marriage contract was valid in law. I laughed and wept when I saw the lovely creature sitting in the alcove. The hair on her head must not fall under the scissors before my picture was painted! Thus did I swear to myself. I sent her a laughing look, and she smiled back. Again and again I tried to capture the contour on the canvas, but my outstretched hand was shaking, I could not hold the charcoal, and the white canvas seemed reluctant to let the first black marks be made upon it. In the half-darkness of the room the womenfolk behind me were agog to hear whatever would come next. Every breath was audible. Awe overcame me when, as in the Holy of Holies in the Temple, I saw the maiden dreaming in the alcove a rosebud in one hand, a pomander in the other. Contemplation, and the intoxication of love pressed towards violent union in my soul, a spiritual tempest aroused by the mystery of that girlish apparition. Zephyr-blue, rose-red, and gold blended together in the brocade of the trousers clothing the crossed legs. From the little waistcoat, embroidered with twinkling silver spangles, the deep décolleté of which permitted me to see her little breasts, nestling like a pair of doves in a nest of muslin, my glance roamed further, only to be captured once again by the charm of the hieratic head-dress she wore, gold, enamel, and filigree work such as the jewelers make locally, crowning her black hair, whence my eye gradually slid off to the duller, more ordinary colors of her relatives' garments. The fight emanating from the bewildered girl cast a secondary radiance upon these women, like the last ray of sunlight touching the earth already veiled in deep night. The light also played in the folds of the rugs on the walls and on the floor, the enchantment of love gradually fading out, glimmering a moment longer among the velvety shadows, then to be extinguished in the background.

After at first keeping her face averted, doubtless in order to conceal her maidenly shame, she turned her little head to me defiantly, whereupon my heart began to thud and tears came into my eyes, because her large eyes looked at me so enchantingly that I thought I could not bear it for long. She could not understand what I kept on softly whispering all this time, the flattering words with which I sought to woo her, words not meant to be heard by the women craning inquisitively over my shoulders. The thing happened before I stopped to think how, with the few crumbs of Arabic that I knew, I was to say that her gaze bent full upon me was reducing me to utter confusion. 'Oh, your eyes!' It had slipped out before I could help it. Ah, how gladly I would have left it unsaid! The girl blushed deeply, the blood in the veins of her little firm throat making it swell, and the bud dropped from the hand that she raised to free her breast from the stuff enclosing it, as though she felt a burning pain within her. The women began to make a noise and to weep and the girl swayed on her feet as they led her out of the room.

For more than a month I made vain attempts to see my model again. They lied to me, they made excuses. I traveled back to Tunis, made myself popular with the vendors in the bazaars, bribed them to betray to me the name of the family of the boy to whom the girl was promised. I spoke with the boy's father, who had his office next to his corn and seed warehouse behind one of the gateways in the rectangle of walls that shuts off the sarcophagus of the Marabout from the bazaar, from the noisy life of the streets. The merchant was not unapproachable, although his extensive business left him little time for other things. He was willing to help me and sought an explanation for the Caïd's refusal. Perhaps I should have refrained from making contact with the authorities? What — he said, shaking his head — could one expect of those worthy people in Djerba, his kinsmen, who were just as superstitious as the fellahin themselves. Then I met an emissary of the university in Jerusalem, who was visiting all the ghettoes in the world and making a collection. He was lodging with the merchant, and the merchant introduced me to him. The emissary had not yet been on Djerba and was very willing to make the trip there in my company, but he had only a shrug of the shoulders for my offer to have the synagogue restored at my expense. It was of course my own affair, I could do what I liked with my own money, he said, though, frankly, his university was in greater need of support. As an enlightened man of the world the boy's father deplored the fact that his co-believers on Djerba were a prey to fatalism that not merely made them bad believers but also bad debtors in matters of business, no better than the natives themselves, who — he said in conclusion — did not keep up with the times. With pride he indicated his extensive correspondence, to which he then proceeded to devote his entire attention, for which reason I took my leave of him. The delegate of the university did in fact come to the girl's community with me. But the girl herself had meanwhile been spirited away to the mainland, in order to hide her in Sfax, to save her from being pursued by me. And once again I succeeded in tracing her. I knew of a private aeroplane, belonging to Monsieur d'Erlanger, who had his country residence in the vicinity of Carthage. I was determined to put an end to these intrigues and to kidnap the girl. It was easy to make contact with the pilot, but the plane was at the moment under repair — it was one of the first aeroplanes ever built. Junk! Already, so to speak, made obsolete by modern techniques, which have meanwhile advanced with giant strides — or, more accurately, on giant wings! There was unfortunately nothing to be done — what a pity! I paid for the wine, and the mechanic took his leave.

Meanwhile the sun was burning ever more madly. Whenever I passed by the marketplace in Houmt-Souk and saw the incredible pyramids of lambs' heads, with flies swarming over them, I was nauseated. They are accounted a delicacy among the natives, but to me they looked like pyramids of human heads, their eyes staring at me. I was almost demented with all my plotting and planning as to how to trace the girl. I was incapable of doing anything else, I walked around as though under a spell, and the thought of her haunted me day and night. Once I even bought up all the fish in the market, a big basketful of weird creatures, freshly fished out of the sea that same morning. Until the flaming ball of the sun went down I stared, instead of painting, at what gradually became a gelatinous mass. 'You mustn't make an image of anything that casts a shadow!' That was what the emissary had said to me. This is no longer a law for the Jews, but it is still observed among the Arabs, who are permitted to make only abstract patterns. And the Jews on Djerba were in no way different from fellahin. In the coffee-house I heard of a sorcerer who concocted not only love letters for those unlearned in the art of writing, but also love philtres. I was prepared to believe in the strange effect of certain herbs whose juice, if mingled with food and drink, makes a virtuous maiden compliant to a lover's will. An intermediary was found and the magic potion tried, but without any effect.

Another time that faithful friend of mine, the deaf and dumb

Negro chauffeur, took me to see a relative of his who lived on the outskirts of the Negro quarter. His dwelling, built of old petrol-cans, lay hidden behind a cactus hedge, and the way thither led past a garbage dump where people threw their dead cats and dogs. In the nighttime now and then one of the Negresses would come furtively creeping along there — one of those who spent the day standing up to their waists in the water at the edge of the sea, washing clothes and singing. In the night they did not sing, nor did they have their infant at their breast or on their back, which is the usual place for it to sleep, and they were shy. I had to wait for a long time until the doctor had finished with these women, who perhaps came for a medicine to save a sick child or to restore their fertility. For the Africans, magic remains the beginning and the end of all wisdom, the motor that sets all thing in motion, because it has power over the living and over spirits. I waited a long time! What secret business had they with the medicine man? Perhaps they wanted to destroy a rival's happiness by means of a thread from her dress. At last it was my turn. The sorcerer stood over a boulder on which the oil, which had been poured on to it for so long, had congealed into a greenish cake the size of one's fist. Then, stooping, I followed him into his low-ceiling consulting-room. The gaunt elderly Negro with the gray side-whiskers squatted on his heels. He pushed a wooden stool forward for me, because I could not manage to take my ease in the same way as he. After casting a searching glance at me he rolled a little package up in the skin of a sand-lizard and wrote magical hieroglyphs on it. When he had finished, he waited to hear my wishes. The beauty of his expression was not impaired by the texture and color of his skin, which was rather like blackish-gray ashes. I was struck by the dignity of his features, by his resemblance to Michelangelo: even the broken nose was not missing. As a boy, a long time ago, before the time of the French occupation, he had been sold into slavery here — he had been born in the South — and he had also been three times to Mecca and nevertheless possessed the ancient wisdom and was a member of an African men's secret society. As if involuntarily, his black fingers toyed with a few white moonstones, which gleamed in the darkness. He had already heard my story, and being a sensible man he had not taken it lightly. Allah has ordained who shall come together with whom! Only unbelievers laugh at love as a folly. Is it a matter for laughter when the hot wind rises or falls? Could he force the girl? For I did not want to go on living without her! There was nothing I would not have done, yet there is nothing to be done with a father who chooses the fat son of a rich merchant in Tunis for his daughter's husband without her setting eyes on him before the wedding. I had learned, incidentally, that she was reluctant to enter into this marriage. Like a sick man, who finds relief from his sufferings in the ever new pain they cause him, I sought out the community, without any hope of success. Now that the people had ceased to fear me they threw stones at me. Indeed, they even went so far as to mock me, and the women made obscene gestures when they caught sight of me. All this I told the doctor. He scooped up a handful of sand from the floor, told me to wet my handkerchief with spittle, and then threw the sand into the handkerchief. I was to return some days later, as soon as the moon was favorable. He would accompany me to the girl's house. I became confident for the first time since this misfortune had befallen me. When the appointed night came, the black man was waiting for me at the place where we had agreed to meet. He got into the motor-car and sat beside the driver. When our little car crossed the sand towards the white village in the moonlight, the black man told me I was to take the handkerchief with the sand in it and throw it down at the threshold of the house that had so long been locked against me, not to utter a word and, as soon as the girl came up to me, to take her by the hand, lift her into the car, and drive off instantly. During the trip the magician sat there in front of me, in silence, not stirring, almost invisible, cloaked from head to foot in a white woolen garment. It was icy cold. The market-place was deserted, and the car made a fearful noise in the narrow, bumpy clay street. When I listened to the sound of the engine it was not to reassure myself that it was working properly: I had the notion that I was the only living being on earth. Not even the desert foxes were barking at the moon. The car positively flew along, an automaton. It was like a dreary weight upon my heart — that dead word: automaton. Was it really possible that I was already suffering less?

Only when we turned the corner did I begin to be afraid that the beating of my heart was louder than the noise that the car made, and I thought everyone must come running out. Yet I firmly believed in the doctor, who had knowledge of secret things and had power over them, over the ghosts that one conjures up for oneself in one's helplessness. The nearer we came, the more tightly did I clutch the ball of sand, and when he gave the sign, I flung it, striking the wooden threshold as I had been told to. My aim was good! At that very moment the heavy doors opened soundlessly, and across the bare courtyard there came the girl, walking in her sleep, with closed eyes, pale, and with an expression of suffering on her face — she walked towards me with faltering steps, one hand outstretched as if she were groping her way. I seized her hand. Then suddenly my own enterprise, which I had planned for so long and with such passion, seemed to be quite senseless. It was her shut eyes that made everything now strike me as so unnatural, that made me want nothing more from this being whom an alien will had forced to come. And therefore I called out to the sleepwalker, who opened her eyes and staggered backwards with a faint scream, letting go of my hand. When the car started again, I just had time to see the girl going back to the house, without even turning round. The gate remained open. When the Arabs speak of eyes, they always make a sign to ward off evil. I brought the whole disaster upon myself that time because I did not make the sign that wards off the evil eye.

Nature began to breathe again, a faint breeze was stirring the trees, as it always begins to do before dawn. The doctor flung the hood back from his face and looked at me, smiling.

THE SEVENTH LETTER FROM THE TRAVELER

I

Ireland 1945

For a long time I had in my possession a Phoenician silver coin. Through how many hands must that coin have passed! Through the hands of the money-changer precisely, swiftly counting the takings at the table that he brought to the marketplace in the morning . . . through hands of men robed in purple and costly linen, who heedlessly dropped it into the hands of a beggar covered in sores, hands that raised it to the lips with a blessing for the giver . . . or hands paying it in wages to the foreign seaman . . . Carthage hired mercenaries from the farthest lands of the globe, or pressed foreigners into the service.

On the obverse the coin bore the image of a leaping horse. One could still make out the wild creature's worn contours; the stallion seemed about to burst right out of the circle in which the artist had set it in characteristic movement for all time. How often this coin must have escaped the fate of being thrown into the melting pot. Barbarian hordes harried Northern Africa, one horde after another taking possession of the Phoenician Empire. The urns and the unburied bodies of conquered and conqueror alike crumbled to dust nearly two thousand years ago, just as the realms that followed upon the Carthaginian Empire have long been reduced to ruins. All that is told by my silver coin, which escaped destruction, is that silver money was once current there in Carthage and that there were perhaps also horse races for the mob, to keep them in a good mood.

Now, recently I happened to see a newly minted half-crown of the Irish Free State, on which there is also the image of horse. The horse is said to be man's noblest conquest. Perhaps there were reasons of State for alluding to some almost forgotten local meaning attached to this noble animal, as a symbol of something that is past and gone — something that has already passed into legend, that is rediscovered in myth and fairy tale — just as choice has also fallen on gryphons and chimeras, the noble eagle of the skies, the lion, the King of the Beasts, and finally the horse.

But since the nominal value of modern currency is nowadays arbitrarily decided by the State and is purely fictitious, because it is no longer related to any content of precious metal, so that such a coin is minted from ersatz-alloys and on a conveyor-belt — why a horse? Perhaps to show up the breeders, who destined the horse for the knacker? Anyone who has watched the horses on the freighter sailing from Dublin to the slaughterhouses of Antwerp, and seen how often they die on the voyage, does well not to let himself be reminded of the breeder, lest his blood freeze in his veins.

The Amazons taught the Homeric heroes how to master the horse. In legend the horse often became a winged being, bearing its feminine rider as on the wings of the wind into all four quarters of the sky. Did the Gorgon, that frightful female with the fluttering hair, cause panic among the Greeks? The Gorgon was the embodiment of those mounted *dames sauvages* who came in their throngs from Pontus, ordered armies of women, sworn to hatred of all men, sending out their whistling arrows from the bow so swiftly, as they sat on the back of their galloping stallions, that anyone who caught sight of them always re-membered their faces as though framed in a nest of twitching vipers — supposing he survived the frightful encounter with the Amazons. The horse played a demonic role from Pontus to the cradle of archaic Greece. Among the Gauls and Celts proph-etesses would sacrifice the horse — it had to be a white palfrey — at a time when those tribes were already incorporated in the Roman Empire. Even today the French and the Belgians ascribe to horseflesh the virtue of blood-building, while the English do not eat it — except perhaps in Parisian restaurants, where they are not told what it is.

In England horse-racing became a great sport under Cromwell. As Rome took horse-racing from the vanquished Gauls, so England did from Ireland. In our own time this sport is losing the character of a popular amusement; it no longer has the gaiety that affords stimulation wherever that taste for gambling and danger and taking sides can have free rein, as in the Palio at Siena. England is going to the dogs, as the increasing popularity of dog racing proves. Dog races are no longer a sport in this sense, because the crowd's gaze tends to be glued to the numbers of the totalizator. The word 'sport' comes from '*desport*' and '*portare,*' to carry to all four points of the compass. But if one cannot speak of a Roman horse in the same sense in which one speaks of a full-blooded Arab or distinguishes between the Spanish and the Nordic breeds, that does not justify one in hastily assuming that in the Roman Empire, when Rome was becoming the economic center of the world, the horse was only used to carry burdens, like the mule, ox, or ass. That would be too hasty an assumption. The network of Roman roads, linking all parts of the world, cannot be compared with modern methods of transport, the railway, the steamship, or the motor-car, to which England owes its economic supremacy in the world — they must not be compared merely because the familiar sound of the word 'Empire' tempts one to do so. The Roman Empire must be regarded as a unique historical phenomenon. It is necessary to take the unity of horse and rider as the basic unit of a measure that the historian must apply in his historical appraisal of the Roman Empire. Horse and rider are a political unit, just as horse-power is a unit of energy in physics.

In ancient Rome the only citizen with full rights was the man who provided a horse for military service; only when mounted was he an integer, like the centaur of myth. He was the smallest unit in the State. But the Roman did not behave like the beggar on horseback. He did not take life easy. He became a missionary; the network of Roman roads linking all parts of the world was merely a means to an end, intended to bring the whole world under Roman law, which is based on principles of universally valid justice, the same for all nations in the world, a natural law, that is, in harmony with Nature. Whether it was a thoroughbred, a mule, or a donkey on which the centurion sat, the missionary knew what he was after. If one wishes better to understand an historical event, it is also advisable not to confuse Rome's political mission with the tasks besetting a modern economic empire, such as England or other sovereign States. It is recounted of the Scottish missionary in Africa who talked himself dry preaching against the Negroes' sin of drunkenness, that he accidentally pulled a bottle of whisky out of his pocket. But in that pocket one would also find iron nails, cogwheels, ships' screws, railway tracks, and other products of industry, together with raw materials such as coal, ore, wool and cotton, but no idea like that inspiring the Roman Empire. The fact of a surprising awakening of religious zeal in the early years of free trade in the British Commonwealth is generally contemplated through the eyes of a romanticist, but it was the missions that opened up export markets among the heathen children. Romanticism does not lead to clear thinking. The equation will not work out if one tries to see one and the same political manifestation in an equestrian statue such as, for instance, that of Marcus Aurelius, and a mounted policeman. For while the Roman legionary was bringing the barbarians the gospel of the future State, with its justice and eternal peace — just as one tells fairy stories to children to keep them quiet — the modern democrat exalts the idea of the State in such a way as to turn himself into a puppet even although the strings by which he is worked lie in his own hands.

Every morality wreaks its vengeance on those who violate the principle inherent in a social convention. This would demand that one should voluntarily keep to the rules of the game, on the assumption that one can throw up the game as soon as it ceases to amuse one. People forget that even the conception of the State as a person in the legal sense is a fiction. If it counts for anything more than a mere playing with words, the confusion between subject and object creates an effect that the citizen does not envisage, namely, that the state, which is our better knowledge, is lost. In society a joke is told, which nobody understands. Privately everyone regards himself as the one idiot who has missed the point, yet no one dares to admit it openly. Let us just consider the events of the most recent times, which each of us is old enough to have experienced himself. The sovereign States waged world wars, signed peace treaties, and set about social planning, as though all this would have no effect on the individual human being's fate. An immense ever-growing number of people who lost their spiritual *terra firma* together with their native soil are driven along the highways of the world, perishing in concentration camps that grow yearly in number. For this peculiar political situation the individual has to thank the fact that the causal nexus is no longer clear to him. If one does not ride oneself, but sets the State on a high horse, the citizen goes to the dogs. Analyzing the Zeitgeist would be a job for a psychiatrist. What in the modern citizen is only a neurotic complex and the symptom of a morbid syndrome becomes the norm and the substance of the history of the modern world.

To come back to the Roman races: seven racing chariots had to go round the course seven times, and it was the same in ancient Gaul and Ireland. The finish line was represented by two pillars or poles, which were crowned by strange egg-shaped symbols, visible from afar. The modern Englishman is so busy that he does not notice when daily, morning and evening, he dashes past the same symbols in the form of a closed lotus, a pine cone, a thyrsus, or even of a perfectly ordinary egg, flanking the gate of his front garden, outside his little semidetached house. Now, a symbol preserves its ancient meaning even where it has degenerated into mere decoration. Does not the Englishman also say 'my home is my castle,' although he knows that this has for a long time been a mere figure of speech? One cannot take out of a pocket anything that has not first of all been put into it, and in the same way the symbols have to serve so long as the thought in which they originate remains unchanged. Modern man tries to cope with the danger of becoming conscious, not merely where the natural functions of the body are concerned, but in general where our human nature is concerned, by averting his eyes from it. It is unjust to cite Christian other-worldliness as an explanation of this much more obscure problem; it only illumines the matter in part. Now, this harmless ornament that we deliberately overlook in our little front garden has a hidden meaning, of which — as in the case of stereotype phrases — we do not become aware, but which suddenly overwhelms us when we are least alert to the danger of becoming conscious. Because we are startled by the unexpected obscene implication in a joke, just as in a caricature a hitherto unregarded detail, the nose, the paunch, are emphasized and given point, suddenly taking on a life of their own and making the caricatured person irrelevant and comical, because of that, I say, we are on guard against taking the symbol on the garden gate for what it actually means — the sign of the eunuch condition of the modern citizen — for else we would become suspect to ourselves. Socrates tells us: The only virtue in life is clean thinking. Why does our hypocrisy not bring us into conflict with public opinion? Perhaps because every deviation from the norm — that is, from thinking as the Zeitgeist wishes — causes us embarrassment, rather as if we were to run around naked now that it has become second nature to wear clothes. We lose our moral balance instantly when we slip on the famous banana skin. The lie about life ceases to be a lie as soon as it becomes a habit.

Why, actually, do we play cat and mouse with ourselves, first-seemingly without any special purpose — putting up a few of those oddly egg-shaped things outside our houses, and then overlooking them?

After carnival comes Ash Wednesday. Under the greasepaint of enthusiasm with which we sacrifice ourselves to the State there grins the inner scepticism; yet we pretend to ourselves that reason must be silent because the State is our destiny. Admittedly, even in the Roman Empire the mob made self-mutilation during the races the main focus of the State celebration of carnival; and in disguises and obscene travesties, in libertinage and high foolery before the whole public they celebrated the *ver sacrum*. In the blood-soaked arenas of Rome and Byzantium youths exuberantly castrated themselves; that was why these egg-shaped symbols were put up at the end of the race-course in those days. Since the introduction of conscription the *ver sacrum* is celebrated not only at carnival and not only by ecstatic youths. In the modern State, however insignificant it may be on the map, the claim to absolute sovereignty is implicit. I repeat: Morality wreaks its vengeance on the partner in the game who violates the principle inherent in a rule of the game, a rule based on the voluntary principle.

I crave the reader's patience if in this somewhat prolix introduction of mine I have stretched the idea of the riderless horse too far. The nag has meanwhile gone the way of all flesh. But the story of the modern democrat thrown by his steed has, fundamentally, little to do with my story, which I now mean to tell, and serves rather to discover how far one can go without straining the reader's patience to the breaking point.

On the reverse of my Carthaginian coin there is a plant. That plant aroused my interest even more than the horse on the obverse. What importance it must have had if it was chosen by the specialists who conducted their manipulations with the Phoenician currency, to figure on a coin that was valid everywhere in the economic realm of antiquity. Let the reader bear in mind that that economic realm extended all along the North African coast, past Egypt and into Asia Minor as far as the Greek archipelago and back round the Balkans to the West, along the Italian, French, and Spanish coasts and northward as far as Ireland.

This plant was surely not a foodstuff. Edible plants have indeed been cultivated to such a degree of perfection that they no longer have the slightest resemblance to their primal form; yet no single species of grain — to take only this as an example — has ever been forgotten or died out since the Stone Age. I am no botanist. As a layman I would say that the plant rather resembled some ordinary seaweed. The reader may be presumed to know that, thanks to their business acumen, the ancient Phoenicians were well able to cope with the new middle class of officials, slave-overseers, and officers of the standing armies in the countries economically opened up by Carthage and were capable of building up a worldwide trade adequate to the needs of this new class. Of what kind can the wares have been that kept supply and demand in such a favorable relationship to each other that a worldwide commerce was solidly based on them and a monopoly could be founded? As social history reveals, jewels, weapons, and utensils for these new classes were no longer made of gold, electrum, and bronze, as they were previously for rulers and the nobility, but of the cheaper brass and zinc, and later of iron. It is likewise well known that this nation of seafarers could see further than the ten fingers of the greedy hand can reach, for the Phoenicians did, after all, invent arithmetic. It was the establishment of the decimal values numbers that first enabled them to perform the four classical arithmetical operations as easily with the largest figures as with the smallest fractions. This latter was necessary for the turnover of cheap industrial products, when, as in our modern shops, substitutes and imitations were to be palmed off on the populace at large. The populace must provide a profit. It was the Woolworthian principle that the Phoenicians also applied to their mass production of a certain very mysterious article.

Are we here, perhaps, on the point of discovering a secret of this Semitic people's productivity, one of which no economic expert has hitherto dreamed, no matter whether he adhere to a capitalist or to a communist school of economic thought? If so, every scrap of evidence that seems to contribute to the recon- struction of the situation assumes the highest importance, even where the general public is concerned, indeed, for everyone who has acquired a certain training from much reading of detective stories. Only acquaintance with all the facts that must be taken into consideration will enable the reader to form his own opinion.

If I am not mistaken it was Herodotus who mentioned that the Carthaginians used a kind of seaweed for manuring their fields. This at once struck me as rather implausible, although as a writer of travelers' tales Herodotus usually had fairly good judgment both of men and of things. To me it seems excessive to suppose that a sea-faring and commercial nation with a keen eye for the main chance should have racked their brains about methods of improving agricultural land that could be had for the taking and which was in any case tilled by slaves. So it may not be entirely a waste of time to take a closer look at this supposed agrarian industry. I am not wandering from my subject if for a moment I amuse myself by pointing out that in earlier times the distinguished dead used to be painted in the color of life, as is proved by finds in the sepulchral chambers of Egypt and all ancient cultures from the Land Between the Two Rivers to Ireland. This was done in order to deceive the spirits of the departed, at least for as long as the dye lasted. And in the same manner food, drink, slaves, and servants were also provided, first *in natura*, later symbolically, so that the dead in the realm of shades should not go without any of the good things that the earth provides. Thus spellbound in the realm of shades, they left the living in peace. In the new empire of Egypt, however, the living also painted themselves with ocher, as can be seen from the frescoes. This was done for the same reason that the wild Scots and the North American Indians used red for their war-paint. Gradually the color red acquired a metaphysical significance, which may be connected with the spreading of the dualistic religions of Egypt and the Near East, which were beginning to dominate intellectual life everywhere. Dualism is a mystery that has always been of lively interest to the Oriental imagination. The idea of assuring immortality, rebirth, or resurrection by means of magical incantations, rituals, and secret potions became known throughout the world of that time through the ubiquitous presence of armies and fleets, coming and going always with merchants and traders in their train. Wars do not merely promote progress in science and technology; religious propaganda also takes advantage of such times of universal restlessness. As today so then too there were world wars between the empires fighting among themselves for domination of the world. Victory assured the monopoly of trade in an economic territory enlarged by conquest, which also favored the introduction of the stable gold and silver currency that the Phoenicians first invented. Money henceforth remained the basis of progress and prosperity, until sovereign States in most recent times went back to the barter practiced by primitive societies. Although gold and silver slip through the fingers more easily, primitive peoples in

Australia still to this day use millstones for money. Speculation in real estate began to develop as soon as it could be expressed in money values. For this purpose laborers were bought from victorious generals' prisoner-of-war camps, an innovation to which we have returned in modern times, for it is a practical measure. A planned economy is buoyed up by the hope that a wave of prosperity will last forever.

Red dye was originally meant only for the warrior, whom it imbued with faith in his invulnerability and in eternal life, giving him courage and lending him magical power over his enemies. Although belief in immortality is also the psychological basis of the idea of resurrection, it is not to be dogmatically identified with the belief in a beyond as such. It was only towards the end of Roman domination, when the misery and wretchedness of this world was becoming insufferable to all, that this belief gained universal acceptance among the masses. As a consolation prize Christianity, the Koran, and the Enlightenment preached the doctrine of a Paradise in the beyond — or of an ideal state of things on earth some time in the future.

Herodotus was a man with all the talents of a modern foreign correspondent, and so, whenever the situation did not permit an appropriate testing of the facts, just like any other reporter he resorted to merely passing on what he had from hearsay. It is to him that we can trace back the rumor that red dye was obtained from the murex. On the basis of my own researches I assert that purple was obtained from the seaweed represented on my coin. I submit my solution to an unprejudiced public, which may survey the evidence itself. Let us imagine ourselves in the situation that prevailed at, say, the time of the Punic Wars. It was a favorable juncture for the missionaries of a belief in the beyond. Is it not therefore logical that the Phoenicians were the first to have the idea of investing their money in the mass manufacture of red dye? No sovereign State in the world, even though it be the most Christian on the whole globe, or the most progressive, or a 'Volksdemokratie' voluntarily cedes a monopoly. Least of all is this to be expected from a reactionary power such as the historical sources compel us to consider Carthage to have been.

We can safely assume that the history of the manufacture of the red dye is not a mere rumor, but a *canard* deliberately broadcast, a story that Herodotus was fooled into believing so that he should, in all good faith, make it more widely known. *Une blague*, that's all! How is it that serious scholars have brought themselves to repeat this fairy tale so often, this story that a reporter traveling around in those foreign countries should, merely for the sake of his *beaux yeux* have been entrusted with that extremely important secret on the keeping of which the weal and woe of the Carthaginian Empire depended? After all, what security measures were needed in order to assure, at least for a time, this and that great power's monopoly of the manufacture of atom bombs and hydrogen bombs! Peasants who had become landless were recruited to form standing armies in the pay of the warring great powers. Each soldier bought the red dye symbolic of life. The Carthaginian manufacturer would positively have had to invent belief in immortality in those days if it had not already existed. Did not Christianity itself owe its spread to the existence of armies, as is proved by the great numbers of martyrs in the Roman legions? However, the lords of Carthaginian commerce miscalculated when they thought they would keep the monopoly of purple dye for themselves alone and forever. The Romans' reason for waging war against Carthage, namely, the immorality of the latter, must be regarded in its true light: the war was fought for the monopoly. My theory is that the Phoenicians must have obtained the red dye from a seaweed quite easy to find, which made it possible to manufacture it in profitably large quantities. It is true that when it is burned the ashes can also be used for manure. But such a use must not be inferred from the image on the coin, for the Phoenicians were commercial seafarers and not agricultural experts.

Why did Cato daily in the Senate urge the destruction of Carthage? In the Third Punic War Carthage was razed to the ground. With its extirpation the Carthaginian people had expiated a 'collective guilt'. Nevertheless, the red dye symbolic of life became ever more expensive. The Phoenician dye-works worked under cover abroad, as Höchst Chemicals tried to do in the Second World War. There was, for instance, the independent city of Tyre, a source of annoyance to the Romans. There the Phoenicians worked under the protection of Philip II of Macedonia, who as a result was never again to sleep in peace. in fact, they there manufactured the dye from the extremely rare murex, which is fished on the coasts of India. They could prove that it cost them more than they made by it. At that time it was only Roman Senators, Consuls, and very rich people, like Arab oil kings in the Yemen nowadays, who could afford such luxury. Those cunning people in Tyre went on working at a loss rather than yield their secret. After Tyre had been razed and Macedonia had been conquered by Rome, the dye-syndicate's secret became generally known and the monopoly ceased to exist. This was followed by a crash on the stock market, so that now the Romans had to employ Draconic measures in order to protect the Senators' privilege of wearing the red toga. Even the threat of the death penalty cannot stop the spread of a fashion if the ladies will not cooperate. Red became popular, whatever divine Caesar promulgated in Rome, and has carried the field to this day.

The history of the red dye symbolic of life runs like a scarlet thread, like Ariadne's thread, through the political tissue in which past and present are woven together in our thoughts. Whereas on the one hand strange ovoid shapes outside the houses in England are the symbol of the citizen's unmanning, a symbol handed down from the past, the red rag, on the other hand, that is borne ahead of us, has become the symbol of rebellion. Those who will give their lives in their enthusiasm for some utopia of the future do not die out. This teaches us tolerance, which is supposed to let everyone work out his salvation in his own way.

My private curiosity has often enabled me to liberate myself from prejudices that are as natural to a rationalistic era as superstition was to the Dark Ages. A favorite parlor game consists of imagining what the history of the world would have been like if this or that had not happened, or had happened differently. Similarly it is no less amusing to those with a sense of curiosity to seek problems where for other people they simply do not exist.

On an Egyptian potsherd of the Middle Kingdom, which is in the Louvre, there is a Phoenician seafarer depicted with a few brush-strokes. Together with other wares, not further specified, he carries on his ship a bale of plants, to the importance of which an inscription especially testifies. According to the catalogue this is to be translated as sylphidium, but this interpretation is followed by a query. My conjecture is that an Egyptian potter is much more to be relied on than the economists who impose their modem economic theories on an obscure past, without being able to lure the secret of purple out of its shell. In accordance with my interpretation of the bale of plants on the potsherd I must reject Herodotus's report as erroneous. The extraction of the juice of the plant was of course not as it was in Ireland at the time. When the invasion of England was being planned, it was considered a home industry, but now it must be regarded rather as an industry working for export. In much the same way as the Japanese cultivate pearls, the purple-dye plantations must then have been established in shallow sea-water. And we must regard the seafarer on the potsherd as one of the many captains of an extensive Phoenician shipping company controlling all the then known seas, an employee of an efficient priestly organization. The entrepreneurs were unwilling to take risks — pirates, shipwreck, and even more the perishability of the final product, the purple dye — and that was why they transported the raw material, the bale of dried seaweed, which had no value. However much was lost, enough and to spare was left to supply the many colonies owned by the Phoenician commercial world, where a competent local industry was able to manufacture the purple on the spot. Let the professional historians dispose of this explanation of mine with a wave of the hand, as the idle speculations of a layman — I take my stand with the cobbler who said the foot must fit the shoe.

II

A coincidence, similar to that which caused me to take the first and the second step in search of the secret of the plant on my silver coin, literally pushed right into my face a proof — which anyone can even now investigate for himself — of the rightness of my assertion, when I happened to be staying on a little island on the west coast of Ireland. I owe it to a little donkey, which kicked out with all four feet when I rolled down a slope with him, my arm round his belly, until we both bumped our heads into the goalpost of an ancient Celtic race course: the ovoid crown-piece, which lay in the shallow water at the shore. Now, I should not have met my half-wild donkey had not Napoleon I once had a Spanish cargo of these gray animals dispatched to the west coast of Ireland. There they were to serve as transport animals for the French Army, with which the Corsican was planning to invade England. Napoleon I did not get to England. He was less successful than Caesar. The donkeys remained in Ireland and went wild. At this point an historian of the pragmatic school would be at the end of his resources, because he would — in the black and white manner that I cannot sufficiently condemn — deduce a victory for democracy from the fact that Napoleon I was decisively defeated by Wellington. Which democracy, consequently, since Napoleon I was a reactionary, must be embodied in the British Empire. That is the way things go if one generalizes and gives up contact with what stares one in the face. Is not economics itself an example of how the taste for generalizing causes one to overlook the sole solid fact that emerges from all history, namely, that the future is never decided by one or the other possibility but always by a third? As regards the casting of light on my secret, the historical result of the Battle of Waterloo is therefore quite irrelevant and the importation of Spanish donkeys into Ireland decisive. Even a donkey that has gone wild remains a donkey, just as a human being remains a human being. We regard donkeys as comical, perhaps because we think that in this so very congenial animal we sometimes perceive features that it has in common with man, who is not quite domesticated. Or perhaps we only laugh at donkeys because man, who is sometimes described as an animal that can laugh, prefers to laugh at others rather than at himself!

First, however, I shall relate in what manner I made the acquaintance of the little wild donkey, a gone-to-seed Prince

Hamlet of ancient breed, who, scarcely more than a few hours old, found himself in Ireland facing the question: 'To be or not to be?' Ireland, the Emerald Isle, is green as the color of hope. In my experience this is the only promise made by Cook's Travel Agency that does not turn out to be a mere romantic fancy. The Flood there takes place daily. The mists rising out of the ground, from the now saltless sea-water that has gathered in thousands upon thousands of bogs, ascend unimpeded to an incalculable height, where storms mix them with the clouds that have made the great journey by air from America. From that height cascades of water fall without cease. That is why Ireland is the Emerald Isle. In an instant every blade of grass, each hill and mountain lights up with an iridescent sparkle of raindrops, with a rainbow over them.

There loomed up before me, like one of the Valkyries in person, a tall, red-haired Irishwoman of prehistoric aspect, skillfully leading her little mount along the giddy meanderings of the path up the steep cliffs. In addition, she was proudly carrying on her head a heavy load of seaweed. The little black donkey-hooves performed acrobatics worthy of a tightrope-dancer. The women work, while the insignificant-looking men sit at home drinking whiskey and talking politics.

Since there are only a few roads leading into the interior of the country, one must grope one's way through the bracken, which is many feet high, with a long staff such as shepherds carry. The spongy ground is treacherous, with fathomless depths. it was after a cloudburst, and the gray sky was still hanging down in folds, heavy as a curtain, when the wind blew the fringes aside, and there was light! The sun shone upon the damp world through the rift in the clouds, and then the curtain of the sky tore asunder. Even before this I had thought I saw something white in the depths of the water, and now suddenly, down below me, stones gleamed as the sunlight touched them. Among these stones I discovered the big white alabaster egg. But what had become of the second stone belonging to the goalposts of a race course? I decided to look for it as soon as the rain was over. It seemed I was not the only prudent person who had thought of drying his wet skin among the boulders piled up in bygone times. A whole family of donkeys had got here before me — and the father donkey pulled a long face on seeing me arrive. Doubtless he was well acquainted with human beings and felt the blow of the stick in his subconscious! He was the first to leave. The mother donkey's udders were still full, but she warned Hamlet against human beings by withdrawing from his nuzzling lips and trotting off likewise, round the corner. The baby, being still inexperienced, did not understand the hint. His face seemed to be all eyes — big, shining eyes like those of a child of the sunny races in Spain, North Africa, or Phoenicia. His eyelids were darkened with blue eye-shadow; just so do the fair ones in Arabia improve on Nature, making the eye seem larger. There were still some drops of milk trickling down his muzzle, which was as velvety to the touch as a mole's skin. This little donkey was still so weak that he could not yet walk properly on his four legs, much less run. All day long I scarcely met a single living being, so my heart was well stocked with the spirit of fellowship. Yet there was one thing that differentiated me from the donkey, namely, that I employed human cunning in approaching him: the cunning of the hunter, who kills animals. But I was far from having any evil intent. I stalked him upwind, even drawing the young creature's attention to me by proceeding on all fours, like himself, as I came nearer and nearer to the stones against which he was leaning. Nor did I fail to rub myself with fragrant herbs, in order to get rid of the accursed human smell, then stretched out my hand, grasped his head firmly, and planted a tender kiss on his donkey mouth. The animal struck out with all four feet — what a stampede! In a flash his parents were far away! With the little donkey in my arm I rolled down the flattened grass of the slope, until we were both brought up short by the second stone egg. There we were awaited by the tramp whom I had hitherto not noticed in this grey atmosphere, so entirely was he one with Nature, in a way that no domesticated citizen can be.

The tramp willingly accepted my whiskey after he had dried his tears, for he had been helpless with laughter. A great deal has been written about the Irish habit of whiskey drinking. For the

English Puritan it is explained by the Catholic religion, which he considers a somber superstition to which the Irish are addicted. A foreigner will refuse dishes that he does not know, whether they be bird's-nest soup, wethers' eyes *au bleu*, rotten eggs, or baked grasshoppers. The idea of a nation's passionately drinking a whiskey distilled from fermented potatoes is disconcerting to a Puritan accustomed to whiskey distilled from fresh barley. The tramp told me how the notorious potato blight, which makes that fruit of the earth unfit for human consumption, had first occurred in Ireland in the middle of the nineteenth century. People must live. So they distilled whiskey from those potatoes — too good to die of, too bad to live on. In France, likewise, at the time when there was neither bread nor cake, people at first refused to eat the potatoes that had just been introduced from America. People are suspicious of what they do not know. But without potatoes the Parisians would not have had the strength to raze the Bastille to the ground.

Anyone who travels in one of those high, two-wheeled gigs that they have there, with seats facing each other, on ill-fitting axles, instead of bowling along metaled roads in a civilized automobile, gets thrown about so much that he will never forget his journey to Ireland. There, too, he remembers the many fire-ravaged barracks of the English militia, who controlled the country from strategic positions on the hills before Ireland became a Free State. It was after the liberation that I came there. The tramp still remembered vividly how the English mercenaries drove away to their motherland, the breakfasts stolen from the Irish larder, along those same roads where people crawled and died of hunger before they could reach home. From him, finally, I also learned that in the time of the third Napoleon, when the Germans were, as usual, trying to get to Paris and the French were trying to get to Berlin, there was a great demand for the red dye with which the stuff for the *poilus'* red trousers was dyed in the year 1870. That war came too early for the revolutionary inventions in the chemical industry. So it was only the peasants of the west coast of Ireland for whom it was a windfall. They were still using a very ancient method of getting beautiful red dye from the ashes of seaweed. With it the women dyed the wool that they spun at home. Yet just as war-profiteering is never a lasting blessing even for neutrals, the result was that the covetous peasants neglected their fields so long as there were showers of red goldpieces with Napoleon III's portrait on them pouring into the house. Nor did the women, busily stirring away, like witches, at the red dye in big cauldrons, have any time left to take the seaweed as manure to the fields menaced by the ocean.

What linked me to the red-haired tramp was his fiddle, which prevented our legs from tiring. We danced along the road, he teaching me the jig. Besides this, he knew by heart the history of all that had ever happened in his country and could recite genealogies and stories of the princes and the bards. It was from him that I heard the story of the red trouser material. He confirmed, on the evidence of oral tradition, what I have read, namely, that when the Scots invaded Ireland in ancient times they used to adorn themselves with the violet juice of a certain seaweed. At one time, he said, this had been the general custom among the Celts. I could have learned still more from him, but our ways divided.

What then were the facts about the dye that Tacitus was so struck by among the old Teutons, whom he — unlike Cato with regard to the Carthaginians — surely did not intend charging with any immorality? Did he not laud their virtue by contrast with the perversions at home? Is that dye to be explained as protection against the weather? Soldiers and sailors tattoo themselves, after all. Certainly the clothing industry had not yet reached the level of productivity to which it has attained nowadays, but to make up for that there was then no rationing in wartime. If my theory about the red dye being symbolic of life is to be rejected, the use of cosmetics could only be explained as the expression of an allergy to water, which would not be gallant towards the ladies. To me my assertion that for people who are prosperous the color of life is a symbol of the permanence of their prosperity and, for other poor devils, a promise of a better future in the beyond, seems to be still the most to the point. Lipstick and cigarettes make one forget one's hunger.

An Obituary for the Amazons

In England, in the nineteenth century, there was a movement to obtain equal rights and the voting franchise for women. In the Second World War, admittedly, the Suffragette movement did not bring about the realization of the rights of man, but it did achieve conscription for women. That modern neuter, the robot in dungarees, in the collective State, needs no human rights; and, with that, lipstick also becomes superfluous, which brings the story of the red dye, symbolic of life, to an end.

EASTER ON CYPRUS

I WAS SITTING IN A TAVERN on the island of Cyprus, longing for the cloudburst to be over. If these had been tears falling, what a long weeping it would have been! I wondered whether the rain-whipped mops of half a dozen ragged palms outside the brick arch would soon allow me to get my bearings again, which I had lost in the labyrinth of malodorous alleys that apparently all lead down to the harbor, where I should have to pass through another archway and again ascend a steep flight of stone steps.

The walls of this ancient citadel of the Lusignans or Turks — incidentally quite devoid of antiquarian charm — were so close to each other that anyone who had to ascend barely had room to squeeze past anyone descending. Should I go back the way I had come? No! I was heartily thankful to have found the way, in the dark, out of that quarter. In the red-light district a puritanical morality provides for the visitors' safety and hygiene — presumably not without a sidelong glance at the taxes paid by the girls there, who are all registered with the police. In raggedly curtained windows the unmoving idols sit with legs apart, waiting for the approach of someone at whom hundreds of suddenly animated shadows clutch, quarreling for possession of him, promising him the bliss of the houris in Paradise, and spitting at his retreating back as he edges away. As I ran, I had scratched one hand on one of those razor-sharp agave leaves, and it was bleeding. The lacrimose gramophone record from the land of the Nile pursued me, and yet the years of my inexperience lie far in the past. Once upon a time, behind a fluttering, flowered curtain girlish hands were practicing a tune of Schubert's on the piano. Once upon a time — it was on a Sunday morning in spring. I did not find it very difficult to get over that fit of sentimentality. Besides, the gramophone record was badly scratched. At every revolution it uttered a howl like the little dog Fifi belonging to the lady in the first class of the ship in which we had come. It was really funny; later, when I was sitting in the tavern, I thought I could still hear that howling. Now she would be taking her little dog to bed with her, now patting it, now kicking it out of doors. I, too, would have preferred to go to bed in my cabin, with the prospect of dreamlessly sound sleep, instead of having to sit all solitary in a tavern, for I could not understand much of the Cypriots' gibberish. I shall not easily forget that night, or the cloudburst either. It had not been pitch dark like this before I found the tavern. It even seemed as though the storm was passing; only from time to time it lashed out, with a mischievous blow, at the wretched palm trees. Here is Nature working off her bad temper on the shaggy vegetables, I said to myself. On picture postcards of exotic atolls, dreamlike trees slant in the life-generating warmth that rises from the moist womb of earth, in the background snow-peaked volcanoes and mysterious temple precincts. It wasn't like that here. I should have thought twice about traveling in the summer, because of the plague of flies, then too the really infernal heat on board, and not least the pungent smell of too many unwashed human bodies. Loaded on a ship from whose hold no breeze could ever blow away the stench of rotting fish, rancid oil, and freshly sulphurized sponges. Furthermore, I had to reckon with a traveling companion who liked to poke his nose into things that were no concern of his. Finally, I had not paid for a first-class passage in order to stumble over rats or yet worse things. And down below they economized to the limit on light. Emigrants are not all that particular about cleanliness. But the steerage, where the emigrants were stowed, had a great attraction for my traveling companion, for to the purser's vexation the number of steerage passengers had increased while we were on the high seas, though without anyone's having come aboard without a ticket. 'It makes the trip cheaper,' my friend, the 'emigrants' patron, declared, rubbing his hands. What was wrong? Hadn't I invited him to join me on this journey to the Promised Land simply for the reason that I wanted to give him a chance to taste that measure of happiness in living life to the full according to his capacity, which is the due of every human being? He simply went crazy at the thought of being able to kiss the soil that his forefathers had trodden. Every port brought him nearer to the National Park that, as is well known, Lord Balfour had reserved for the Jewish people, to which my traveling companion belonged. Nobody can accuse me of being lacking in toleration of other people's views. Yet one really ought to be able to see beyond the end of one's own nose. Take for instance his naïve idea of a providence guiding the Chosen People, which had arranged things so that Israel was on the very edge of the oil fields for control of which several great powers had just been fighting a world war. I couldn't help thinking of the stooge who plays the front legs of the camel in the pantomime and who is kicked in the pants by his partner in the hind legs every time he gets out of step. If I looked forward to having some fun at my traveling companion's expense, that was no crime, was it? Fate had singled him out to be always the unlucky one. Didn't he himself say it had been bad luck for him being born at all? That was a moot point, for in his case the doctrine of natural selection was still awaiting confirmation. For the present he was sweating it out in the ship, where I had left him to his own resources. The storm would not have cooled the air in the harbor, and the angora goats that had been taken on board during the voyage would not have sweetened it. Only that morning I had been struck by the fact that he was rapidly losing weight in spite of being plentifully fed on board, and it wasn't that he was being pursued by women, who, as everyone knows, think of nothing else.... Anyway, the lady in the first class spoke only French. I couldn't help laughing at the idea of even imagining my friend in a 'gallant' situation . . . his thick, red-haired calves emerging from an old-fashioned nightshirt, from which he refused to be emancipated in spite of my objections that it was no suitable garb for any traveling companion of mine. A

glance in his shaving mirror ought to have told him why he was
unlucky in love. Those cotton-wool earplugs against drafts, sticking out of his ears like corkscrews. Oh no!

Far be it from me to try to justify myself to anyone! Besides,
I have sufficient evidence that, as it were by way of a compensation provided by Nature, he always managed to beat
disaster to it by a short head. He was the first to appear at dinners
given by rich Jews, where he had been asked only as the thir-
teenth. This about the thirteen, incidentally, I had not learned
merely by hearsay; in Cairo I had been asked out with him.
Whatever one may think about the Chosen People's humor, I'm
no spoilsport either. But I do not at all relish being the one at
whose expense other people laugh. On that point I tend to be
rather sensitive. He had pressed me, saying I absolutely must accept the invitation, the party simply wouldn't go without me. Of
course I didn't think anything of it when, during dinner, I was
asked to turn on the light. Now, whenever someone tells a joke,
I regularly miss the point. Why should I be coy about just
stretching out my hand? I thought to myself And so I turned on
the light. Afterwards, on the way home, I asked why precisely I
had been asked to do it. Because a pious Jew is not permitted, to
do this on the Sabbath. Why not? It makes him unclean. My
traveling companion was laughing at me. It would be some time
before I forgave him for that. 'I had hoped you'd laugh it off over
a bottle of wine,' he remarked placatingly. 'What if I don't!' I said
furiously. Since then my heart had hardened against him. I hadn't
finished with him yet, hadn't yet wiped him out as if he were a
sum wrongly done on the blackboard. It's only since I've been
sitting in this tavern that I can be quite honest, although this isn't
so easy, for in my breast, too, there dwell those supposed two
separate souls of which one might say, as of the Roman augurs,
that they can't look each other in the eye without grinning. I
have already said that my friend was rapidly losing weight. Was
he expecting that in that hotbed of a ship he would be reduced to
the salt of wisdom, by which the commentators of the Talmud
mean the radiant dove of pure reason, whereas other teachers
mean the bride in the Song of Songs? I was really not seeking a

quarrel with him on purpose, but there are limits even to my patience, such as when, as so often, he would lift up his nasal voice in a sing-song:

> Thy navel is like a round goblet,
> which wanteth not liquor;
> thy belly is like an heap of wheat
> set about with lilies.
> Thy two breasts are like two young roes
> that are twins . . .

'Oh, for God's sake! Can't you stop checking the inventory?' I bawled at him. There is nothing more certain to set all my nerves on edge than intimacies of that sort, which nothing in our relationship entitled him to indulge in.

'All right, then, they were two young roes, and twins at that, and there were two thighs, with all the rest of what belongs in between! If you aren't capable of clearing up this problem on your own, kindly seek information elsewhere. Whatever your bride of Zion may happen to have been equipped with, I didn't start wearing long trousers yesterday either. I don't need anyone to go totting up what goes to make up a female.' Since meanwhile an announcement from the captain for the passengers began to come over the loudspeaker, I had no chance to say any more to him. I had not dared to hope that we would put in at Cyprus. The British consulate was probably still open, so it wasn't too late to see about what I wanted there! My impatience increased as the oil-driven turbines thudded more and more slowly, the funnels belched forth black smoke, and finally the derricks were swung out over the quay. Once more, and faster this time, the engineer set the ship's screws turning, this time in the opposite direction, and once again foam was churned up. The seagulls dirtied everything, clumsily flying, oil-spattered, out of the greasy wake now rippling out into the brackish water. We landed. I frankly admit that my traveling companion's attachment to me had often driven me frantic. My strict refusal to let him accompany me on certain errands to the consulates in the ports where we put in had time and again caused him to have the most absurd suspicions, which I was not at liberty to dispel if I was not to betray myself. There he was already, his Kodak slung round his neck. 'What do you want to go photographing for in this god-forsaken dump? So as to be able to paste a souvenir in your album at home, showing that you too have been where Aphrodite first set foot on Cyprus?' I sneered at him. What did he think, anyway, that he was going to do with all that stuff, the photographs of dancing girls, camels, pyramids and then all that trash he'd gone buying in the bazaars, the damascened daggers and swords, which were Japanese imitations made for export, Moroccan leather cushions that the moths came flying out of the moment one sat on them, and finally that pickled Egyptian cat? I grabbed all this trash from under the beds and threw it in a pile at his feet. 'Tomorrow we will be in Haifa, your destination, where we shall part as agreed. You'll be kissing the soil trodden by your forefathers, and I shall be regretting a calamitous summer holiday, so I advise you to stay on board now and pack your suitcases. Doesn't our cabin look like a carnival? It's not my job to stop you from wasting your money. These souvenirs! After all, it's your own money you're throwing away, not mine.' Naturally this scene had been distressing to me, because he gazed at one with those watery blue eyes of his in such a way that one ought to have forgiven him his devotion. Once he had even followed my tracks in the sand and actually saved my life. Remembering it now, I couldn't help laughing at the involuntary drollness of the thing that had happened to me in Old Biskra, with the Kabyls, who take every tourist for a homosexual. These curious ideas they had probably gotten from a well-known writer who was living there at the time. I should not have been able to ward off the attention of these horse-breeders for long, and they would finally have throttled me in the darkness and flung me into one of the muddy ditches in the oasis. Even if I had been Chaplin himself, this time he should not know me by the size of my shoes — thus had I sworn to myself. For, after all, my fate depended on my visit to the British consulate.

I racked my brains, trying to think of a way of slipping away unobtrusively. The arrival of a steamer is always a source of much popular interest in a harbor. Porters and vendors of wares — how they all fought among themselves, even before the boat was properly tied up. And how long the steerage passengers' passport formalities took! Some were hailed by members of their families or by friends, with violent gesticulations and much shouting, as soon as individuals could be recognized by the crowd seething on the quay. Greeks in their colored fez, Turks in their white fez, popes with long black beards, in caftans, Jews likewise in caftans and with side-curls... eunuchs in loose trousers caught in at the ankle, still in the fashion dating from before Kemal Pasha. What a difference the use of a knife does make between them and the Chosen People, I thought. Nobody seemed to be in a hurry to deal with the cargo. At this rate it could go on for hours. The angora goats were picked up in bundles, by their big curly horns, in the hooks of the crane standing on the wharf. For a while they dangled in mid-air, their sulphur-yellow eyes flashing out some obscure Morse-code in the violet atmosphere that heralded a thunderstorm, and then they were stowed away in the hold, which was already stuffed as full as a flour bag. They were to be used for developing a new breed in Palestine that would yield finer wools. What things such emigrants do take with them! It was as if they had been trying to recapitulate the Exodus from Egypt. And with every passenger more fleas came on board as well. First there had been the fleas in Marseilles, which one had not noticed while buying one's roundtrip ticket, thinking all the while only of Notre Dame de la Garde glimmering all white on the rock, until with slightly misted eyes one saw it blurring in the distance. Then there were more fleas in Morocco, Oran, Algiers, and Bône. In Egypt, however, there were special ones, a sort that had been mummified together with the cats of yore. They say that cats' fleas don't bother human beings, but this is not so — so far as I had the opportunity of observing from the experience of my friend, whose blood is sweet.

How was I to get rid of him? 'It just occurs to me that I must go and apologize to our next-door neighbor. I drummed on the wall in the night because she was groaning in her sleep, and that pest of a dog was barking, as well.' I am never short of bright ideas whenever it's a matter of attaining my ends. But my friend did not let me out of his sight, so I resolved really to knock at the door of the next cabin, which was opened without delay. This comes back to my mind in the tavern, because the scratch that caused the howl on the gramophone record reminded me of the confession made by Fifi's mistress. I almost fell through the doorway, where she stood as though she had been expecting me. I am not made of stone, and she was an undeniable success in her négligé. What was more, her hairdresser must be an artist at his work, if the Titian red of her loosened hair was not indeed Nature's handiwork. I merely wanted to draw her attention, tactfully, to the fact that in her sleep she was in the habit of uttering cries for help — thus I lied. 'Who would turn a deaf ear to such cries?' I said, slamming the door on the intrusive fellow outside. 'Please sit down, but turn your face to the wall until I have slipped into a dress. Just one moment! What delicacy on your part, offering me your sympathy and advice! I am just waiting for the steward with the drinks. Don't you agree, there's nothing like it for the nerves before dinner? I sleep so badly.' She said this loudly enough to be heard by the fellow outside. Obviously she was entering into the spirit of my little game. My traveling companion would never have dared to speak to her. I said it was unpardonable of me to put my delightful neighbor to any inconvenience, and I refused to listen to her apologies for having disturbed my own night's sleep. It was rather, I said, her dreamy eyes that were to blame for my sleeping badly. And yet, I said, although there was only the thin partition wall between our cabins, she remained as infinitely out of my reach as the stars in the sky. She turned white and red, yet she seemed in need of more encouragement. The stratagem of literally bursting in upon her like this seemed to promise success. It is true that she shifted her chair away from the bed, as though unintentionally, while I was all the time working my way nearer to it; yet she had abandoned her hand to me. 'Go on with what you were saying!' Coming back to the purpose of my visit, I felt it permissible to suggest that it was the influence of the full moon on a nature as hypersensitive as hers that kept her from sleeping. Should I draw the bed-curtains, to darken the cabin? 'It was not the moon,' she confessed in an almost inaudible voice. 'It was the steward.' I looked at her with embarrassment. 'How on earth did he get in here in the night?' I objected. 'I never lock the door, for fear of a fire breaking out.' One must forgive her these tears, I thought, and forgave her also the steward with the drinks. From these eyes one could tell that the little mouth that went with them would not be capable of saying 'No' for long. These supple hips — in such soft arms no man could remain without feeling. Even a ship's plank on the high seas does not try to withdraw from the grasp of him who tries to seize it. With malice in my heart as I thought of how my traveling companion did not have so much luck, I saw my chance of easily conquering the fair dreamer. After all, she was no green girl. Coming closer, I could admire the particularly tasteful choice of the pattern of her nightdress — tiny bunches of roses.... Like a connoisseur I felt the gossamer-thin stuff between my fingers, while she breathlessly followed the progress of the siege that was menacing her virtue. She blushed. Then suddenly something went wrong. It was like rain drenching a fireworks display. 'The moment I came in I had the privilege of observing that your nightdress revealed more than it hid. This by contrast with the veiled image of Sais, of which the ancients tell.' 'What do you mean?' She looked at me aghast. Perhaps she did not care for a discussion of the mysterious gnostic doctrines of salvation current among the old Egyptians, in the situation in which she found herself, yet that did not seem to be sufficient explanation of her dismay. With widened eyes she wildly tore herself out of my embrace, falling back, step by step, from the bed, as though she there saw an apparition looming up out of the deeps. I once saw something like this as a ballet intermezzo, but it seemed to me that my neighbor's talent was really wasted on the role of sleepwalker. It shook my confidence in *la grande nation*, whose second nature is said to be logic, if an appeal to reason was to be unsuccessful, considering that my beauty had only one veil — and that the last — to lose, instead of Salome's seven. For the beauty herself I seemed to have become as thin air, and this was something that told me to take myself off in time, back to where I had come from — which I would have done, had not the steward with the drinks that moment appeared in the doorway. He put the drinks on the table and then turned down the bed for the night, somewhat ungently expelling Fifi, who had been unobtrusively sleeping under the quilt. The dog set up an ear-splitting yap-yap of protest. Thus wrenched out of her somber thoughts, the lady in the first class gave the officious young Ganymede a stern glance, commanding him to be gone. Thereupon she lifted up the accursed lap dog, whose paroxysm passed off only when it had been removed to the bathroom. The scene had made an impression on me. I wanted to leave it at that, and to vanish, but she held me by the sleeve to keep me back. Before I went — the lady whispered — I was to hear her strange story. Of this confession, during which my thoughts drifted off to my much more urgent business at the British consulate, I at least heard enough to gather that she had evidently worked out a theory according to which her lap dog was under the influence of some sinister ghostly power. 'The dog hears her master's voice.' This happened as soon as anyone came close to her bed, with intent to perform actions not within the scope of a spirit, which is not of flesh and blood. It so happened that all this was also connected with a veiled image — which also spoke, for she had heard its voice as distinctly as mine, as though it were the most natural thing in the world, much as one person takes two lumps of sugar in his coffee, another three. The picture had been painted by a well-known artist, commissioned by her husband, an invalid, whom his doctor had advised to put his affairs in order and make his last will and testament. 'Darling, you can't fool me!' These had been his last words, but his widow had attached no importance to them. Why, after all, should she? Death haunts many people who have no religion, and the thought of it goes round and round in their heads. With a fleeting glance at the bed, from which no dog need now have driven me, she continued with a sigh: 'At the hour when he passed away I naturally draped my dear husband's picture with black crape.

When at last I was about to go to bed, late that evening, expecting to sleep well after all the agitation of the day, and after I had been blowing on Fifi's soup to cool it for her, my little dog suddenly began barking and prancing around me as if she were demented.

'Could someone be coming to see me so late at night? I was not expecting anyone. Just fancy — the first evening after all that had happened! My glance happened to pass over the draped picture. Who can describe my horror when I saw the mourning-crape undoing itself and dangling, floating in the air for what seemed an eternity. Oh la la! the dead man *was* looking at me reproachfully! I need hardly say that nothing in the world would make me to go bed alone now, I was so upset by this message from the beyond. Had the spirit designs on my little dog? The strange thing was that she too would not be pacified, although I took her in my arms. Who shall say that such a little animal has not as much claim to sympathy as a human being? She cannot put her needs into words as we can, but you should just see her wagging her tail when I let her get into bed with me. Defying the deceased, before his very eyes, I took Fifi to bed with me. After all, I couldn't be expected to stay awake all night. At this, to my great surprise, the black crape drapery floated back on to the frame, into the position in which I had previously fixed it with drawing pins.' 'And Fifi?' I asked. 'Fifi went to sleep at once, but what is still more remarkable is that the apparition did not occur again after I hit upon the expedient of taking Fifi to bed with me every night.' 'Only Fifi?' I asked. She reproached me sternly for my frivolity, yet gave me to understand that at home she did not live in a one room apartment, like a nun in her cell. It was her lap dog that annoyed me, because she was in the habit of feeding it with scraps from the dining-room table and on plates that were used by everyone, without anyone's daring to protest against this deplorable custom, which is, alas, so widespread. Perhaps she had told me this ghost story only in order to engage my interest — or did she take me for some shy novice whom the handmaids of Venus blindfold with a silk stocking? It was all up with her coyness. But my time was up too — which did not permit of my any longer playing the dragon-killer who would liberate the virgin — or rather, the widow — from the rocks of her fixation. Gently I tried to part from the fair creature who was now resigned to her fate, forgetting even Fifi as she threw herself back on the soft pillows, thus prepared to cushion the fall that comes, as we all know, after pride. The separation cost me the less effort since the dog had evidently once more heard her master's voice and came dashing out of the bathroom, as though shot out of a gun, with much infuriated barking. 'Are you afraid Fifi might bite?' she wept. 'Why did you have to bring the accursed wretch on the voyage with you?' I shouted from the door. 'A psycho-analyst knows who ought to go to bed with whom. It's his job.' I nearly knocked down my traveling companion, who was waiting outside. Oh, the consulate would be shut by now! As for the dog, which was clinging to my calves, I cold-heartedly and vigorously kicked it overboard. Its mistress must have had a fine opinion of me. Luckily for her, she fainted in her négligé, at sunset. Even the steerage passengers drew closer. The captain, a broad-minded man, allowed them to come up on the sun-deck in the evening every week-end, to hear the wireless concert. Every-one stared, struck with awe at what became so obvious in the still intense light of sunset that etched deeper shadows against a tender background. No doubt the gentlemen in the first class took care of the poor woman. It isn't every day one gets the chance to play St. Martin by covering another's nakedness with one's own coat. As for the little dog, which, I subsequently learned, survived its bath as if it had been a dolphin — one could rely on the harbor police, or, failing them, on the flotilla of English torpedo-boats maneuvering at no great distance. An Englishman will not pick up a wallet that someone has lost in the street — perhaps with the last of his money in it — one mustn't interfere, but he will risk his life for an animal, for instance fetching a cat down from a chimney where it has got stuck. A Frenchman, on the other hand, keeps a dog more for the purpose of striking up an acquain-tance with someone on the other side of the street, when the chance occurs.

Well then, how did I get rid of my traveling companion? While I was elbowing my way through the crowd of steerage passengers embarking in Cyprus, whose passports were to be scrutinized on board ship, I thought I couldn't believe my ears. The captain was now announcing over the loudspeaker that owing to unforeseen circumstances the ship would be remaining in the harbor overnight. An inner voice told me that I would spend this night ashore, to be on the spot again first thing in the morning. It would hurt my traveling companion's feelings, but nothing bores me as much as having to explain my actions, especially when it is a matter concerning me alone. What should force me to be ready with succinct explanations, as though it were a matter of filling in a form for a life-insurance policy, or income tax? I simply can't stand being obliged to give an account of myself in matters concerning nobody but myself. I was ready to start a quarrel. If I had not scandalized the lady, there would have been time enough to go to the consulate and get back in good time before nightfall. Let him sleep on board, then — he had no nose for the intensive odoriferous activity on the ship. I was in a rage by the time we reached the gangway. Then I saw my chance. 'Look over there at what's sitting on the sea-wall, *la jolie petite*, a harbor whore, still no more than a child, the very image of Cinderella, straight out of the fairy tale.' I had succeeded in diverting his attention. 'Just a moment while I take a picture.' When he aimed his Kodak at her, the girl began screaming for all she was worth, and before he could get his black cloth over his head, she had flung her skirt over her face, leaving no doubt as to her sex. 'A subject for the gods! The very raw material of primal creation!' Thus I encouraged him, and at one leap I had landed on the other side of the barrier, whereupon I went dashing down the gangway and disappeared amid the crowd on the quay. 'You're not being quite honest,' my inner voice told me. 'Here you're about to be caught, *flagrante delicto*, chasing after a little bit of skirt.' 'Horrid insinuations! just a lot of beastly malice and nonsense,' my other self retorted. What was the point of having qualms about offenses not specified in any code of law? This teasing on the part of my conscience, or whatever it was, was something I already knew all too well. My purpose was nothing more or less than to offer chivalrous support to the little creature because she was crying. That is the truth, naked and unadorned. Where was any evidence that she must be one of those girls? — well, you know the sort I mean. As if, anyway, there were only such and not also other kinds of girls on Cyprus! If there were only enough bread in the world to fill all bellies — it's only hunger that drives them onto the streets! What is such a half-grown child doing roaming around the harbor-quarter at a time when other people are already asleep? In a place full of filth, flotsam and jetsam, street girls' belongings, blood-stained by sailors going for each other with knives as soon as the taverns close. . . . The good shepherd carrying the little lost sheep home on his shoulders — that was what came into my mind — feed my lambs — *pasce oves meas* — how unsuspectingly such a little lamb may graze beside the abyss, until someone comes and invades its little patch of grass. Isn't that true? Then it would be all up with that little innocence, that little bundle of nerves, that heart unversed in the ways of the world — a heart that begins to beat faster and yet faster, overtaken by panic, then stumbling, and finally falling a prey to the wolf! I liked the idea of following the girl. Without a care, simply off on an adventure. It was like the good old days. After some vain search — for dusk had fallen — I had to abandon the pursuit, because I met the lady from the first class, accompanied by several gentlemen who were returning to the ship. They too had stopped. I therefore said good evening to them, for here I was on my own ground. Why should I dodge this capricious widow? 'Are you angry with me for my scandalous behavior on-board?' She shrugged her shoulders but did not walk on. I said 'good evening' once again, bowing low, which annoyed her. She told me outright that she knew very well why I had no time to thank the gentlemen, who were walking ahead, for having pulled the little dog out of the water into which I had thrown it. Nor was anyone still in the dark about my visits to the red-light districts of our various ports of call. But she did not mean to give me up, she would try to reform me and cure me of this weakness — her voice trembled slightly. 'It's yet another relapse, just the same as with malaria!' I was taken aback but nevertheless accepted this suggestion. It was news to me that my fellow passengers had evidently spied out my secrets. However, lest this lady should hear yet more romantic rumors about my promenades on land, I decided to confess to her in confidence that I did in fact avail myself, without a qualm, of the opportunities that Mrs. Warren's profession offers to single men. 'Fundamentally you're such a complete stranger that it's a matter of indifference to me what you do. Dear God, if only I had never set eyes on you!' She did not weep, but she had turned pale. I did not understand anything about ladies, I was beginning to discover, although her interest could not fail to flatter me. 'Look, dear lady, at that church over there — yes, that one straight in front of us. It is dedicated to the Virgin. In ancient times it was the temple of Aphrodite that stood on the site. Virgins sat outside it, and by no means only virgins of the lower classes, and they did not leave that place until they had given themselves to some stranger — to anyone at all, whoever happened to have the inclination. Afterwards he had to throw a coin in her lap, for the temple treasure. Ah, you are horrified! My dear lady, let me tell you that life consists of prejudices — indeed it does! A person who always had to consider whether he would act thus or thus would be like Buridan's ass, which cannot decide between two bundles of hay and therefore starves to death. As is well known, Herodotus told his contemporaries this story, gaily and quite without embarrassment, after he had been in Cyprus.' The lady from the ship had listened patiently, yet she scarcely dared to raise her eyes as she said: 'Sir, you overreach yourself.' 'You see, dear lady, this can't befall me in the company of daughters of joy. They follow the divinity's commandment, and to this day they do not let the stranger depart unsatisfied.' I knew it wasn't decent of me to make such mock of her. Nor did she any longer look like a widow who knows her way about with men, but more like an inexperienced girl earnestly thinking about something she found it hard to understand. Was I only trying to shock her? And now I noticed for the first time that she had made herself up to look her best for this expedition ashore, with a new permanent wave and a somewhat transparent blouse. Had she been expecting to meet me? Now, she had taken hold of a button on my jacket, drawing me closer so as to look into my face. She was short-sighted. I looked round, then I kissed her. 'Although I have not deserved your indulgence,' I said hypocritically. *Sotto voce*: 'I wanted to steal the key to your heart out of your elfin hands. It takes more than a coquette's tricks to undermine any inborn romanticism. That is why in the company of others I act the villain, in order to unmask myself to you alone.' To this she replied in an equally low voice: 'If I only knew what to think of you! You eye the most innocent attention I pay you, as though you were peering through the glass of an aquarium — and then instantly make yourself invisible again like the polyp in the water it has darkened.' She herself laughed over this delightful simile, and she then remarked, with a glance at her dainty watch, that it was high time for us to be going back to the ship together; the gentlemen were no longer waiting. Of course, she said, her story about the draped picture was also an invention. 'And about being a widow — did you make that up as well?' 'The widow's veil is like the nun's coif, both practical and becoming — a symbol, if you care to take it as such,' she said roguishly and took my arm. It was an ivory tower for a virgin, which, to confess to the truth — she said — she was: a self-respecting girl, which was why she had no intention of throwing herself away on the first comer! What vexed me most was that the story about the veiled picture was taken from her unfinished novel, which was to go to the printer as soon as she was sure of the impression that the manuscript made on others. She wanted to make me acquainted with the whole work in the course of our time on board ship. Well! The role of the imaginary reader was not exactly a flattering one for me. So she had thought all this out so subtly in her naïveté? No, this could not come to a good end. 'To return to Herodotus — I'm prepared to bet that you wouldn't dare to inform your contemporaries of your experiences on Cyprus — as he did?' If she had never had a real shock in all her life, at least now her hair seemed to stand on end like that of the Inquisition's victim at the first touch of the flames, when I craftily promised that I would myself speak to the man who printed the ship's newspaper and would get him to publish, for the entertainment and edification of the passengers, the story of how and why the little dog had fallen into the water. 'You won't come by any literary prize in this way, but neither will it make any publisher fade away. Isn't that so?' I laughed caddishly. Unfortunately we had meanwhile caught up with the gentlemen, and the gong was also being struck for dinner, which nobody wants to miss when he has paid for it. What a good thing that I had resolved to stay ashore. With so many legs taking the ship's gangway at a run, I lost sight of her. Even supposing I had caught her last glance, it would not have boded any good either to me or to any possible posterity. Many sensitive people believe that they can feel a malevolent look even on their back. It must have been quite easy to make me out, against the grey of the harbor wall, in my white tropical suit, which I had recently bought in Cairo, and not off the rack either. I cut a pretty good figure in it. But perhaps she did not bother to turn to look at me again. The French have enough practical common sense about people not to be sentimental — and they also have good appetites.

And so I stayed behind on my own in Cyprus. I shall be here all alone in the gathering darkness, I thought. This was not quite true, for meanwhile the stars had come out. The Milky Way was glittering spectrally in the midst of that infinite graveyard of worlds — as the poet has it — over me the naked astral disk of the moon with the yellow patch in the middle, a cloudiness as in an egg that has been incubated too long and that will itself outlive the maternal womb. If the indifference of the cosmos excited me, how much more so did the harbor wench, who was no mythological figure and for whose sake I was prowling around Cyprus in the night. Actually, how does it happen that a rational being will suddenly begin to behave on the pattern of those old broadsheets with pictures of a topsy-turvy world where the rabbit turns a gun on the sportsman? What craziness on the part of the author of the universal comedy, to destine one to be a chaser of skirts! Not even the earthworm goes about it differently. Plato would have done better to explain the erotic instinct on the basis of that example, more or less as follows: what was originally a unity was split into two, which is why the halves everlastingly feel the urge to unite again. Was not even the first human couple predestined to seek Paradise in sexual union, which was the reason for their subsequent expulsion from the Garden of Eden, this again being followed up by the divine commandment: Ye shall increase like the sands of the sea! Similarly, after the Punic Wars the Roman Senate ordered the mob to copulate instead of distributing more free corn and sending them to bed with a Mickey Mouse. This brought about the decline and fall of the Roman Empire. Naturally I regarded it as unseemly to be, as it were, a witness of the intimate hour when eternity was here preparing to bring forth a new star in the skies. Is it absolutely necessary to take any notice of that? I was overcome by a sense of oppression; that is what the thought of eternity does to me — eternity, which rolls the globe along before it as the sacred scarab does, so long as there is no lack of dung.

I ought, long ago, to have got myself a bed for the night. Perhaps now it was too late? On the far side of the square there was a hotel, which was recommended in my guide-book. It reminded me of the papier-mâché architecture in a bankrupt film studio, in this diffused light in which the East now seemed so queerly faded and washed out. All that was missing was that film-technicians should suddenly come dashing along, bundle up the scenery, and start building up a set for the next film. In my wallet I still had the travel agency's prospectus: The wonders of the Orient, on the threshold of which the tourist stops off to visit Cyprus. It will be an unforgettable experience — visits to three-star sights — hotel rooms, meals, and tips included in the price! The night life here was not so attractive as in Paris, either for tourists or, it seemed, for the inhabitants. The Consulate would not be open again until ten in the morning. The foolery had gone on too long. Anyone else in my place would long ago have realized that this Mediterranean voyage was a failure and have cut his losses. I watched the alien countries and their inhabitants gliding past me with no more interest than one feels when leafing through illustrated weeklies in a dentist's waiting-room, or like one who sits staring at the screen in a cinema and who has reason to dread the moment when the lights go up, because the police are on his heels. I really ought to read myself a stiff curtain-lecture; I shouldn't always be going off the deep end like this. The consuming fire in the flesh and bones should have been burned out long ago! God knows I've no reason to be afraid — what should I be afraid of? Perhaps afraid of picking up a certain letter from the *poste restante*? The case was indeed as simple as that. As if I didn't get enough letters, bearing the most various addresses — and as if I didn't occasionally show some of them to my friends, or perhaps even carry one of them around in my breast pocket for a while. It's simply ridiculous to be afraid! Sheer nerves! This is what happens when one's under too much of a strain. Nerves! just as I said. It's nothing but the result of an insufficient supply of blood to the brain if such a strange sound is perceptible, starting up somewhere deep inside and continuing — despite all the efforts one makes to overcome one's fear — to the point where one begins to lose consciousness. Nobody thinks about fear — I would be crazy to get worked up now when I no longer have any need to make a secret of the thing, when I can confess to myself what a bad way I'm in. Let's be honest for once, at least with ourselves! Certainly, it's about a letter, the contents of which I don't even know yet, a letter that possibly hasn't ever been written. After all, why should the young lady write me a letter? Isn't the whole thing the most perfectly ordinary situation in the world, in no way different from that of any rejected wooer who is kept in the dark either on purpose or because one has long forgotten him?

That ear-splitting sound — how could I have been so mistaken about it? — it came from that cart over there in the otherwise empty square, its wheels simply huge solid wooden disks, which revolved with a grating sound that did not seem to disturb either the two Cypriots tripping along, their short white woolen ballet-skirts covering narrow hips, and red pompons bouncing on their felt slippers, or the span of oxen slowly but irresistibly drawing the cart. They had collided with the knight's gravestone. Too bad for poor Humpty Dumpty, an advertisement outside the antique shop without which no Cook's hotel is complete. Here the American schoolmistresses who save up for

years for the journey to the Promised Land lay in their supplies
of necklaces of fake gems or scarabs. However, the American
tourists had recently left Cyprus in a hurry because of the Wall
Street crash. That was the closing number in the big parade that
had begun with the election of a president who promised the
whole world 'normalcy'. Now the Elks, Templars, and Knights
of Columbus who had marched along in showers of confetti and
glory, adorned with medals, with swords of honor and flying
banners, behind the crash of brass bands and the tinkle of jingling
johnnies playing the campaign tune, would not be collecting
antiques any more. Nothing but ex-millionaires' cheques, old
newspapers, burned-out light bulbs, shooting stars?

The Indian watchman, tall as a tree, had been awakened by
the crash and started up out of the proverbial millennial sleep of
the East. He rubbed his eyes and yawned into his big, blue, bushy
beard — what a lot of white teeth he had! He rose from the mat
on which he had been sleeping. Obviously it was a long time
since he had received any wages from the hotel that he was
guarding, otherwise he could not have been so thin. Now he
would have to get on his bicycle instantly and dash off in pursuit
of the careless Cypriots whose fault it was that the worthy
Crusader was now lying smashed to smithereens. He had made
his way here in response to what St. Louis said: We shall send the
Tartars back to Tartarus, where they come from, or they will
send us to Paradise! Perhaps the hotel watchman knew where I
could get a bed. This hotel here, which sported three stars in
Baedeker, and which had once been a mosque, had obviously
gone bankrupt, for after ringing the bell I waited in vain for
someone to open the door. The silence inside that incorporeal-
seeming dome was spectral. Involuntarily warding off a sense of
unreality that threatened to overwhelm me, and which seemed to
emanate from the stones and from everything under the earth, I
tried to get something out of the man whose expression was a
mirror of changing moods — dejection, melancholy, helplessness,
and then again amusement. 'You speak English?' I asked. I
glanced at my wristwatch. 'Half-past nine? It's been dark for so
long!' I showed him the time. 'Perhaps because the days are still

quite short. Darkness comes on fast. He was evasive and averted his gaze from me to look at the sky. His face was blue too, as though dead, or rather, like the moon that the two white oxen had borne away between their great big horns. What odd people one meets here! I thought. Of course, one is on the threshold of the Orient! Suddenly the Indian salaamed and swarmed up a bamboo-pole into the air. For a while longer, through the many-colored panes of glass in the dome under the stars, I could watch his white turban growing smaller and smaller. Then I pulled myself together! We're not going to let ourselves be taken in by magic. Far better get drunk. And I sought and found the tavern, also because it had suddenly begun to pour.

For quite a while I had been sitting in the tavern, regretting that I had given up my bed in the cabin and also thinking of my neighbor with more indulgence — I would even have put up with Fifi as a sleeping companion. 'Bow-wow-wow', I went, imitating Fifi — perhaps somewhat too loudly. And again, bow-wow-wow. I couldn't help it when I thought of the sad doggy gaze on the label of His Master's Voice records. Then suddenly something happened that aroused me from my doze. Someone was pushing me away from the bar, so I removed my new straw hat from there and put it on the chromium steel chair on which it was too uncomfortable to sit in my wet clothes — which was why I was standing. What was he saying? He wasn't used to being rudely treated in a place of public resort? The abrupt transition from a waking dream to a concrete situation, the risk of perhaps getting a stiletto between one's ribs — one knows that these Mediterranean types are easily carried away by their temperament — all this was not exactly agreeable. Admittedly I had barked at him. And what of it? Since he had not joined in the doggy concert, he was not the cur I had, in my half-sleep, taken him for. There are enough known borderline-cases of a telepathic nature, cases of minds entering into rapport with each other, indeed even people living at a distance from each other, who do so, circumventing all the usual means of long-distance communication such as the mail, telephone, telegraph, and television. So why should the dog Fifi not also send messages to me? I didn't feel too easy about the whole thing, so I simply denied it all out of hand. "What? Did I get you right? A barking ghost — you can't be serious, chum!' I laughed in a jolly way, as if I saw how funny it was. Every educated person knows all too well — I continued — that our ear is capable of perceiving sound waves only up to a certain pitch. Nor should one overlook the possibility of self-deception, or indeed of chance, as an important factor. Actually chance had so willed it that in the darkness, when I was making my way to the tavern, a dog had snapped at me. I displayed my bleeding finger, which the man ignored. 'Why — you wonder — do I prefer to sit the time out in this tavern until my ship, which you may have seen in the harbor, has finished loading? I think of continuing my journey on board that ship tomorrow.' To my relief the fellow's facial muscles seemed to be slowly relaxing. Yet there was still the danger signal in his hard, amber-colored eyes, the pupils of which had diminished to the size of a pin-head. A half-caste, I decided, one whose head has been turned by England's liberal policy, so that he is now stuffed up with pan-hellenistic ideas, but whose blood doubtless contains an admixture of all the races extending from Nineveh and Babylon as far as the African bush where today it is Karl Marx's long-maned head that looms instead of the lion's. Might he not be an *agent provocateur*, a member of one of those revolutionary secret societies who has as much regard for the sanctity of human life as for an empty cartridge case? How exciting to imagine that, and on a holiday trip into the bargain! in order not to arouse his suspicions I therefore had no choice but to show this Maltese, or whatever he was, that I myself was well able to cope with doctrinaire agitators. Only was I thus really ensuring that I would come out of the adventure safely? 'God forgive me,' I therefore said chattily and brightly, 'my summer holiday trip was a failure from the start. It's enough to make one lose heart when one thinks what nonsense one often mistakes for a revelation from heaven — when in fact, man, who is made in the image of God, is of a foolishness equal only to that of the ape. Which is, as we all know, the basis of Darwin's revision of the story of Creation. Therefore it must be our noblest task, as serious thinking people, to set systematically about the reform of society!' He remained obstinately silent, only letting his tongue flicker nervously over his sensual, rather negroid lips, which were greasy with the thick Cypriot wine to which he was constantly applying himself. 'The greatest happiness of the greatest number! Yes, that's the slogan, though no one has yet seen that Paradise on earth — nor, for that matter, the one in the beyond either. Comrade, let us drink to that. I happen to have a copy of *The Times* in my pocket — a bit out of date — look at it for yourself! There is the first-hand report of a successful experiment made by the celebrated Russian, Professor Pavlov.' I held the newspaper in front of his face. 'Here you have the proof, if any should still be required. A sausage was dangled in front of a dog's nose, with the result that saliva began to gather in its mouth, although the head was already severed from the body. All that was necessary to make the experiment successful was that the dog should previously have starved to death. This experiment is based on an epoch-making idea. Measured against the importance of this idea, even the great French Revolution looks pretty farcical. An ideal has come tangibly within our reach — the celebrated chicken in the pot, for which the little man's mouth has been watering since the time of Henri Quatre. It was with the demand for this chicken in the pot, which has meanwhile had time to go bad, that the little man stepped upon the political stage, and since then he has been there waiting for the fulfillment of his just demand.'

The bottle of red wine was beginning to dance, but I was too carried away by my own eloquence to take any notice. 'Don't let your head hang, comrade — progress will be victorious over blackest reaction!' It seemed to me that everything was beginning to float in the air; it seemed as if I myself had become weightless as my flying thoughts. It was as though the force of gravity had ceased to function in me and, to make up for that, had doubled in the chairs and even the bar itself. And yet the bar was firmly set in the cement of the floor. Nothing would stand straight any more. The wine bottle tipped over, and the wine ran over the bar. But when the bricks in the walls began to crumble and the aluminum pier supporting the ceiling began to bend, just the way

I once saw a strong man bending a horseshoe outside the National Gallery in London, and when the ceiling itself came down and a short circuit set the beams on fire — I thought it was time to take a closer look at things. Everyone had fled from the tavern with the exception of my neighbor, who kept casting sidelong glances at my straw hat every time he thought I wasn't looking. 'Is it an earthquake?' I asked in dismay. No answer. So I picked up my straw hat from where it lay on the chair, intending to get out of there. I did not put my hat on as fast as I had to remove it again, because the red wine that had spilled out of the bottle, and which had collected in it, was running down all over my face. Now I won't put up with being laughed at by anyone, no matter who it may be. So, turning up my collar, with the most exquisitely courtly and yet somewhat icy demeanor I waved my hat in a wide arc, in salutation, and with a measured tread passed out through the door. Outside, however, I ran as fast as my legs would carry me, although the severe earth-tremor was not followed by any others. I abandoned the young man, with whom I had — not without having to overcome some reluctance — placed myself on an equal footing, to his amazement at the tellurian tricks played by this island that was, as has already been mentioned, the place where the goddess Aphrodite first set foot on dry land. Now I could even see the harbor through a rent in the mist, because the storm was dying down. Yet what I first took, through the gray veils of the mist, for the flashing of the lighthouse signal — now stronger, now paler — must — the supposition shot into my head — be my ship, which, borne away on the waves, was now floating far out at sea! My ship! In a really excessive fit of desperation I sought an object on which to vent my rage. To be left behind on this bewitched island, this damned earthquake-ridden sand-pit — there was no enduring the thought! Fool of a womanizer that I was to go dashing after a buxom little creature who then fooled me, and there was the ship disappearing, and with its going, as it were, the wire had snapped that kept me, the puppet, jerking. How long would I have to stay here waiting for the next boat? Perhaps even until the foam-born Paphian herself again rose naked out of the waters before the eyes of all who had nothing better to do than to stare. Nowadays it is only Scandinavian girls who do that without batting an eye. So I gibed at myself. For now certain thoughts again began to take their familiar, disastrous course; and it was precisely in the hope of repressing them that I had set out on this summer holiday! Once the mechanism of memory is set working, there is nothing to stop it from going back into one's earliest childhood. To begin with, at a time when I was still going to school, there was that wax figure of a girl in a glass box in the Panopticum, whose breast rose and fell gently as though in sleep. God preserve me from memories! Let's rather think of little — what was her name? — anyway, I wonder what became of her. What a pity I lost her! If it did suddenly give me a pang of a kind I was all too familiar with, like an acute physical pain, the sort of jab one gets at the dentist's, then it was really caused only by the somewhat tardy reflection that all I had glimpsed of the dainty little creature was her naked belly — where Nature displays her mystery — with the astonishing result that I was spending my time here serenading instead of going back to the ship. How should I have recognized her? And so what was keeping me? Why had I purposely missed the boat? — not, surely, because I had already meant to wait outside the British Consulate till dawn, contemplating the flag of Albion that rules the waves — the flag drooping on its thin steel wire, motionless, a wet rag, indifferent as a shroud over all hope. Neither Aegean myths nor waterspouts can put the gods back into the atmospheric strata they have deserted. My summer voyage was futile, because I am simply defenseless against certain memories. While even childhood imaginings lose their gigantic outlines when we come to riper years — as though waking from a bad dream — we go in quest of reality in order to assure ourselves that we are no longer dreaming. In vain! Something else counteracts that endeavor, something that hovers as a shadowy intuition on the threshold of consciousness. As though a door would not open because there is someone on the other side holding the handle tight. Undeniably it is I myself, I am the opponent, looming as a mere outline, like a silhouette or a picture from which the colors have faded. The right expression would be: I am beside myself. This phrase usually implies criticism, even admonition, but all I wish to emphasize is the fact that what is happening to me is inexplicable, indeed fateful, something that will inevitably seem fictive and hysterical to those who have not shared the experience, who have not gone through what I had to go through.

With my hand on my heart I can tell when my heart stands still; my hands begin to shake at the thought that I must now sign my name on the form before the clerk will look and see whether there is any mail for me. Only a few more hours of such anxiety and suspense, and then everything is over and done with, so far as my life goes. My fate will be sealed, because first of all there may be no letter from her, secondly there may be a refusal, and thirdly she may have sent a letter to the Consulate giving her consent to marry me! Well, there are people who can talk and argue about love; some consider it a passing infatuation, others a beast-like war of the sexes, generating hatred that extends beyond the grave. This is merely half a confession. I haven't the time to go into this further.

To think there was a time when I used to be flooded with incomprehensible happiness that depended on the letter-writer's gracious mood! Perhaps she never wrote the letter I am expecting? Once I had the privilege of watching her, leaning over her shoulder as she dealt with her always extensive correspondence in the leisurely, scrupulous way that was characteristic of her. I am a man who lives through his eyes. After all these years my imagination still takes fire at the recollection of that luminous figure, sitting at her escritoire late one afternoon in Paris, in a dress that was the blue of a ripe fig. In that tranquillity I absorbed into my very soul the innocent sight of that young girl who was to remain forever beyond my reach. What would I not have done in order not to be so unworthy of her! A ghastly fear overcomes me lest even my memories of those happy days should ever fade. So must death overtake one, and one fights against it to the last moment. Forgotten — that means being dead! The reader perhaps thinks this ludicrous? It is indeed enough to make one laugh, and I myself join in the laughter, although the mirth does not come from my heart but is tainted with gall. Ha-ha-ha! What a grotesque idea it is that goes so naturally through my head — it's like being a criminal with the rope already round his neck, who realizes that he has no more personal obligations, and that by leaping from the stool under the gallows he can take care of his death for himself. My head is in God's hand no longer! I said to myself, staring at the closed door of the Consulate.

While I was awaiting my sentence, just to pass the time, I took a cruel pleasure in frivolously blackening the innocent memory I had till now borne in my heart of the picture that that young lady presented, seated at her desk. It is true that in Paris I had already been jealous of the noble families — scattered all over the world since the Russian Revolution and most of them living very wretchedly — who were in intensive correspondence with her. Nor was I any less jealous of her two brothers, whom she so idolized and who were to be started on their careers by this girl's energy, although she was scarcely out of school. Her mother had connections with the great fashion-houses in Paris, London, and New York, and her idea was that they should open a salon in Helsinki for such of an aristocratic clientele as could still boast of a certain wealth.

Again I could see her, placating me with a glance, with a sigh of relief piling up the letters on the desk, already in envelopes. I am only reporting the way I believed that I actually saw it. Was it still myself? Was it my eyes that deceived me? She had risen from the desk, and then she seemed suddenly to remember some trifling thing that had slipped her mind. She had almost forgotten to answer the insolent letter from Annecy that she had of course thrown straight into the fire. She had done so even without reading the letter, in which I had expressed the hope of being allowed to speak to her just once more. Probably she had called the maid back, bidding her wait while she scrawled a few hasty lines on a sheet of letter-paper — blue paper, a lady's vertical handwriting. She had finished with me. Forever! Wasn't that it? With a faint tremor of her aristocratically flaring nostrils she put the letter on the silver salver, adding it to the pile of those to be posted. Her little pout of girlish hauteur will have seemed — to the party in the drawing-room next to the room where she had been writing, to this dozen or so handsome, well-dressed young people who were all engaged in lively conversation — the charming smile with which one greets civilized people who belong to one's own circle. The heavy *portières* over the double doors were closed. I am the only person who knows the other side of the medal. This smile does not lull me into deceptive tranquillity. Not me! I screamed into the darkness, into the night, screamed as loud as I could, impotent in the face of this diabolic visitation. My strength is at an end! I can't go on! No wonder that the interior transformation had to happen then, the miracle that tells the palsied man to throw away his crutches. That letter must never, never reach my hands! A merciful warning emanating from the deepest unconscious layers of my being told me not to step into the trap. The naïve hope that my long, my all too long agony might some day touch her heart had long ago made way for resignation. Submitting to my damnation, I had to laugh at myself, as at the clown in the circus who tries to sit down on a chair that is pulled away from under him. I shall not go on enduring this humiliation. I shall turn my back on the Consulate. When I had taken this final decision, I had a still better idea. According to the Greek calendar, the great Easter festival began at dawn, and no single shop, no institution, no consulate, not even a post-office would be open anywhere in all Greek territory. So I was all unexpectedly in a state in which one doesn't know which side of the mirror one is on. Here I lie sprawling on these steps, and anyone passing by will take me for dead — my other self pinched my nose, raised my eyelids, moved my legs, and — sure enough, I had stood up and there I was suddenly running as fast as my legs would carry me, out of the clutches of death.

How could I have let myself be so taken in by that tourist publicity with its technicolor tints? Basking in the sunlight of the legendary Orient, on terraces ablaze with intense light. . . embracing life . . . dancing in the vineyards . . . all that the prospectus heralded. . . . The more I reflected on it, the better pleased I was to have at least got rid of my traveling companion

without more ado, even if not with a light heart. As of the Prince
of Denmark, in the play *Hamlet*, where the best clowns are to be
found, I might have said:

'. . . this deed ... must send him hence
With fiery quickness ...
The bark was ready, and the wind at help...'
'Ay, marry, why was he sent to England?'
'Why, because he was mad; he shall recover his wits there;
or, if he do not, it's no great matter there.'

   Retrospectively I had to beg my traveling companion's
pardon, for this Mediterranean trip had not been his idea at all.
I had had to talk him into it. Yet for a long time I went on
thinking that it was not at all a bad idea to put these infinite
expanses of water between the young lady and myself; for thus
I was cunningly dodging the verdict that was suspended over my
head like the sword of Damocles. How long, I wondered, had I
waited in every harbor to see if there was an answer? The law is
not so hard on the condemned prisoner, for at least he is told the
day and the hour of his execution. I was no longer in the slightest
afraid of an answer such as I deserved. She prefers not to see me
again! Polite, but clear! Good manners have become second
nature to her. Not for nothing was her mother lady-in-waiting at
the late imperial Court of St. Petersburg. Before the Revolution
there were still noble Swedish families living on their extensive
estates in Finland, where there are few people, and infinitely
many forests, and lakes opening like windows into Nature. A
sensibility that is alert to receive impressions owes its first and
most lasting instruction to Nature. That is education. This is a
complementary addition to the subjects that young girls of good
family learn at their boarding schools. In every port of call I had
inquired whether there was a *poste restante* letter, one — what was
more — in a blue envelope, with the address clearly and decisively
written in a large, vertical, ladylike hand. Each time I had given
the consulate at the next port of call as my forwarding address.
The whole journey was indeed a mere pretext, as I realized even

in Marseilles, where I thought I observed the young clerks positively laughing at me before I had even got outside the door. This letter never came. I had to make do with the rubber-stamps collected in my passport every time it was checked — the way someone else keeps adding to his postage-stamp collection. While my fellow-passengers gazed open-mouthed in unceasing raptures at the sights and reveled in the adventures that one experiences in foreign countries, I can safely assert that for my own part I spent the whole voyage more between heaven and hell than on the water.

Day was breaking, and I was wandering aimlessly around in this malaria-ridden harbor-district. Why should she write, anyway? And yet? And yet? Could it be any trouble to her to dash off a few non-committal, formal lines, some sort of acknowledgment of my farewell letter? I had been waiting for it for two years. That's twice twelve months. What would have been the end of it if the post-offices had not been closed for Easter? I should still have had to wait a while longer in the queue, until the man in front had finished his business at the counter. Then my fate would have caught up with me, the fate from which there was no escape. All this must be carefully taken into consideration. How ashamed she must have been of my shameless behavior, how ashamed that her mother should know of it! I have come to realize what damage I did at that time. How long she let me feel the cold touch of the steel set to my breast before she plunged it into my flesh, tearing open this wound that shall not ever heal. Ah, destiny — there it lies concealed behind that girlish brow — all that lies in store for me! Truly she is not without feeling as are those immovable cold marble goddesses! This I knew, and I deliberately hurt her! Her eyes were moist when we said goodbye, and I offered her my own silk handkerchief, in order to mock her to the last. I was still lingering over the imaginary picture of myself being called to the post-office counter — the man in front had pocketed his documents. Lucidly, in full possession of his consciousness, when the rope no longer holds the falling man in safety, but snaps, he resolves to break the connection of his own free will and so plunges into the fathomless deep — *dies irae, dies illa* —the world is covered with a rain of ashes.

One must leave one's yesterdays behind one, casting them away like a pinch of salt flung over the left shoulder. One must know how to shut one eye at the right moment — better still, to shut both eyes when Poseidon's raging bull rises out of the wine-dark Grecian waters. With the words 'Yours to all eternity' on his lips a man sank below the arc of the world over which sun, moon, and stars pursue their tranquil course. Thus, or in some such way, the poet will tell the story; he would engage Homer and the bellowing bull of mythology in order to lure the reader away out of reality into the Grecian dreamworld that corresponds to the travel-agency's prospectus. Nevertheless — the coastal waters were here too shallow for throwing oneself into the sea and committing suicide. While I was considering this, the fellow I had met in the tavern popped up beside me. In his outstretched hand he had a big blue moth that was just struggling out of its chrysalis. The creature shivered faintly as it spread its still crumpled wings in the air, as though about to fly away into the beyond. What happened next is far from elevating. All in all, who's interested in hearing exactly how I came to fall into the water? 'You want a girl?' was the way the conversation began. But a girl was the last thing I wished for. Then color came into his over-alert face with the negroid lips that I found insuperable. I wonder where he spent the night! Had he a stranger before him of the kind who understands love in the Grecian way? There are situations in which one fears the twilight. The South had made this fellow more precocious, just as I had the advantage of him in regard to experience. Nobody will ever be able to discover what a jumble of elements go to make up such a primitive nature, a human being that is still solidly locked in primeval times and nevertheless feels quite at home in a world of jazz, Coca-Cola, and Hollywood. He never steps outside his prescribed role. He only shakes himself, like the mule shaking off flies.'You're in luck — I know a jewel of a boy!' With a swift but unmistakable gesture over eyes, breast, and hips he whispered in my ear, although there was nobody to overhear us. He came close up to me, and I made a movement as though to escape, whereupon he grabbed me with one hand, sliding the other into his cummerbund. However, what he produced was not the expected stiletto but a little package, from which he shook some grains of white powder onto the palm of my hand. 'Best quality,' he assured me. 'Just what I'd run out of' I said, thankful to perceive a way of escape. The price was not too high considering the heavy penalties on illegal trading in drugs. I bought it and even went further, in order to send him away in a good mood. I admired the tattooing on his fingers, arms, chest, and back, which were done in black, blue, red, and green, a dragon circling with its tail in its mouth, mermaids, pythons, the Greek flag with its dove and olive branch. 'Artistic?' he asked. 'Ministers, professors, and the workers' union have the same. 'Only one can't get it off again when one's tired of it, isn't that so?' He said he also had a very handsome drawing on his abdomen, if I would like to see that too, and he was already preparing to undo his cummerbund. I suggested that he should show it to his wife, whereupon he flung me into the water.

Poseidon, a bellowing bull in the wine-dark Grecian waters, did not bear me off to the realm of shades. It was not even barking dolphins that waked me. I say it was presumably the salt water that beat so thunderingly against my ears, and the screaming seagulls that espied me on the shore at Paphos, where a last tumbling wave left over from the night's storm cast me up unharmed, as the whale once spewed forth Jonah. The fellow from the tavern had vanished. *Moriturus te salutat,* I said like the gladiator dedicating himself to death in the arena, and, standing up all dripping on the sand, I prepared to resume life at the point where I had hoped that I had lost it. But this is easier said than done. One pinches one's nose to make sure that one is still oneself. Even one who has been given up for dead and who returns to life needs some time to adjust himself to everyday life. Even pinching one's nose takes time; it takes time for the nerve to convey the message from the nose to the brain, where it is perceived. Without this perception of one's self one can wear the handsomest nose in the middle of one's face and still not be sure that it is one's own. Here was the hitch in my attempted suicide. Science nowadays proves succinctly that the hearing of sounds, the seeing of objects with light and shadow, in fact every sense-perception, and finally also our identification with our ego, takes place in various parts of the brain. There one has my problem in a nutshell. What I'm now trying to say is: If one asks a normal human being where the sun, the moon, the stars, or even Almighty God is or are, without hesitation most people will point to the sky or to their own breast. Right! I myself had so long believed I could base my identity on possession of a straight nose, blue eyes, and an oval face, as is recorded in my passport. However, since I have been beside myself I cannot expect anyone to take me for the person I am, without coming under suspicion of trying to put something over on myself or somebody else. But where then am I supposed to be, now that I am beside myself? One surely doesn't evaporate into thin air? Such things come out only with the aid of spiritistic conjuring tricks, when certain manifestations, say in the form of whitish, plasmatic substances, issue from the medium's mouth and from other parts of his or her body, these substances regularly being diagnosed by persons of unquestioned scientific reputation, as being gauze veils, cotton wool and similar nonsense. The devil take it! What was happening to me anyway?

I must try to remember how it all began. I was talking about a letter that I never received. That letter, her answer to the infamous farewell letter I had written, must never come into my hands. That I was resolved on. Whatever I had done, I passionately insist that I had no cause to be proud of having thus treacherously put to the test the confidence of a young girl who had liked me very much. I swooned with longing for her. But when she wanted me, I pretended that I didn't want her. Since then she remained beyond my reach. Living only on the memory of her had become a habit with me, as if it were my daily bread. Unfortunately one can't entirely rely on the accuracy of one's memory. Even though I daily tried to recall everything that had happened, one thing or the other would sometimes loom up very vividly all of its own accord, and what I had forgotten would suddenly come to mind again. Having come to know the young lady so well — ah, if it had only been no more than that! — an episode without complications, an episode that everyone will think perfectly ordinary — everyone, that is, who has ever done the same thing and from the first moment fallen head over heels in love.

It was in her cousin's house near Dresden that I saw her for the first time. It was the winter at the end of the First World War, while I was still convalescent. But no, I soon caught myself being let down by my memory: I had already visited her once in the boarding house where she was staying in London, and that was before the war began. She was holding a huge box of chocolates in her hands. She had never seen such a thing before. Except from her brothers, she had never before received a present from a man. I remember thinking that I must tell her not to rhapsodize about her brothers so much. One also had to be careful not to mention her father. Such a blunder could have been committed only by someone not familiar with the rules of the game. At that time the young girl's family circumstances were already to some extent known to me; I had been informed about them by her Swedish cousin. Afterwards I frequently used to muse on what it is like when one is dead: can one still wish for anything? Perhaps one would wish to see that girlish face just once again, with its nostrils flaring with hauteur — just once again, even if only for an instant, as it had been the first time! That may be foolish; after all, when one's no longer alive everything is at an end. But the way it is with memories is this: one thinks one need only press a button and there they'll be. Only it isn't the same any more, for even memories lose color and fade. One grows modest. But I couldn't forget her utterly — no, I could never do that! It's true that bitter memories stay longer. Why can't I help lingering over them? Now it also occurs to me that I must correct myself yet once again. For even before that I had seen her once in Paris, looking into the brightly lighted window of one of the dress-shops in the rue Castiglione, with her cousin, a lady whom I had met in Sweden and who now introduced me to her. The girl's coat was definitely not warm enough for that icy winter's evening. The half-grown creature must have shot up too fast, for her dress scarcely reached to her knees. Yet that hair could be found together only with such blue-gray eyes. It was plaited and wound round her slender head like a huge tiara. As her cousin laughingly told me, the girl's hair was so long that she could stand on it when she took it down. 'Without shoes and stockings, I hope?' She let this pass without comment. She obviously did not think it suitable that I should try to make myself popular in such a way. The heavy plaits made her head ache; her mother would understand if she had her hair cut when she left school. I was horrified to think of this ritual mystery being performed — if it had to be performed at all — not by the scissors of a priestess of the virginal moon but in a vulgar hairdresser's shop. Perhaps I said something of the sort, yet I have never forgotten her glance, which seemed to say: 'Don't I know you better?' Almost certainly she had seen through me even then. Nevertheless she subsequently overlooked much that I did wrong — perhaps more so than I deserved. For it was after all quite deliberately that I behaved as badly as I could whenever I was sure that it would come to her ears. I am not sure whether she didn't already know me better, although the blush crept into her face that fatal night and how quickly she managed to hide it in the torrents of her loosened hair.

Thinking back, I honestly find no cause to boast of having seduced many a pretty girl in my time. Among other things that occupied me then, I was after the daughter of a merchant who had come from Moscow with his family. Everyone in town knew how unscrupulous I was — not because I was calculating, but out of pure thoughtlessness. Anyone who took up with me simply had to take the consequence. It was not my fault. One's made the way one is. I'm heartless. So I was astonished to see with what elaborate cunning and with what courage a girl of good family would aid her seducer to achieve his ends, even though he was the most unsuitable person to provide a springboard for the adventurous Nathalie. Fortunately for her, as though by tacit agreement among all who had known of it, the affair never became public knowledge. Afterwards I had to repent of having smuggled the young Russian girl into my room. And this had been in the night of 12 December, of all nights, on the eve of the Festival of St. Lucy, while I was spending the weekend as the guest of the young Swedish couple with whom we were both on terms of intimate friendship. This night is dedicated to St. Lucy, who sacrificed her eyes for the blind, and it is the longest night in the winter, a night that they celebrate in Sweden as bringing forth light, for which reason they keep vigil all through it. The music had ceased to play in the ballroom flickering with the light from hundreds of candles, and the guests were taking their leave, laughing, clinking glasses, and wishing each other all happiness. It was still some time before the last carriages and sleighs had driven off with their merry passengers, the sleighbells tinkling gaily and the snow whirling up around them. Nathalie had already slipped away unobtrusively, straight after dinner. At last I too could retire to my room. I was tense with curiosity to know who would be the light-bringer — the girl who, according to Swedish custom, appears at dawn at the bedside of the guest of honor, bringing him coffee and cakes, which she presents with a new year's kiss. According to custom it must be the prettiest virgin in the house. What they said of our hostess's seventeen-year-old cousin from Finland was that she had grown into the loveliest creature since I had seen her last, a mere child, in Paris. But since I was chasing after the Russian girl, I had not yet encountered her. What seemed impossible to those who said our hostess preserved calm in even the most difficult situations now seemed a fact — she nearly lost her composure that night. I saw a light in my room, and in my bed I found the Moscow merchant's daughter, whose parents were known not to tolerate her having liaisons. Like one of the prudent virgins, she had not hidden her light under a bushel but had put her candle on my bedside-table, in order to wait for the right bridegroom; but she had got tired of waiting so long and had gone to sleep. It was tempting to consider letting the novice make her sacrificial offering so long as Morpheus still let it be painless; but at that moment the door quietly opened. The Swedish lady of the house, whom I nicknamed Humming-Bird on account of her fickleness, was standing in the doorway, holding a guitar on which she struck up a tune while the light-bringer sang the song. With the crown of lighted candles on her head, her loosened hair falling right to the ground, and with a brimming goblet of champagne in her hand, the graceful girl from Finland paced round my four-poster bed with the impenetrable demeanor of a figure on an icon. She ascended the step and pulled the curtain aside, thus discovering that I was not alone. 'Is he asleep?' Humming-Bird asked, following her into the room. On a Swedish girl's lips the word 'yes' always sounds like a sigh, no matter whether it signifies the granting or the refusal of a request. The white-clad girl with the candles alight in her hair, now standing very close, bent over me and gently raised one of my eyelids with her fingers. I was found out for the second time. She had discovered that I was only pretending to be asleep. I am not worthy that anyone should raise as much as a finger to help me, I thought. It simply served me right; I had richly deserved it. Then she tipped the goblet like a priestess making a libation and poured the contents over my face. Laughing, the two conspirators vanished, as though they had just played a clever trick. And Nathalie joined in the laughter!

No, it was disgraceful to have brought the seventeen-year-old girl to my room in these circumstances, I raged. The trap into which I had so wantonly gone had been sprung, as at a tug on some invisible wire. I simply could not understand how it was that the mysterious alarm-mechanism of reason had so suddenly ceased to function in my mind. 'Are you thinking of the girl from Finland?' she asked me. 'I don't know *what* I'm thinking of,' I hissed at her. 'That's a lie!' she said reproachfully. In an out-and-out paroxysm of fury my hands were automatically closing tighter and tighter on Nathalie's throat, for obviously she had betrayed me. She closed her eyes, wholly concentrating on what was happening to her. I'd make her laugh out of the other side of her mouth, I swore. Luckily for her I emerged in time from this state of grotesque insensibility. Outside in the snow black-birds were quarreling about a worm, or one had got into the cat's clutches. Nature is merciless. But a line must be drawn somewhere. 'A little more and the curtain would have fallen upon a melodrama,' the Russian girl said scornfully. The whole thing had been what the English call a blackout. After I had been wounded, a similar cerebral reflex had been produced in me hundreds of times by the sudden flashing of an intense light into my retina. Evidently the unexpected light falling into my eyes from St. Lucy's crown of lighted candles had caused a similar reaction. When Nathalie was already applying herself in good heart to her breakfast, she said: 'Perhaps it is fitting to suggest that now, at the end of the war, when the streets are full of men mutilated in all sorts of dreadful ways, you shouldn't make capital out of a bullet wound in your head.' I myself was not completely satisfied by my explanation of my odd behavior, yet I knew no better one in a time that had no sense of drama and which had also lost its sense of humor, that liberating faculty. Boastingly however I declared myself prepared to go to the Russian girl's parents that very morning and sue for her hand. This merely in order to get the wretched affair off my chest! I was too anxious about her reputation, she said, twinkling at me roguishly. Yet it was now up to her, she said, to keep me from taking a rash step. At that moment the voice of reason at last made itself heard again in me, like the bell ringing at the other end after the line has been cleared. For, she said, she was far from being the sort of girl to tie herself for life to someone who had nearly throttled her. '*Tu me faisais peur! Trop embarrassant de mourir par la main de l'amant! Trop vieux cliché!* So let's drop the subject. The girl from Finland has turned your head. It's time to go and pay your respects to her. My feminine instinct tells me that you're head over heels in love with your nocturnal visitor. Since one doesn't get anything in this life by just wishing for it, I'll take you to her door myself.' For all her gaiety, I thought to myself, Nathalie had her little head screwed on the right way; she was capable of making resolute decisions and ready when necessary to show herself a good loser. I began to admire her again. Yet I was even more grateful to her for not making a scene, a thing that I profoundly abominate. With a conscience by no means clear I now took leave of her.

Frankly, I was eager to pay my respects to the young lady from Finland, whom I had not spoken to for so long. First of all I went to the florist I usually patronized and ordered my favorite roses, that aristocratic Maréchal Niel, for the following weeks. 'These roses have become rare. Pray accept them with the grace of the era that bred them.' I thought I was outdoing myself. The young lady ignored the flowers. She was looking at my hands, which were trembling, which was why I tightened my grasp on the stems. 'I am glad of your visit — but what brings you to see me so early in the morning?' The fragrance of my roses was spending itself upon the air in the room. Perhaps it was because of the shining eyes into which I was gazing: I was awkward in this schoolgirl's presence. Actually it was bold to appear before her after that distressing encounter the previous night. The thorns were pricking my fingers. 'I wish it had never happened,' I stammered. I had to try to pull myself together. The floor seemed to be giving way under me, rippling out in great circles. She put an end to the alarming silence by saying: 'They say it's an angel flying through the room.' I shook my head violently, although that was exactly what I seemed to be seeing. Or rather: the angel with the flaming sword at the gate of Paradise. It is incomprehensible to me that, when a fact seems plausible enough to the rational mind, for instance such a fact as that the sun is shining brightly — and so long as facts do remain the final criterion of truth — anyone should think of simply denying such facts out of hand. Such a fact, for instance, was the gaze of this proud seventeen-year-old! One might perhaps argue about whether it was outshone by the brilliance of the sun, or whether fresh-fallen snow on the mountains might not be still whiter than her cheeks, or gold deep within the mountains more sparkling than her hair. Yet what is incomparable is the line of her finely etched nostrils; for me that is beyond dispute. Still, because I too have my pride, I did not tell her that; on the contrary, I remarked that it was a wonder that all the flattery and compliments that had come her way on her début in society — all of which her cousin had proudly recounted to me — did not turn the head of a young lady who had only just left boarding school. Lightly she parried this by saying: 'I'm afraid I cannot flatter myself that I have noticed you in my entourage. On the other hand, I have not missed you.' 'Allow me to justify myself to you, mademoiselle . . . .' She cut me short. 'if your visit should be in any way connected with the episode of last night, then it is our common friend to whom you must justify yourself. Return to her, in heaven's name! Nathalie's exotic nature demands no more than an adventure with the Don Juan of our goodly capital.' With a faint cry she bent over her escritoire. 'A blot on the calligraphy! It is my graduation certificate!' Now I didn't mind making my situation even worse. I started up. 'Damn it all, I don't take the merchant's daughter seriously!' As if playing a game, I turned all cards face upwards. I had the idea of becoming engaged to the merchant's daughter only because it came to my ears that people were laughing at me for my infatuation with a young lady whose father I was old enough to be. 'Has Nathalie also turned you down?' she asked me scornfully. I flinched under her scorn as under a flick from a whip. Was she trying to provoke me or was it something else she had in mind? 'I love you unto death!' I burst out, and immediately regretted it. 'You'll survive it,' she said curtly. But when I went to the door she added in a lower voice: 'Never mind, just keep on trying.' I was speechless. Presumably she took my silence for a failure of presence of mind. It still astonishes me to think how I could carefully weigh in the balance a remark flung off thus carelessly. 'Do you wish me now to take my leave?' I stammered. 'Yes — no — I don't know — yes, for I didn't sleep in the night, I had a headache. Today I am going to have my hair cut. Wait a moment, I have something more to say, so long as we are undisturbed. I have now finished my schooling. Mamma is expecting me in Paris, where she is buying supplies of lace, spangles, semiprecious stones, and plumes, such as are now fashionable. I love to work with things that are radiant and delicate. Mamma and I mean to open a fashion house at home, in order not to have to go on being poor relations of our Humming-Bird.' 'When do you leave?' I asked, hardly able to get the words out. 'Tomorrow.' 'So soon? May I follow you?' 'There would be no sense in it, for I shall have no time at all for personal matters.'

I suppressed a cry of desperation. She took my hand and wiped away the little drops of blood with her handkerchief, which she let me keep. 'In the summer we shall have a holiday, perhaps we'll see each other again. Give me your roses now. The poor things are dying of thirst, I'll put them in water.' Her eyes were moist as she took the flowers. 'For the new year,' she said, kissing me on the lips. Her breath had the fragrance of fresh-fallen snow. 'Mademoiselle Snow-Fragrance,' I said. The phrase appealed to her, although it was not an original idea of mine, for in Finland girls are often given names such as Bird-Call, Pebble-Sparkling-in-the-Sunny-Brook, Cloud-Drifting-over-the-Lonely Road, and the like more. The door opened and Humming-Bird came in with a telegram from Paris. 'What a joke!' she exclaimed in that high voice of hers when she caught sight of me, and she wrung her hands. 'Oh the incorrigible fellow! That handkerchief doesn't go with those socks.'

Some months later my patience was rewarded by a telegram signed: 'Your Snow-Fragrance.' I flew from Therapia to Geneva and thence traveled several hours through the night by car, until I found the house where she was paying a visit — where, however, I was only able to see her alone for some minutes in the open air. The thaw had begun. There was still snow on the mountains.

The following summer I learned that the ladies were having a very busy and exhausting season in Paris. They were therefore favorably disposed to accept my suggestion that they should recuperate at Annecy, which was not too far away, before returning to Finland. I have always been adept at instantly making myself liked. My attentive manner to elderly ladies, even where I was solely concerned with gaining my own ends, made it inevitable that in the very first hour of our reunion at Annecy I was able to persuade the young lady's mother to move from her modest *pension* in the center of that provincial town and take rooms at my hotel on the lake. Napoleon III had built the place for the beautiful Spaniard. My means and my wish to be in the closest proximity to the daughter decided me to pursue a line that experience had already proved a successful one. The only time when I ever observed anything like a telepathic faculty in myself was when I asked the old lady if I might take her daughter dancing. 'She is wearing her first ball-dress in the evenings. You will do better to dance with her instead of always just looking at her. She is still so young.' And was the old lady so sure of what her searching gaze told her, that she was prepared to give up an illusory future in the bush for the sake of the bird in the hand? That evening I conducted both of them to my table — decked with my own flowers — in the large dining room, which was adorned with a monumental portrait of the Empress Eugénie by Winterhalter. At dinner the mother wore pearls. 'If one doesn't wear them, they lose their luster. But this necklace is really meant for my daughter. It's all that I shall be able to give her.' I nodded in such swift agreement that she must certainly have thought I had not understood what, though still unspoken between us, was bound to be put into words before long. Why did she survey me through her lorgnon with the peremptory air peculiar to a lady who had been holding receptions since the days of Queen Victoria? 'My daughter has taken a fancy to you, *mon dieu*! You are also in love with her, *naturellement*. But you have known each other too short a time for your wishes yet to go hand in hand.' I pricked up my ears. 'Perhaps mademoiselle is still too young to be betrothed?' I suggested, groping my way forward, at the same time folding my arms in order to show that I regarded 'going hand in hand' as a mere figure of speech. I considered it necessary to make my point of view quite clear right from the beginning, perhaps also because I could not help admiring the way the old rebel (as we jestingly called the old lady among ourselves) made a beeline for her object. 'I freely confess to you that I never regretted having made just such a romantic marriage when I was still very young.' I asked her to consider whether I was not after all too old, for I was almost old enough to be the young lady's father. At this the daughter wrinkled her little nose, which always disarmed me, and said: 'To make up for his being much older, I'm a head taller than he is. So we're even.' I swore that there was only this young lady in the world for me. '*Certainement*,' the mother said in confirmation of her daughter's remark, and instantly devoted her entire attention to the wine list, where I believed I could recommend one vintage quite particularly. 'Trés intéressant. A wine that I must try.' In this choice the daughter had advised me. It was a Bordeaux that would make her mother sleepy. When the dance music began, the party at the next table broke up — an English couple, their son, and his friend, both of them insignificant — and it was fortunate for us, for the two young men had begun to observe us. After they had sufficiently discussed several important subjects, such as what the coming season promised in the way of partridge-shooting, fox-hunting, and a return to the season in London, and were left with nothing more to criticize on the menu, although they nevertheless dined heartily, they decided to dance. 'You mustn't frighten off the young men. My daughter will lose her chance of some amusement if you go on casting such murderous glances at them.' I managed to be a moment faster than one of them. Rising from the table, I saw that the young man was obviously on the point of introducing himself; but he abandoned his intention. Let him go and count the stars in the sky, if he felt that way inclined. My partner danced like a schoolgirl, which is indeed what she still was. When we returned to our table the neighboring party had already gone, and the wine was also beginning to have the expected effect.

We wanted to go down to the lake, and the daughter waited considerately until it seemed the right moment to put forward our wish. With something of an effort her mother succeeded in making us believe that she had not been having a little nap. 'I was only sunk in thought.' She began to wake up again. 'To whom, I ask myself, should I rather entrust my daughter when I have gone? One who is too young? Nonsense! I have no fault to find with you except that you go about things too systematically. There's no little trick *que cet intrigant ne mette au profit pour monter ses affaires.*' With this remark she quite won my heart. 'There is no point in overlooking the fact that she has two brothers who are students. There is *la petite fille*, and there is, of course, myself besides. We aristocrats do not seek for reasons when we wish to give. I have done for *ma petite fille* all that a mother can do. She has a good figure and has enjoyed the best of educations, in a school for the well-bred daughters of noble families. She is an innocent child.' With a deep sigh she rose and took my arm. 'Well, we shall see how the cat jumps, as we say in Russia. You are responsible to me for my daughter! She is our treasure, our whole fortune.' In a matter-of-fact way she contemplated her dainty handkerchief, with which she had dabbed at her eyes — which were not moist. 'Let me think it over quietly. At my age one needs little sleep. And tomorrow we have the whole day before us. We shall not come down for *déjeuner*. I shall take my daughter for a long walk, but we shall be back for *diner*, which you will meanwhile order, in consultation with the mâitre d'hôtel, in the same excellent style as this evening. There's no nonsense about the cookery here — it's just good, nourishing French food. *Merci pour cela*,' she said benevolently to the discreet head-waiter, who bowed low. 'Let us talk no more tonight. I feel the fatigue that is natural at my age.' I was permitted to lay her stole round her shoulders and to press the button for the lift.

Once among the old trees in the park the two of us worked out how we would spend the next day in order to make it last as long as possible. The yellow flowers of the broom-bushes along the lake-shore poured forth their sharp fragrance. I knew of an inn that could easily be reached by steamer. In the water one could see vestiges of lake-dwellings. That was for tomorrow when I was to meet her with her mother as if by chance. At this hour the park belonged to us alone, and we hastened through it in every direction. Along the paths stone statues on marble pedestals, outlined in the moonlight, watched like old friends, soundlessly and very solemnly, over the lovers wherever the curtain of old trees was drawn back. We talked only in whispers, and in German, because that language harmonized with the nocturnal atmosphere. At that time German tutors had become more popular even than French dancing-masters in Russia, because the Russians who liked to travel abroad were thus able to hear, while strolling in the gardens of watering-places like Baden-Baden, or in the Black Forest, in Alsace, or in Switzerland, the familiar sounds of a language that they were accustomed to associate with romantic raptures over the beauties of Nature. The young lady's father — whom one avoided mentioning — was one of those who had left his fortune 'at the tables' in one of those watering-places surrounded by resin-scented forest. I believe he is still alive, living all alone far in the North, keeping a boat.

She was delighted with my notion that she should stand on a pedestal from which the statue was missing. We found the fragments of the statue itself in the midst of nettles and creepers. 'Only when your face, which looks like marble in this moonlight, begins to change expression shall I be able to believe that all this is not a dream.' 'That you shall do,' she said and let me lift her on to the stone, which rather confused me lest she should consider it just as much a joke as her mother's projects. Spine-chilling awe befell me when all at once the silk she wore, its blue now bleached snow-white by the moon's rays, slipped from her shoulder, so that she resembled the statue of Diana lying in the bushes — on which meanwhile, as on the path among the leaves and on the stones, the dew had fallen. The air trembled. Where the folds of her dress had fallen open one feminine breast swelled forth, at which we both stared awestricken, for, like the pine-cone on the Maenad's vine-wreathed thyrsus, there was a dark bud springing up there. It must have seemed no less amazing to her — that this should be happening to her before another's eyes, and a man's eyes too. At first she laughed like a child; then she became quite still. Her slender fingers stirred as though trying to trace the lines of the miraculous flesh. Then even her hand lay still upon her breast. But her eyes shone with the same glimmer as the stars in the night-sky above us. She was gazing down at me. Her mother was long asleep. A voice of conscience told me: I am not worthy of the gift. What was it that her mother had said? We nobles from the North never seek for reasons when we choose to give. I thought I heard voices in the distance. Overcoming a certain dread of touching the marble goddess who had come to life, I helped her down from the stone. It was quite unthinkable that anyone should be allowed to see us now. And she too realized now that she had shown more of herself than even she had previously known. Hesitantly we looked for the path to the lake, where she wanted to bathe. It was quite out of the question, I thought, oppressed by the memory of the fairly clear hint given me at dinner. Considering me a suitor was just an *idée fixe* of her mother's. '*Va donc, vite, ma petite fille.* Soon the two of you, I mean you and he . . .' And then she had been too tired to continue the conversation. Now I knew this happened only in fairy tales, and it could happen only to a dream-prince. *Trop expansive*, that was what her mother was.

She had swum out quite a long way while I was waiting beside her clothes, when one of the youths who had been at the next table at dinner emerged from the bushes that covered me. 'It would be very unhealthy for you to go in for a swim now!' I said hoarsely. 'So sorry,' he said and disappeared with all speed, as though he were wearing the red-hot slippers that Snow White's stepmother was made to put on. I think I had stepped rather urgently on his thin evening-pumps. I had also brought a bath-towel from the hotel, and she let me dry her with it. In doing so I behaved as if what I was touching were Praxiteles' honey-colored marble, and she lauded my tact. This amiable acknowledgment of my devotion was not so entirely deserved, for the proud girl was well able to keep me at a distance without hurting my feelings.

It made me more than happy to be called by her, even if not to be chosen. The bath-towel was still dripping when I pushed her into the hotel lift and slammed the door, sending her upwards before the eyes of my rival's parents, who had been there first. Through the metal bars of the door a mischievous smile thanked me. It was the last smile I had from her.

During the sultry morning that followed a particularly violent thunderstorm broke; sheaves of lightning and rain set the lake in turmoil, its colors changing like the eyes of the giant kraken that I had once watched in its impotent rage in the Naples aquarium. I had already been waiting for a long time, lurking behind a pillar in the corridor while the other hotel guests emerged from the breakfast-room, singly and in groups, and gathered in the winter-garden, intending to go for a walk as soon

as the usual thunderstorm, which came up as regularly as it
passed over quickly, had cooled the atmosphere. So it was too
that morning. I could not see my ladies anywhere among the
throngs of people ready and eager to set forth. Presumably they
had gone out early. Nobody was late today. The thunderstorm
spent itself as suddenly as it had burst. Going out into the open
air I craned my neck, trying to see over the heads of groups
receding into the distance, and incidentally noticed the young
Englishmen running down to the lake and beginning, with much
jollity, to bale out their boat. It was anchored close to the
embankment. Now I could see them drawing up the anchor and
cleaning off the weeds. They sat astride the low wall, over which
there were still occasional waves breaking. Now they must have
caught sight of something, for they paused in what they were
doing and called out to someone. The wet stones were shining in
the sun, which had just come out, radiant as if it had suddenly
dried up all the clouds. With glaring vividness, as though it were
a picture developed on a Kodak plate, I still see in memory what
I then beheld. There was the young lady in a wet bathing-
costume that she had, frankly, long outgrown, while her mother
was preparing to photograph her in that provocative garb. She
must have called out to her daughter, telling her to walk up and
down the narrow wall to get dry. My God, what an ugly feeling
it left me with! Of course there was no money to spare for a
suitable bathing-costume, for there were those brothers, and then
there was Mamma herself, and the girl came last of all! Then why
hang about precisely there, where those two insufferable fellows
were pretending to be so busy, although doubtless also throwing
off an occasional *risqué* remark? I could not hear so far, yet it
seemed to me that the ladies had also laughed. I wished I were
dead then and there, struck by lightning — wished I had never
been born! In my desperation I would say frightful things to this
procuress of a mother. I had no heart to approach Mademoiselle
Snow-Fragrance in this condition. Yet it must be! I rushed to the
wall, breathless. I could not have walked along it without growing giddy and stumbling. That was how it was. Where were they?
I slowed up and peered over the wall to where the two young

men had already got their boat afloat. They took no notice of me, which was just as well, for my face must have been contorted with fury. For as far as I could see over the water there was nobody bathing, only the boat rocking in the water, which by now was again quite clear. Where the gentle wavelets rippled the sand by the wall, they slightly raised and lowered the torn twigs, leaves, and water-weed. There were still some pools full of thick mud. Only an hour ago this transparent lake had been seething like the crater of a volcano, and the night before it had borne a naked goddess. Such details as that of the bathing suit that was too short for her I remember as if it had been yesterday. That was why she had not put it on the previous night, she said. Of course it was all right for me to go with her when she went for a swim. *Bien drôle*, the thought of being embarrassed by me! The idea would never occur to her! In the North nobody was embarrassed by nakedness. All year long one waited for the sun and the sea-bathing, because it was healthy and made one cheerful. Admittedly, there were people whose only thought was to be smart, whether in their clothes or without them. A girl has her pride and knows how to deal with smarties. So it had been an hallucination? How gladly I would have believed that my over-strained nerves had played a bad trick on me; but I was afraid of going mad. I went senselessly running on, further and further, then leaped into a taxi in which I drove to the Swiss frontier, and then, changing my mind, I drove back again. Outside the hotel I engaged the taxidriver to take the two ladies back to Paris the same day. The young lady was less shocked by my description of the episode than I had expected. 'Don't I know you better? I'll persuade Mamma that she has urgent business reasons for going straight back to Paris.' But as soon as she was seated in the taxi together with her mother, I wrote the fatal farewell letter and also left the hotel. Of course I took the next train and followed the ladies.

II

Further and further inland I went running, after the macadam highroad had come to an end, running barefoot because my damp canvas shoes had become insufferably hot. Past medieval storehouses where Greek and foreign shipping-lines now had their offices, I reached the open country. The sun was blazing ever more intensely, and here there were no more houses. I fell down in the white chalk-dust, which instantly closed over me like water. There is no clock to tell how long I lay there. I had only visual impressions, above all that of this hostile light from the noonday sun, now vertically overhead, which I was trying to escape from before it blinded me. Not far from sunstroke, and without a hat at that — I must have lost it in the night — half fainting I groped my way along the steep white walls of the quarry. Even with my eyes shut, my eyelids roasting, basted with sweat, the flickering of the hot dust was anguish, as I searched for some irregularity in the terrain. Was there no shadow or coolness anywhere? When I had descended to the bottom of the quarry where the rough stone came from for building these Mediterranean towns that I had recently been seeing, I thought: this is the threshold of the underworld. Just so must it have been: a city without windows or doors, houses blind and dumb, houses outside which one can shout oneself to death and no one will ever answer. How comfortably off my traveling companion must be now, lounging at his ease in a deck-chair in the shade! I thought of him with envy while my brain seemed to be melting. Oh, I shall still make something of my life! It's not because one wants to live eternally, and one isn't growing any younger — but I don't mean to grow any older here on this bewitched island. I shall take the next bus back and go down to the ship! Somehow the door-bell came into my hand, and I pulled it. Faintly, like the telephone ringing in another room, I heard the sound of it. It must be good to be there inside. The rocks must have opened even as I risked opening my eyes. I was able to see into a cool vault, heard a girlish voice chanting a counting-out rhyme, and saw the girl, scarcely more than a child, playing ball. Making the ball bounce back from the wall and passing now one leg, now the other, over it, she caught it skillfully behind her back, in a tambourine that she held there, her arms crossed. Seeing me standing there amazed in the doorway, she missed, and the ball rolled to my feet. 'Amalthea!' she called. Another voice, a deeper one, asked: 'What is it?' 'There's a tourist at the door — he'll be asking some more of those funny questions that nobody knows how to answer,' the child said perkily to the older girl, perhaps her sister, whose face was all I could as yet see in the background. The extraordinary garment that she was wrapped in aroused my curiosity because it was neither a pinafore, a shift, nor an apron, nor anything of that sort, but more resembled a horse-blanket such as was hanging with other pieces of washing on a line stretched diagonally across the vault. Then I heard the person, whoever it was, coming out. How strange the footsteps sounded, I thought — not really human at all. When I could distinguish her shape more clearly, I still could not really make out what sort of creature she was. Seeing me so obviously speechless, she laughed. To the child she whispered: 'Tell him goat's milk is good for children because it's full of vitamins.' Now I felt nausea rising. Yet her smile was touching, even though I found it distressing that she should show more naked leg than a respectable girl ought to. Modestly she at least tried to conceal the little rosy udder with her hind legs. 'I don't want to bother you,' I said. 'I just wanted to try to telephone and find out when the next bus stops, and where!' 'There's no telephone here. Where is it you want to go?' she asked, drying her hands on her wool. She wrinkled her nose in a superior way. 'I'm sorry, I can't stay here, standing about with nothing on, as you can see. My only dress is in the wash.' 'Well, you see, I just wanted to bring the ball back,' I stammered. 'That's all right. Give the child the ball.' Then she gently pushed me outside — and disappeared, as did also the opening in the wall.

   When my traveling companion cross-questions me, as he inevitably will, I shall simply stick to the story that I saw a damsel clad in purest white, a veil over her head and a long-stemmed lily in one hand, and shall recount how with the other hand she gathered up her train and with the tip of her satin slipper kicked a tennis ball that had rolled to my feet. Who could foresee that the ball would roll in that direction! Swearing with my hand on eyes, heart, and loins, I shall assure my friends that this damsel sent the ball flying round the corner, where it then lay still. No more than a hundred paces further on — there was the bus-stop. The damsel was taller than I. How different everything would be if one were only married, I thought. 'I must think it over,' she said, as though she could read thoughts. 'Good,' I said, for I had plenty of time, and so had my friend aboard the ship.

Around the corner there was a gray stone building like a little temple, with a portico of Greek columns, but also with a totally unsuitable chimney on the roof, from which smoke was issuing. How absurd it seemed here, with no other building far and wide in all this dusty solitude. I had seen this temple before somewhere — yes, it had been one hot day in the East End of London. It was in May, and the air was bursting with humidity. Walking along those endless shabby streets of identical houses full of dry rot, which eats its way, green and pink, through the cement, making these slums look like mangy cats, I had been struck by something that I could not help thinking of now. There was an alehouse, and next to it a brand new public lavatory with two entrances, marked 'Ladies' and 'Gentlemen.' In front of it a somewhat decrepit old lady reposed, dead drunk, in the gutter, wearing a crumpled bonnet that had seen better days. The flat-footed, kindly giant of an Irish policeman, whose tall helmet made him look even taller than he was, stood gazing at her helplessly. The Irish have a dignity all their own, even when lying drunk in the gutter. 'Don't touch me, I'm a lady,' the aged person said forbiddingly. But on the other side of the street there was the building of which I have spoken, built of the same gray stones as this temple and also with a Greek portico and also with the tan chimney on its roof, with thick black smoke rising from it into the blue sky. In every house in the East End they start frying fish and chips in the morning, in mutton fat. But over the portico of the building from which all this smoke was densely rising there was the word, in gold letters: Crematorium. 'The bus ought to be here any moment now,' the damsel said. 'I seem to have been waiting for an eternity,' I said, whereupon the damsel turned away and departed as she had come, playing with the ball.

I was glad to see the bus approaching. The nearer it came, the faster it rattled along, and so it naturally went dashing past the stop, so that I had to go panting after it in the dust. In response to my shouting and waving the driver finally came to a halt. How I now longed for my traveling companion! Perhaps it was only because, as I have already hinted, he always managed to be a nose ahead of his fate, whereby the automatic trundling of destiny was slowed up as if by the well-known grain of sand in the machinery. But what I enjoyed about this bus trip was that I had spared my friend this at least. Even today, as I write the story down, it makes my conscience lighter to think of it, for it is not so long since I was one of a few friends attending his cremation in New York. Today I don't mind saying frankly that his intentions were always of the purest and entirely harmless. His mission in life was to leave the world a better place than he had found it. True, he did not succeed in that, but even when the Creator of all things rested on the seventh day and surveyed his Creation, all he could say was that it was good because now it couldn't be changed.

There were so many passengers taking the bus that it seemed as if nobody wanted to stay at home that day, as if everybody had taken a holiday from everyday routine. They were all in high good humor. The driver kept on blowing his horn in the most superfluous fashion, and with a sudden spurt he had at once increased speed beyond the limit, in spite of the fact that the road was uphill. We went positively flying round sharp bends, faster and faster, as though it were a matter of knocking down all of the bowling pins at once — in this case the milestones, which stood out in relief against the dusty gray precipice, like white sugar loaves. I wondered with some anxiety whether the drivers of rickety old vehicles like this had their vision tested before they were granted a license to drive a human cargo. On trains, at least, one can insure oneself against accidents. I hoped the driver was going to see the pothole straight ahead of us, where the embankment was just crumbling away, collapsing in a cloud of dust into the abyss. And to think that the brake drums must be full of sand! The grating of the axles went through the very marrow of my bones! There was one front wheel hanging in empty air. . . . A little bird flew up. Without being able to explain it to myself, I knew: If that little bird hadn't been there, there would have been an accident! I told myself; Once we're over this, it'll be all right. Tally-ho! And we were over it, and it was all right! I can't stand the sight of blood! The thought that something might happen — all would then be over, anyhow — could itself bring about the accident as we flew, fast as thought, over the yawning chasm. Hasn't one heard of people being killed by falling out of bed, just because they had a premonition of the same thing in their sleep? The little bird was an integral part of the wave of happiness in which I subsequently lost myself — all the more blissfully because I had managed to keep my wits about me. I felt myself to be like the flying bird, all lucidity, with the heights above me and infinity ahead of me. For the first time this journey was purely refreshing, a real holiday, and this even though the bus was bumping me about somewhat. I had at once taken a seat that was politely given up to me by someone who assured me that he preferred to stand. Tourists are welcome everywhere, so there was no reason to stand on ceremony. Incidentally, I shall return to the subject of this gentleman, since willy-nilly one could not fail to notice him because of his big blue beard. He was the living image of the Typhon in the little museum behind the Acropolis, except that the latter has no hat on his head — a hat, moreover, dashingly pushed back off the forehead. I notice a lot of things, because I live through my eyes. If I consider it aright, Amalthea's deformity — oh, excuse me — Amalthea's unusual figure was also very noticeable. just imagine: a girl with four legs! It takes a certain freedom from prejudice to prevent one from finding such a thing funny — it positively calls for an amount of philosophy not at the command of most tourists. It was reason enough for those sisters to live in retirement. I have no doubt that she wore her horse-blanket — as soon as it was dry — proudly as a queen wears the purple. I thought of her body, white as a lamb's — no, as a goat's! Nor can I pass over the fact that she gazed after me, waving her little tail instead of a dainty handkerchief

All men are brothers! That is a splendid principle, particularly in harmony with the sense of well-being now filling my heart. It may be only a platitude, but in all fairness I must here point out that this elevating principle, that of the brotherhood uniting all men, would not be universally valid if one were to forget the female sex. That was why I liked to remember dear good Amalthea. But just as I was dwelling on that memory, the atmosphere in the bus became quite suffocating, which did not disturb the other passengers, who were all earnestly applying themselves to the food they had brought along with them for the journey. There were hard-boiled eggs rubbed with onion, pickled fish and olives, over-ripe cucumbers and melons, and all of it was swilled down with resinous wine out of goat's-bladder bottles, and brandy, which tasted like furniture polish, that was handed round and partaken of without improving the eaters' breath. So a faint distaste for these people began to stir in me because they could not overcome their brutish limitations. Fortunately my attention was diverted by a quite charming scene going on outside — a vagabond girl with a dancing bear, which an old fellow was whipping on to further exertions. She was playing the tambourine. The windows had been shut not because the passengers could not bring themselves to watch cruelty to animals — only an Englishman would write to *The Times* about such a thing — but because of the girl's insistence on coming to the windows to beg. 'What fun — just look at the praying mantis raising her thin brown hands as in prayer.' I thought: The praying mantis and the dancing bear could be made into a wonderful story if one were able to write it. Since the worthy Aesop the tradition was to endow animals with human attributes for our entertainment, until that Puritan, La Fontaine, suddenly gave the matter a modern turn by attaching a moral to the story as Darwin attached a science to it.

Obviously in this instance the good shepherd was too late to carry his lamb on his shoulders. The Lord who provides for the lilies of the field.... Yet even the highway somehow provides for its girls, with fresh air doing its part towards their survival, as one could see. However, what I did not like at all, now that I looked more closely, was that the bear had no nose-ring, whereas such an animal should always be led by one. If anyone were to ask me about the wild animals in the zoo, I should be able to describe them all, just as one sees them through the bars, each according to its nature. But it makes a difference whether such a brute is kept safely behind bolts and bars or goes running around loose. 'Yes indeed, sir! A child's life endangered by that brute!' I screamed at my neighbors. It was impossible to hear, through the closed windows, what the little girl was saying. Her lips were moving, and she was crying. It was a good thing that the gentleman with the big blue beard opened the door of the bus in time to get the girl in, and with my own hands I slammed it against the brown bear, which was going for the girl, grunting, with open jaws. 'Get going, driver! How else are we to be there in time for dinner, before nightfall!' All the passengers urged the same thing. Still, I don't want to close my account of this episode without explaining why the bus had stopped. First, in order to let the engine cool down, and secondly and above all because just at that point, where the road cut between steep walls of rock, this traveling circus had stopped right in the middle of the road. To be precise, there was only one single, dilapidated wheeled cage for the one beast of prey. A mule was rolling merrily in the dust, whinnying, unresponsive to the kicks and blows it was receiving and the myriads of flies that would obviously soon be devouring it, it was so old and so covered with sores. Nevertheless, as soon as the mule-driver, who had a moth-eaten lion-skin slung over his naked torso, was able to push the little cart to one side, the bus driver stepped on the accelerator and speeded on.

The waif measured me with a glance, the way one assesses an American or someone whom one takes for an American. 'Would the gentleman kindly pay the trifling sum for my ticket?' She said it with the sort of winning smile that gladdens the heart, even though it is not intended for anyone in particular. The round black eyes of all the men were fixed on this immature creature, who resembled a falcon poised for flight, which breasts the air as though itself as light as air, and so off into all four winds. The little girl was not heavy, and she sat quietly; incidentally, she was not so little. She looked no different from most such half-grown girls. But my tranquillity was at an end. I felt like Punch and Judy in one person, battered and flung this way and that by the jolting bus. Yet these blows were nothing in comparison with the batterings that the two antagonists in my breast were giving each other. For my purest intentions and my bad conscience were skirmishing with each other. The little girl, who at first sat dreamily gazing into the distance like patience on her monument, until she was given something to eat, had now fallen asleep. She had gone to sleep quite unconcerned by the fact that she was sitting on a strange man's lap. When one is hungry, conscience will approve of whatever fills the empty stomach, from which one school of economists has drawn the conclusion that an empty stomach is the only cause of a bad conscience. I had leisure enough to muse on this. Besides, it diverted my attention from the young creature, who much attracted me. I make no attempt to show myself in a good light; but the gentleman who had given up his seat to me was certainly not plagued by such scruples. His face was flushed, his eyes sparkling with lechery. How comical a man seems when he is undressing a woman in his thoughts! To make up for that, for all the alertness of his Phoenician eyes he will never discover wherein the real mystery of the relation of 'I' to 'You' consists. Ah yes, my good Monsieur Typhon with your big bluebeard! Not even if you were a tripartite figure, like the bluebeard with the scaly fishtail in the museum on the Acropolis! Someone like you will always continue to be like a fish in a glass bowl, bumping your snout against your own reflection. If he only knew how ridiculous he looks with this lust in his eyes, which it makes the like of us downright embarrassed to behold. No, one simply can't expose oneself like that in public. The fact that my own face was becoming flushed was necessarily connected with the principle of purity and respect for women that is sacred to me, and thus with the responsibility that had been wished on me in this bus with all these men around. The little girl's skirt was definitely too short — it didn't cover everything! Naturally I at once averted my eyes, also because the little girl jabbed me with her knee. An attack of conscience seems to me much like influenza: one person gets it, another doesn't. Bluebeard was all of one piece, and his eyes never strayed from the little girl. He wasn't ashamed to say that he could positively eat her up. And yet there was nothing so very special about her; she was just a wild young animal, glowing from having been in the sun, mixing among all these strange men as casually as she had previously been scampering about in the dust of the road with that savage beast. Somebody must have cut off her thick black hair with a pocket-knife! So was it really surprising that even my ingrained reserve, which I owe to my origins in a cooler climate, was no match for the attractiveness of a feminine creature that was, moreover, the only one in that omnibus? Ignoring the witless remarks made by my fellow-passengers, I stealthily sought the child's thin brown hand, and I don't know why, but I suddenly couldn't help thinking of the harbor-prostitute. I had lost her in the crowd, though I had indeed run down the gangway pretty fast; she had too big a start, that was it. The moon must have been shining brightly enough for her to see me fairly distinctly in my white tropical suit and straw hat. Well, that's over! Enough of that — no memories! Let's not go back to the beginning again! I'm no hero, and I'm afraid of what is waiting on the other side of the door and is about to turn the handle. It'll be better to listen to Bluebeard; that will be less oppressive. Time seemed to stand still — let the moment last forever! Even the telegraph poles, which went positively flying by as we traveled, seemed to have stopped for all eternity, although they were made of feelingless concrete, and the wires of cold metal. Couldn't one practically hear the wires whispering: 'Be content with what you hold in your hands?' For what else does anyone say over the wires but: 'Well, we'll see how it turns out in the end?' There are a thousand things that are preferable to a terrible end. And some day the winning number will drop into this or that person's lap. Lord of the dead! Give us a holiday — touch wood — no memories, not even any more of the bitter ones! I began to tremble. What did I now care for the crooked paths that lead to happiness, the winding stairs, the obscure nooks and crannies in ports of call that have long become nameless! I could no longer tell one thing from another as it all went through my mind, all the more since even the other side, the conscious side, no longer held together, no longer answered. To come straight out with it in plain language, I was beginning to forget what Mademoiselle Snow-Fragrance actually looked like. So then that was the end?

The little angel on my lap positively didn't weigh anything at all. Yet the wench was not really any longer a child. But adults must know what things are like behind Adam's ribs! What was wrong?

Bluebeard is telling a story. His story, which I shall reproduce as briefly as possible, has no moral; it is long and broad as a cowpat that someone accidentally steps into. I must leave it to the reader, if he craves a moral, to find it for himself. It goes without saying that Monsieur Typhon was a man of the world. He instantly transported his hearers to Paris, where there was, inevitably, a lady. It happened that a rich Parisienne, and pretty at that, had not, like her compatriots, invested in Russian railways that were never built. For that, as for the fall of the Czar's empire, it was not the idea of the French Revolution that was to blame; on the contrary, one day the Paris Bourse ceased to back the Russian loan, even suddenly threw the shares on the market, whereupon their artificially high value suddenly vanished and they became worthless. Like her women friends, Bluebeard's lady had a château in the country and a house in Paris, and her boudoir had Oriental carpets on the floor, potted palms in the corner, heavy *portières* hanging to the floor, a sultry semidarkness such as was sung by the poetasters of that epoch, and even the Turkish hubble-bubble beside the plush sofa on which the lady reclined in languorous attitudes familiar from masterpieces in the Louvre. What distinguished her from her women friends was these shares, from the study of which she now looked up in desperation, although, unlike the wives of cabinet ministers and the mothers of sons highly placed in politics, the army, or the Church, she was not speculating in 'Russians'; she had an interest in the economic opening up of Morocco. This was indeed her

only interest since she had discovered that among the Kabyls
there were men of a kind that one would have difficulty in
finding in France. She had no inclination to waste any time
studying anthropology and comparative religion; she merely
followed the dictates of her heart. That was enough! She spent
her nights praying for the conversion of the Mahdi. But should
that miracle never take place, she was prepared to give the
Moroccan ruler her hand, to plight her everlasting troth with
him in the eyes of the God who was Mohammed's and the God
of the prophets, resigning herself to the inevitable in the awareness of serving a higher purpose. We all have the great task of
reforming the world, which is, God knows, sufficiently in need
of betterment. So far, so good. Then came the rising in Morocco.
The lady munificently offered the Mahdi an amnesty from the
French Government and for himself asylum in her château in
Champagne, where she would keep him company. This was not
merely a gesture of condescension and not merely on account of
her shares. She was in fact head-over-heels in love with him; and
he must indeed have been an impressive man. Doubtless he
would also have remained so had it not been for the sole
condition that the lady had to make and to which she stuck: the
Sultan must roll up the Prophet's green flag, the banner of the
Holy War. His answer arrived forthwith, and here is in all
brevity what he had to say in the flowery language of the Orient.
The Sultan shared her feelings (he wrote), yet, as she would
realize, being guided as she was by the tolerant spirit of neigh-
borly love, it would be necessary for her to extend her hospitality
to include three dozen women, the youngest of whom were still
in their girlish bloom. Without this harem he would not come to
stay with her in her châteaus. But this the lady neither could nor
would appreciate, and her answer was, as one would expect,
'*non*'. Her angry glance fell on the door, which was opening. She
barely had time to powder her nose and smile. 'What luck — it's
our Marshal!' The Marshal was on the point of leaving for army
headquarters in North Africa. He was a Frenchman, a brilliant
soldier, and a great favorite of the lady's. Forsooth, the Mahdi
should rue the day when he had sent her a present of a full-grown

Berber lion! Such insolence! And by the mouth of his messengers, who had delivered the wild beast in its cage, depositing it in the courtyard of her house in Paris, he had told her to tame this symbol of the desert before she tried to bring a proud Arab to her boudoir! It was the ideal moment for a call from the French Marshal, who arranged for the animal to be conveyed, provisionally, to the zoo. In the arms of the grievously weeping lady the Marshal was made to swear a solemn oath. She was an angel of devotion, yet crueler than a tigress, with claws instead of rosy fingernails, resolved to tear the living heart out of the breast of him who had scorned her. The Marshal swore by his honor as a soldier, and set out for army headquarters. The lady resolved to put an end to the affair with the Mahdi, and an end such as he deserved! Let the reader picture her distressed condition. Think of the cloying scent that is alone enough to arouse emotions, quite apart from the agitation caused by such unquenched desire. A Marshal of France is no substitute ... still, he would serve his purpose by satisfying her thirst for vengeance. When in the course of time peace had been imposed on the rebellious districts and the rebel leader had to surrender unconditionally, the Marshal had him thrown alive to the very lion that he had sent by way of a *billet-doux* to the lady in her boudoir. It was a simple soldierly way of fulfilling his pledge. This same lion, which had thus become the mausoleum of the last scion of the once so mighty dynasty of the Fatimids, the Greek claimed to have beheld with his own eyes, stuffed in the Sultan's palace at Fez.

There was vigorous applause from all and sundry and a demand that he should tell more stories. My arms were not free, for the girl was lying in them, and the old Turk in front of me likewise merely removed his long pipe in order to stroke his white beard with one bony hand. He scrutinized me sharply and said in a quavering voice: 'You speak English, yes? Yes? Very improper, indeed,' and sank back into his dreams. The remark was evidently directed at the raconteur. I myself found the story trivial and pointless, and so I merely hugged the angel still tighter to my breast. 'I've no idea what you want of me. Let me go, I'm hot enough as it is.' Petrified with amazement, I could only hope that no one had overheard her. Truly I did not deserve such ingratitude. The next thing would doubtless be that the arrogant brat would expect me to apologize, since she was actually imputing evil intentions to me! 'You're a downright menace,' I said quietly but firmly; but I loosened my grip on the child. She smoothed her hair calmly and snapped back at me: 'Don't all men go after little girls? You can't deny you're holding me on your lap instead of offering me your seat.' That was really a bit much. I didn't dream of getting up. Only there was that damned blush again creeping up my neck! This doll of flesh and blood watched me betraying myself. Just amusing herself, eh? 'The little girl's planning to turn a lion into a pussycat! It's not the first time a tourist has had to buy her ticket for her. Every time there's a bus trip round the island she puts on the act with the bear, and anyone who hasn't seen it before falls for it.' So saying, Monsieur Typhon patted me on the shoulder in a friendly way. Now, I don't at all care to have travelers becoming familiar with me. 'Nobody can maintain that I was in any way offensive to the little creature. I wouldn't know why I should be. Because she's sitting on my lap? There was no other seat free! Almost a child, I say! just a little girl!' The vein in my temple was swelling up; I could feel it without raising my hand. I was sweating blood. 'Almost a child, but still, one that belongs to the opposite sex,' Monsieur Typhon said. 'Very improper indeed! You speak English, yes? Yes?' the old Turk interposed, and at this the whole busload of men burst out into roars of laughter. 'In a word, sir, you suggest I was permitting myself certain familiarities that are not suitable in public, no matter how broad-minded one may be!' I was beginning to become thoroughly confused and my voice went up very high, but nobody was listening to me anymore, the men were no longer laughing, merely grunting. It was obscene. 'If that is what you gentlemen are thinking, kindly allow me to explain,' I shouted with the last of my failing strength, 'that my passion for this innocent girl could not be satisfied in an omnibus, because the whole wide world would not have room enough to contain the happiness . . .' I quite lost the thread. Thirty voices or more were shouting in confusion, everyone was jeering at me.

'Innocence — that's a fine story! How young she is, the little Circe! Oh la la! Quiet, quiet! Let him go on.'

The next moment I realized that in the circumstances there was no chance of this coming to a good end. Everything was going wrong, not going straight to its end with that acceleration known to us from the physical law about the speed of falling bodies, but in a round-about way. What, for instance, impelled the acknowledged jester in this company of travelers to insist on giving the turbaned Turk Cyprus wine out of that rancid goat's bladder? Turks don't drink! The Turk called him the son of a goat. Thereupon, and evidently in order to retrieve his reputation in his friends' eyes, the fellow offered to replace the innocent maiden on my lap with the goat that he had at home. I don't know why I laughed. But it wasn't at all bad. The innocent maiden with four legs! Amalthea! My nerves merely flickered, like a fuse blowing. The girl also began to laugh, with one hand over her mouth, and to exchange sidelong glances with the others, who were staring at me. One had to be on one's guard with this mischievous reincarnation of Circe, who transforms men into animals.

The whole company seemed to be plotting something against me. Nobody was laughing now. One after another they came closer, as though there was something about me, whatever it might be, that they wanted to see, and each with sidelong glances at the next, waiting until the first had moved up. Short-sighted though I am, I could bear their muttered comments, and I didn't care for them. The Turk removed his pipe and said: 'You speak English, yes? Yes? Very?' as he pointed at me. 'Is there something not right about me?' I asked the Turk, looking at him sharply as he pointed the stem of his pipe at the little girl. 'Very improper indeed.' What he meant was the wench on my lap! I leaped up from my seat, which the little girl instantly took with a demure bob of her little head. In such a situation one naturally reaches for the place where one's tie is, as though clutching at a straw. My tie had slipped — no, it simply wasn't where it ought to be, it wasn't round my neck at all. This might cost me my head. At any moment now this ominous fact would be twisted into a rope for my neck, by which I would be hauled before the judgment seat of public opinion. A gentleman without a tie on! Stark naked, as it were! Gentlemen, please, adjust their dress before leaving!' So the Turk would have put it, his English being only distantly related to the language that is understood everywhere in the world. For an Oriental, with his extravagant imagination, it is impossible to state the simplest fact in an objective manner for instance, that Mr. So-and-so's tie has slipped to one side. However, he had descended from the bus a short while earlier, whereupon the driver had tried to make up for lost time by redoubling his speed. Fields planted with poppies positively went flying past. The Turk must make a lot of money out of it, with prices what they are these days! I thought. Why had everyone, as if by tacit agreement, avoided making any further reference to the incident? After a fleeting glance at the corpus delicti, which was on the floor, I too did my best to ignore the whole thing, seeing that the others were pretending, deliberately it seemed, to have more important things to think about. I felt some vague danger physically advancing upon me. Remembering the tennis ball, I thought the story would entertain the passengers, and so I told it to them. What a lovely story it was! With forced gaiety I had to confess so much to myself. It was his own fault that my traveling companion was not there to hear it! Had he not gone on long enough, begging to be allowed to come with me? No, no, he needn't think I couldn't get on without him.

If only these people weren't there! Apart from myself, the driver, and the girl there were twelve of them in the bus — twelve, like the Apostles — and all of them not letting me out of their sight. I did my best not to attract attention. The ball must be somewhere underneath the seats, where I could not see it without bending down, indeed kneeling down and groping on the floor under the seats. It was dirty on the floor, and that reminded me of the steerage. Twice a week the ship covered the route to the Promised Land with a cargo of emigrants who had fled from pogroms in Russia, Poland, and Romania. I had no inclination to get my clothes dirty in the steerage. It was his hobby-horse, mere egalitarianism, all this enlightenment, the result of which was that the masses were turned into mere voting-cattle, as beef is turned into soup-cubes. I had taken a good look at these people of his, wretched creatures with backs crooked and shoulders hunched in inherited fear of blows, and with eyes reddened from weeping since childhood. I protested: 'There's a stench of fish', but this hadn't disturbed my traveling companion. I thought his conversation with the old Jew had lasted long enough. The old man merely gave me a fleeting glance through his dark glasses and then, taking no more notice of me, continued to regale my friend. 'Oh, a fellow like that has forgotten, he's emancipated . . .' 'Isn't Israel only casting off its chains in a different way from the Gentiles?' my friend objected. 'But the teachers say the chains were sent as a punishment upon our people for their defection,' the old man said. 'Surely it is your modern world, in which bread tastes dry in the mouth because it could not be sweet manna for the Chosen People, who are yearning for home in the dream colors of the ghetto.' I couldn't help bursting out laughing. 'Dream colors of the ghetto, that's a good one!' My traveling companion scratched himself for embarrassment. My own laughter sounded strange to me, as if it had been someone else laughing. My friend looked like a baby with his prominent belly, his thin neck, and his soft hands. 'Your prescriptions about food are not observed at the first-class *table d'hôte*!' I said mockingly.

I know what I must ask my traveling companion as soon as I get back to the ship again! Not that I'm hurrying at all because I miss him — I can find thousands just like him — hundreds anyway! I must ask him about the tennis ball that the girl in snow-white was kicking along with the toe of her slipper. Can a tennis ball appear out of the air like that, without more ado, and then dematerialize again as though the earth had swallowed it up? After all, the earth only takes the dead into its womb. just let someone try to find me a tennis ball on the floor of a bus, among empty bottles, remains of food, fruit-peel and fruit-stones, lying about in pools of wine! Find a tennis ball! I hummed to myself. And it occurred to me that I had got into the bus by the wrong door, the door where one is supposed to get out, and so I pushed my way forward through the twelve Apostles gathered around me, who were already putting on their cloaks, white habits with hoods to go over their heads. When I arrived at the driver's side, the others were lining up behind me as though to buy tickets for the cheap seats at the cinema in the evening. 'Here's the money for my ticket, which I forgot to get.' I took some nickel coins out of my purse, and the driver dropped them into the fare-box, which, however, failed to make a ringing sound, even after one had waited a while. 'That's foreign money,' said the uniformed man at the steering wheel, whose face I could not see because he had his back turned to me, and with his free hand he took my wallet, in which there was a banknote. 'Please be quick with my change, I've arrived at my destination.'

Whatever he answered could not be heard above the noise of the engine, but also because the passengers now raised their voices in a litany: *Dies irae, dies illa.* For it was Easter, and they were busily preparing to trim wax candles that they would light as soon as the bells came flying back again from Rome. I had no candle, and they began to mutter about this. 'You must realize it's something one prefers not to speak of. But you've been behaving in a suspicious manner here for quite a while.' With these words he pulled out a knife, the blade of which he tested between thumb and forefinger before he began to shorten the wick of his candle with it. 'You must disappear!' the girl whispered in my ear, unnoticed by the others. How is a human being to disappear just like that, without more ado, to evaporate, so to speak dematerialize? I wondered. However skeptical one may be about the consolations of religion, the craving for immortality remains inherent in human nature. One has the sense of it in one's head. Isn't that also why the hole, the grave, the entrance into nothingness is generally marked with a wreath of immortelles and a branch of evergreen? As a thinking person one simply takes steps to prepare oneself in good time. Can a human being have been added to the objective world as one more fact, only to be blown away like gossamer on the wind? I asked myself, all the time keeping my eyes on the man behind me, who took a step backwards every time I looked at him. How much longer did he mean to go on waving his knife in my face? 'You'll hurt someone with that knife of yours if you don't look out! Where are we? What's the time? How far is it to our journey's end?' 'If you haven't a candle, you can't come any further on this bus!' he said, releasing the safety-catch on the door. I opened the door a little and looked out. 'It's beginning to rain. If I have to walk, I shall catch a cold. What is it that's suspect about me? I have a British passport!' 'You can't come to the Resurrection without a candle! You haven't purified yourself of your sins!' An old man began now to complain in a fretful voice. 'Do I not speak as the father of a son who did not return alive from the mountains? And shall we now be content with the blood-money, only because that is the custom?' He began to weep. Voices were raised in the background, saying: 'Do you mean just to let him go? Haven't I told you what you must insist on! He must do penance!' 'It wasn't him! It was one of us who betrayed ... !' 'The name! The name!' someone shouted. I pushed away the man with the knife. Obviously I had been mistaken for someone else. I am no more responsible for the British Government's policy than any other tourist on a trip across Cyprus, but I asked: 'How much is the *blood-money*?' I turned my empty pockets inside out and pulled out my pocket-watch, which I offered them. Someone was holding me by a button of my jacket. 'Have you got the right time?' he asked. 'Don't stand still up there, please — move along,' someone called from the back. 'I'll confess everything,' I shouted back. The man behind me made way for someone else, whose face I could not see under the hood, but who seemed to be Bluebeard, his eyes sparkling through the slits in the material. It now struck me suddenly that they all looked disconcertingly alike, like the Ku Klux Klan, or monks. 'Christ is dead!' 'He died on the Cross for our sins!' someone shouted. His eyes were red. The supposed Bluebeard laid a hand over his mouth to keep him quiet. 'Be quiet! The case ought to be in a lawyer's hands. We must explain how it all happened, from the very beginning.' But the other man wrenched himself free and grabbed me by the collar. 'Shall I tell how it happened? The Savior was tripped up, and so he fell. Then he was beaten. That's what they did. Tripped him up!"We don't want his blood-money in order to grow our tobacco in peace. Does anyone mean to forget whose denunciation set the court to work so fast?' By now I had been pushed to the open door and was hanging half outside, with my feet on the step, preparing to jump off. It was too steep for jumping, but there were olive trees that I could throw myself into, so that I wouldn't fall on the stones and break my bones. 'Hold him!' they shouted, while the old man went on screeching. 'We couldn't even find out where they've buried Jesus Christ. They've buried him somewhere in secret, so as not to make a martyr of Him! This fellow's Judas Iscariot. By treachery he tripped up the Savior. Let's hang him from the next tree.' '*Dies irae, dies illa,*' the monks intoned angrily. I believed myself to be in extreme danger. 'Police?' I thought, when suddenly the bells came flying through the night. Not far ahead, on the mountain-top where the lights were dancing, I saw the monastery. Suddenly all the men in the bus lighted their candles, and voices were raised in chorus — basses, altos, and one jubilant soprano — singing: 'Christ is risen! Christ is risen! Christ is risen!"

There was just a short distance further, the last lap, and the bus was laboring towards the summit, the engine panting and sending out suffocating black fumes. I shut my eyes. I thought to myself: Where unstable people like these in the bus differ from me is that their blood does not curdle. For instance, this Monsieur Typhon doesn't need to shut his eyes the way the likes of us have to, because he doesn't see specters, in broad daylight at least. He's the right sort! He hasn't a bad conscience, as I have. Whatever he does, he will laugh in the priest's face instead of confessing when he's led out to the execution block. Whatever such an unstable person needs — some extra warmth out of the ashes of a dying fire — he'll take for himself wherever he finds it, even from a skinny little half-grown waif! Thus he gets his satisfaction like a proper man. A man all of one piece! Was it possible that I had seen this witch's thin face once already? I racked my brains. What was it, really, that was so touching about her? Heavy tears were rolling from her hard eyes. No, I did not recall ever before having seen this black gaze. Yet I had already once before heard that sobbing of a heart stirred to its primitive depths. A little Mater Dolorosa. 'The letter belongs to me. My letter!' She screamed the words at the top of her voice as I reached out for the letter. Perhaps I shook her a little too vigorously. Anyway, the letter fell to the ground. She had had it hidden under her dress. I was still wondering who in the world could want to correspond with this half-grown little thing that had certainly never worn out a single pair of shoes on the way to school. The thought was too absurd! I also saw somebody deftly bending in the darkness and picking up the letter, which he then set fire to in the candle-flame. The smouldering paper went from hand to hand until all the candles were alight and I tore it from the driver's hands. His fist struck me in the face. It was the fellow whose life I had saved during the earthquake in the night. 'What was that letter? She can't read, can she?' It was a blue envelope, with large, vertical, ladylike handwriting on it. Blue as the bird that fishes on the frozen banks of the lakes in the North! And at this point I fell out of the bus, throwing my arms high into the air.

I had much difficulty in getting down from the olive tree, and all my bones were aching when I struggled to my feet in the dust. Well, congratulations — it might have been worse! I was too stunned to be able to think of getting help for the others. I had to keep on rubbing my eyes not only because of the sand that had got into them when I fell, but also because I seemed to be seeing the scornful smile of the little girl from some other world. That smile was the last certain thing bearing witness to the existence of that world, which was now flying away through the night-sky before my eyes, like Elijah's fiery chariot. There was still the sound of singing: it sounded like the trumpets announcing the Day of Judgment. Then it was swallowed up in the roar of the storm suddenly rising. And then all was still.

Let no one expect me to waste my time hypocritically pretending to feel an interest in the fate of my fellow-passengers. The fact is that I watched the dissolution of that company of travelers as calmly, from my vantage point, as if I had been contemplating some natural spectacle or a fireworks display.

Every catastrophe has not only a tragic, but also a slightly comical side. So what may finally be expected of me is a touch of extravaganza such as has been fashionable since Dostoyevsky produced his Oriental line in Christianity. I owe it to a lucky accident that I saved my own skin. It was, on the other hand, an unlucky accident that the driver lost control of the steering-wheel because I knocked his arm trying to save the blue letter, which was being reduced to a cinder. Nobody could foresee what the result would be. My eyes sought for something solid to focus on, for although I had not broken any limbs, I was still not very steady on my legs. Furthermore, a cypress and several chunks of rock went flying up into the air with the blast. Yes, sure enough, there was something down there belching forth black smoke, and now in the moonlight the serpentine curves of the mountain road began to stand out from the rock, although there was still scree tumbling down and occasionally dust darkened the road again. It seemed as though in spite of all efforts the bus refused to be got back onto its six wheels. How comically like a beetle it was, like a beetle lying helpless on its back, waving all six legs in the air! It needed some resolution to slide down the precipice, peering down from rock-ledge to rock-ledge to make sure of my next foothold. After some time, perhaps after some days, a goatherd would discover the accident and report it at the next hamlet, whence a messenger would be sent for a doctor, whose only task would be to certify the death of all the passengers. He will keep on disappearing into the burned-out vehicle, each time re-appearing with a charred corpse in his arms. This will happen more than twelve times — yes, for there was the driver and then there was the little girl too! By daylight then all the corpses will be neatly laid out in rows, the open eyes will be closed — in cases where there are still any eyes — and the police will arrive on the scene of the accident in order to search the corpses and the surroundings for objects by means of which to identify the dead, money and jewelry being carefully noted. Afterwards it will all be cleared away like a toy that a child has dropped, and the road will again be cleared for tourist traffic. Look the other way, the voice of reason told me — I don't like this story anymore. I was feverish although the night was icy cold. 'When I approached the blazing vehicle, I found there was too much smoke for me to do anything useful, and in any case it was too late. It was only when the fire began to die down for lack of fuel that I thought — yet only for a brief moment — that I recognized the girl's dress, which blew up like a balloon and revealed her face. Actually I did not really see this, only the mocking smile that flitted over the place where the mouth had been, as if to say that the catastrophic end of the pleasure trip had been merely a misunderstanding, and nobody's fault. Yes, this was exactly what her smile seemed to be saying, like someone apologizing for having tried to go out through the wrong door. I believe this smile of the dead is called after the Greek physician Hippocrates. I felt a violent urge to fling myself on that creature who was now no more than ash, so that at least the ash should not grow cold so quickly. But that would have meant being someone other than I am.

At long last a motorcyclist came up the road — a policeman in uniform! My first impulse was naturally to slip away unobserved. My British passport would make him hesitant and would perhaps lead him to think me guilty, for the pleasure-party had evidently been composed of conspirators hostile to British rule. He stopped me and made a brief entry about the accident in his notebook, then asked for my papers. I was actually prepared to confess to complicity, for what had happened within such a short time had blunted my perceptions of the possible consequences. Yes, that was how the land lay! I was just some good-for-nothing tourist, here today and gone tomorrow! This was what I had coldly said to the policeman in answer to his questions, and offered him a cigarette while he took down my 'particulars': where I came from, whether I was alone, how long I intended staying on the island, why I had left my luggage aboard the ship, how much money I had in the bank, whether the name I gave was my real name, and whether I was known to anybody at the British Consulate at Nicosia. This last question I answered with a firm negative, whereupon he shook his head and invited me to mount the pillion of his motorcycle. Involuntarily I made a movement as if to escape, but I gave up the notion. It was futile.

I knew that he could handcuff me if there seemed to be any risk of my escaping. So, surrendering to *force majeure*, I agreed to let him take me to the capital, where I was pretty sure I would manage to get out of this scrape. I only went with the policeman in order to demonstrate my innocence. But the policeman did not seem to be interested in either my innocence or my guilt, and we made the long night trip in silence. On the morning of Easter Sunday he then duly delivered me at the British Consulate.

There, after protracted argument, I got the caretaker to telephone the Consul, after which I was directed to the latter's private house. A slim, correct gentleman offered me a drink and said something about a letter with the Consulate stamp on it, which had been sent to the ship for me! Despite all inquiry, this letter now could not be traced. His wife had written it, having seen my name on the passenger-list. I saw a wooden rocking-horse in one corner of the drawing-room, played with it a little, and asked him to give my kindest regards to the lady of the house, who was now away from home. I declined an invitation to luncheon, for my stay on the Island of Cyprus was to be of the briefest, and I took my leave with many expressions of gratitude.

ANN ELIZA REED

THE DEVIL GIVES MANKIND NO RESPITE; he returns like
a dog to his vomit. We're only flesh and blood, after all, as were
the parents who brought us into the world, and we've sense
enough to know what we're about. There it is, the heart in your
breast begins thudding like a tattoo on a drum, quite uncanny
after so long when you've noticed it no more than the ticking of
a pocket-watch. How quiet it has suddenly become all around the
traveler — gnats, birds, wind and water! All that now reigns in
the conscious mind is mortal fear. Then it is that you espy the
indefinable thing: in the Devil's mirror you see yourself all over
again, but formless, without a body to cast a shadow. When a
human being is stricken with panic and runs away from himself,
the maddened imagination far outstrips every potentiality of
form; for one is possessed by the evil spirit.

    About four o'clock one afternoon I was about to climb a low
hill such as there are many in the West of Scotland, all
overgrown with heather and all as alike as sand dunes in the
desert. I had singled out this one for my goal because it was
touched by the sun's rays falling through a rift in the clouds,
above which the skies loomed high as though it were the New
Jerusalem towering there in the gray, rain-soaked North. In the
very next half hour the mists came down, and all at once those
hundreds of hills, crouching there under the wet clouds, blurred
into purple and seemed to trickle away into the bog. My goal
became distorted out of all recognition, as though the ocean
beyond, which throughout all eternity had been sending its
waves across from the coasts of America to fling them on these

shores, had had the caprice to let this sea wall stand so long only to dissolve it in vapor just as I hoped to arrive at the top of the hill and to dry off up there. For all that week since my arrival I had been wearing the same damp clothes, wading through swamp and those pitch-brown burns that seep through the rushes and under the moss and which one cannot avoid except in bright sunlight, for in the bog everything seems just a shade redder than whatever is next to it. The crofter I'm lodging with will be quite upset! He doesn't let his yearlings pasture here, and even the wise old cattle sometimes sink in and perish. It's seldom that anyone can save a beast once it has begun to sink. The people hereabouts are poor, and losing a cow in this bottomless terrain is a bad blow for a family. My shoes are certainly done for! First one foot, then both. I'm up to my knees in the bog. I have to throw myself flat on this abysmal porridge if I'm not to be sucked right in. I had gone tearing along so breathlessly that I'd forgotten to watch where I was going, and now I no longer even had the long stick I had been carrying, for testing the ground ahead. I'm trapped in the dense mist, I don't even know how many hours it is that I've been leaping and creeping along, or whether it's day or night. There are gaps in the series of my impressions, dark caverns such as the ocean scoops out of the depths, year in, year out, day by day, every hour, every minute, monotonously, ceaselessly. Is it my watch ticking or is it the beating of my heart that I suddenly hear? Seals come forth from the hollow caves to see where the dead fishermen lie washed up on the shore. If ever — all of a sudden and as if by a miracle — a living man sees one of these creatures' gentle eyes gazing at him, these shy people do him no harm, for God's sake, for they take him to be some drowned kinsman manifesting himself to the boatman!

It was only yesterday that the crofter rowed me across in his coracle to the island where his sheep graze summer and winter, untended. Yesterday? Only once a year he goes to shear them, and for a last time in order to slaughter them. The vessel seemed so unhandy, I expected it to smash in the breakers even after it was moored. It took him hours of maneuvering to reach the rock where he lands, and it's so slippery one only just manages to grab the dangling ladder that has to be climbed. I gather that someone once got two lambs (one male, one female) up that cliff, buttoned inside his jacket, but certainly no living sheep ever comes down again. Yesterday I saw my first seal.

Perhaps the crofter is somewhere not far away, with a lantern, waiting for me? Someone might well be shouting and listening for an answer only a short distance away, but a man could yell himself hoarse and the sound would still be swallowed up in this impenetrable mist. In my terror I forgot to be careful. Instead of acting coolly, I made frantic efforts to free myself, with the result that I had now sunk in up to my chest. I began to suffocate, feeling the formless, sticky mass uncannily closing over my ribs. My arms were weakening. I recall having heard that cramp will petrify a swimmer's arms in the very middle of a stroke. It's all up with me! The crofter's wife will be getting no rest in her bed, from which she cannot rise. She wears an old-fashioned lace cap, which frames her little yellow face, and for a long time now she's been bedridden in the little room where the wind howls in the rafters and the damp makes the whitewash flake from the walls. She prays. A half-grown girl, lame in one leg, tends the shaggy little cows that yield brown milk. Homesickness brought the crofter back from America, home to where he had lived as a child until the day when his parents and all the crofters around about were evicted. A whole nation of poor people had been compelled to emigrate, stick in hand and a bundle over the shoulder, as the modern spirit invaded Scotland and the old clan system disintegrated. It was early in the nineteenth century that it became fashionable to import grouse from France and preserve them on tracts of land that were allowed to degenerate into bog. Grouse-shooting in Scotland was a sport that brought the lairds in more than any ground-rent they could charge for the wretched soil — no matter how the crofters might toil and moil! My friend had been lucky, he had been able to identify the place where his parents' cottage still stood, half sunk into the earth, a skeleton from the past. That's where I'm lodging in Glen A—. Even I am so trapped in the groundless ruination of it all that I prefer to shiver in the damp rather than urge my brother Freemason to get the crumbling hearth into working order. We cook on a spirit-stove. It was that special grip of the hand, he said, by which he recognized me as a brother.

No, it's not my pocket-watch thumping, for I haven't wound it since yesterday when the water got into it, that time when the wave broke over the boat. What's the use of knowing the time? There are only two kinds of time, day and night. With tears in my eyes I can feel there is something still alive in me measuring the time that I am still granted. And so then it'll be the end? Hasn't everyone known terror at least once in his life, been frightened to death? No, not quite to death yet, but nearly! Then one becomes another man, in a psychological sense, a man who has to dispense ever more and larger doses of courage in order to escape that cynical self-abandonment which is what life demands with the passing of time. Oh yes, it's indeed another man who gets the better of the Devil by suddenly saying to himself: 'Look, I'm throwing in my hand. I've had my fill. Let this be the end of me.' My patron in Berlin had asked me where I'd like to travel to paint my pictures. Here I'm coming to my end in Scotland, without having painted any pictures, and the collector will lose the money he's invested in the journey. The walls are made of glass, I can see through them. I'm trapped in a glass mountain. Glass mountain ... *Glasberg*.... Glasberg was a London foundling, and London was the city to which the gifted boy owed his education. A number of years ago, being a newly qualified medical man, instead of at once setting down he signed on as a ship's doctor, and since then he had been seeing the wide world. The further the magnetic needle in the ship's compass swung away from the true pole, the less did Glasberg take it to mean *Lasciate ogni speranza!* for his wise head had no need to grow gray over the insoluble equation of *bourgeois* marriage. The infinity of alien skies opened before the bachelor, a cosmic four-poster reproaching those who vainly try to solve the equation by means of two unknown quantities. *Lasciate ogni speranza!* might serve as a motto over the door of a waiting-room, a consulting room, in some London slum! The dowry will stretch just far enough to buy such a practice. There is no hope of ever making the wretched well so long as the wretched go on increasing in numbers! For when private misery becomes the general situation the result is tragedy, and lack of human proportion debases individual courage into social cowardice. How can one think of saving at the expense of wife and children? Poverty has but one cure — money! And then one weary day the slum doctor, idealist that he is, his laurel wreath withered on his brows, surrenders to the common lot, to the destiny of those who are too many, and takes his place in the waiting-room at the end of the queue, giving way to the first of the younger generation *voi che entrate*.

So it was better for Glasberg to remain unmarried. In twelve years all that had come from him was one letter from the East, enclosing a gold ring for the young lady. At sea Glasberg always proved to be a fellow-voyager at once helpful and interesting, especially to the female sex. He traveled with multifarious scientific impedimenta, including a sycamore chest m which he kept an authentic mummy. The hieroglyphs painted on the lid announced that this had been a priestess of Ammon-Ra, one Katebet, of Thebes, in the period of the eighteenth dynasty. Sometimes he would allow a woman visitor to gaze upon this Egyptian coffin. The dead woman's portrait on the lid must have been a very good likeness. On the left side of the abdomen an incision had been made in the painted figure on the lid and the place then closed with a metal plate. Over this was a big scarab, which the Egyptians held sacred.

Equipped for life as a thoroughgoing member of the Peter Pan family, which does not turn a hair at anything so long as it is in its cradle but which gradually, with the passage of the years, reveals more of the happy-go-lucky and feckless character typified as the Schlemil, which nothing, not even the loss of its own shadow, can disconcert — Glasberg interested other people because he did not know what fear was. Fear, so we are informed by a citizen of the Christian island, Dr. Johnson by name, is inherent in human nature and it would be idle to attempt to deny it. Whatever may be the success of the missionary sect of the Brothers of St. John the Baptist, who preach the fear of the Lord (let us call them Johnsonites), they cannot teach a Peter Pan to quake. And that was why Glasberg did not fear the Devil either, when the Devil came for him.

The fact that fate intervened in order to make even Glasberg into a coward, as these unheroic modern times demand, and that this social mission failed of its purpose with Him since he could not be made to shudder over an event that took a truly unnatural turn — that's enough to suggest that he was an unlucky dog. In older times it was the mental attitude that made the hero, and the torch dropped only from his dying hands. Modern herd-morality, on the contrary, demands that we should surrender our faculty of thought, perhaps under the impact of physical *force majeure*, where a man offends against the prevailing system of intellectual conformism. Every epoch creates its own myth, and the myth of mass-man is ours, being appropriate to the idea of progress. After all, even a nursery tale — that of the Lad Who Could Not Learn to Shudder — ends, because of its pedagogic purpose, with a cold shower.

At the time when Glasberg returned to London, young Ann Eliza Reed was about to leave for Scotland with her husband. Since the days of Catholic Prince Charlie the Reed family home had been in Glen A—, beyond the mountains, cut off from the rest of the world, in which the Reeds took no interest and of which they scarcely formed a part. Ann Eliza's husband had steadily enlarged his estate and had reclaimed the bog. To the children that he hoped to have he was resolved to leave land that had been put under cultivation, not rented out to golf clubs. Glasberg, who was in the habit of studying the tremulous life of the present in the mirror of the past, had run into the newly married Ann Eliza again in the Egyptian department of the British Museum and had received an invitation to visit the couple in Glen A— before deciding on his plans for the future. And Reed considered it natural that Ann Eliza should have extended this invitation to an acquaintance whom she had not seen since long before her marriage.

Glasberg spent the whole spring on their estate. But when Reed urged him to remain with them for the summer, he prepared to refuse this renewed invitation because he had left his collection in town, and he had come to London expressly in order to do some work on this collection. Ann Eliza Reed herself begged her husband to let Glasberg go. Since Glasberg had come, their neighbors, who had ceased to call at the manor, had begun to think that the visitor lodging at the croft was a friend more to the lady of the manor than to her husband. Yet Reed, who knew that his confidence in his wife would not strain her reserve to the point of indiscretion and who could see, besides, that Ann Eliza was ailing and in need of care, whereas he was most of the time kept away from the house, supervising his farms, considered this a reason for not letting the doctor go. So it came that Glasberg set up his library and laboratory in the crofter's cottage.

There had been exceptional weather, with no rain for weeks. Ann Eliza had sent someone out to look for her husband on the hillside pasture above the house, known as the Raven's Back; for her labor had begun. The air was sultry, the sky darkening. The laird had told the laborers to press on with the work as hard as possible that day, since there was no more counting on the weather, and to load all the hay on the ponies and get the fodder down into the glen that night. He himself wanted a chance to do some fishing again. His wife had remained alone in the house.

After the doctor had damped down the fire with ashes in order to keep it in overnight and had lit the lantern that he had brought with him from the ship, he left the cottage, intending to go and pay his late-night call on his patient. But as he came out of the door his foot struck against something large and soft. What he saw with horror by the light of his lantern was Ann Eliza lying at the edge of the path. Under her dress, which had slipped up over her knees, her thin legs were drawn tight up to her belly. She was unconscious. Where was now the man whose duty it was to care for Ann Eliza? If she aroused pity and love in one who had no claim on her, then let him be her guardian! That was the measure of Reed. Dismayed, the doctor raised the poor rigid body in his arms and carried Ann Eliza into the library. There being no woman to tend her — for when all hands were needed outside both the men and the women servants slept in the open, sheltering from the elements as best they might wherever they were, in order to be on the spot as soon as it was light — the man himself did everything necessary. He undressed the unconscious woman, loosened her long hair, and laid her in his own bed; and all night long he listened to her heart, which gradually began to beat strongly. He reached out for her breast as she lay deeply unconscious. It would be a long time before Glasberg was to know peace again.

Little by little, like the drip from a tap that has not quite been turned off, the beating of her heart became perceptible, and after a while it was regular. Her eyes were still veiled.

'. . . if I should die tonight, tell my husband what I foresee for the future. We are on the point of bringing great discord upon this house. Glasberg, it is best that you should sacrifice your love . . . that is why I came to you tonight, for the last time. It is my duty to make no enemy for my husband. The first time I came to gaze upon your dead beloved in the chest. If I do not survive the child, then down in the grave I shall do penance for not having been able to give you anything. My body will crumble to dust like that priestess's, without having responded to love. I may not part from the great fool, yet I don't know how I came to have such a husband. I submit to the law that prevails over me, but it crushes me. Is it then to have been my life's whole task that I should not let myself be tempted by the only chance of happiness I ever knew?'

Glasberg kept his fingers on her feverish pulse, and he turned over in his mind the events of these last days, wondering how it could have come about that Ann Eliza lay helpless in his arms.

The previous day Reed had come home earlier than usual, even before the laborers, for he had realized that his wife's life was in danger, and he had wept bitterly. But she had shrieked at him:

'It's no will of mine, Reed, that you should rack your brains over your wife. You have the right to do as you like with your wife, as with your other possessions, so long as she is alive. Just so long as I do not die.'

And she had refused to look at Reed again, turning away as if she were a stranger. The choice that Reed had made, when he decided to marry her, had never really been to his relatives' liking; for, all being more or less closely kin to him, they had cherished the hope of some day calling his property their own. Before Glasberg had come to stay permanently at the cottage, where so much fuss was made of him, Ann Eliza had constantly tried to get herself accepted by the family, who regarded her as an interloper. She had made a genuine effort to take her rightful place in the large family. However, the objection that weighed against her claims as Reed's wife was that they knew nothing of her own family, and it was even said that some Scandinavian countess had borne this daughter in circumstances over which it was discreeter to draw a veil. Since Ann Eliza had inherited not only her light-of-love mother's cameolike brow but also her sense of independence, she had never ceased to nag her husband, telling him that she would no longer tolerate being passed over.

'I came here in order to be mistress in Glen A—, and my maid is treated with more respect than I. Since you are, after all, master here, I regard it as your duty to take up the cudgels for your wife, making her cause your own.'

'Who is it slights you, dear wife of mine?'

'Your father's brother's daughter, that perfect provincial beauty, who can't forgive me because your family had intended her for you. So that you should pay their debts for them.'

'Ann Eliza, my wife,' Reed answered that time, 'then you should not complain. On the contrary, you should bear in mind that your cousin is a more agreeable person than you are.'

But now Ann Eliza felt really hurt. 'Reed, what you say isn't true. My cousin is not disagreeable to anyone except to me. Listen, let me give you some advice. Now do what I say. Just send all these people packing without more ado. I want you all for myself It's my right.'

Reed retorted: 'I don't want to be involved in women's squabbles.'

However, Ann Eliza continued to press her point of view. 'Well then, let me tell you something. In a short time you will have a child. I am about to bear your estate's most precious jewel. Now, so that what is said of Reed may be seen to be true, namely, that he lets women dictate every matter in which he should decide, you must support my cause so energetically that the woman of the house emerges victorious and those covetous kinspeople who have despised me are chastened. Now you know why I myself am close-fisted. It is because I am saving for the future. But I don't want that voluptuous beauty, with her greasy black hair, to be spared anything — that woman you have had your share of, even if today she is more or less another man's wife!'

Reed thought it advisable that Ann Eliza should no longer be reminded of this cousin. He was eager to have the child. So he assured her that he would grant her plea, and he barred his house to all his kin.

Now there was gossip in the neighborhood about visits to the cottage, and people said that Ann Eliza's pride would have a fall and that she was hiding even from her husband's kin; old notions began to be aired again. That very morning her cousin had knocked at the door and asked how the lady of the house was feeling. It required an effort to see the woman who had challenged her. Ann Eliza had been unprepared, and the medicine bottles, the awkwardness that kept her reclining on her *chaise longue*, made her talkative. That was why — for the last time, as she thought — she told them to show her cousin in. Only she did not mean to speak of the child; that was her last trump.

'Gwendolin, our quarrel has ended with your triumph. I am ill. Scotland's damp climate, and no sunshine — I was used to sunshine in my native country and I have not seen it since my marriage. . . . My people have regained their independence, Finland is no longer ruled by the Cossack with the knout. They killed Glasberg's parents! Frankly, Gwendolin, hasn't there been a good deal you have wondered at? Yet it seems to me I shall never again race over the glittering snow in a reindeer-sleigh. Here everything is gray and wet, summer and winter alike. I am crushed by the task of managing such a strong man. You can see for yourself, I grow paler day by day. I did indeed want to get you out of the house, yet now everything indicates that I shall soon have need of you. Your perspicacity surely tells you that this man who is so easily managed by women is more inclined to regard me as a mother than to be a lover to me.' Both women smiled a subtle smile, and each was still thinking her own thoughts when Glasberg came in.

Her pulse is growing fainter again, Glasberg thought in terror. She's falling asleep. Her hand was holding his. He freed his hand gently without waking her.

His thoughts went back to the point where he wondered how Ann Eliza had found the strength to drag herself to the cottage so that she might put her life into his hands. How could things have come to this pass? Glasberg saw himself on the balcony. A haze had come up from the clearing, obscuring the view of the cottage, but over the Raven's Back the late sun was still pouring its glory. Soon it must set, and the last fine day would be over. Glasberg had met Reed going off for an evening's fishing before the rain came.

'I just wanted to reassure you. Ann Eliza has begun to have the first pains, but that's nothing to worry about. As her doctor I shall prescribe rest in bed.'

Making a light-hearted allusion to the rumors about her strange relationship to the doctor Reed had said: 'The two of you have become such good friends that you won't find the time passing too slowly.'

'You think so?' Glasberg had been confused. 'No, I'm sure it won't seem too long. Habit!'

Then the talk had turned to fishing. Only when Reed made to walk on, Glasberg had given him a piece of advice. 'You're Ann Eliza's husband, the only fixed point in her life.'

The fish had put up a good fight and had got away with the line, leaping over the boulders, up the falls, upstream against the cascades and into the other shower that suddenly came from the clouds. With his empty rod Reed had gone after his prey, waving his hand as he turned the corner, and then disappeared beyond the steep rocks further upstream.

'Your husband's out trying to outwit an old salmon — he needs some relaxation after all this hard work,' were Glasberg's first words to Mrs. Reed, lying in the long chair on the balcony.

'And so, as you can see, I am here in his place.' Never had it cost him such an effort to carry the conversation further. He had hoped that the two women's talk, which he had interrupted, would be resumed. But Ann Eliza had looked at him. Loudly enough to be heard by the other woman inside the room, she said: 'Oh, that wasn't necessary, Glasberg. You take too much trouble.'

If he had been capable of it, he would have turned and left. 'How are you? Better?' he finally had to force himself to say.

'I've been feeling sick again, and feverish,' she said, instinctively sinking deeper into the chair, away from him. As she straightened the rug over her, pulling it higher over her breast, her wedding-ring slipped off and fell to the floor; for it was now too loose for her emaciated finger. Suddenly become talkative, turning to Gwendolin, although it was meant not only for the latter, she said: 'How we can't rid ourselves of superstition! How primitive man's customs still cling to us! Thank you for handing me back the ring, dear Glasberg! Isn't it odd how we go on giving each other presents of chains and rings even in these times? And,' she added gaily, 'how the need to take possession of another human being always manifests itself in the same childish way!'

She had been trying to look into his eyes, but they were hidden behind the dark glasses that he wore — just because there was a little scrap of sunshine!

'Why are you still out here on the balcony when the sun has no more warmth?' Glasberg recalled having asked by the way, because he knew her thoughts as well as he knew his own. And, as she made a helpless gesture, he added: 'Why don't you go to bed?'

It went without saying that she could not bring herself to summon the aid of any of the servants, who were needed elsewhere, and she was still less inclined to turn to Gwendolin than to those mutinous servants.

'Well, I'll carry you there myself!' Some such thing he must have said.

'No, no!' There was such a note of panic in the cry that Glasberg had hesitated. Yet the next instant his happy-go-lucky, mischievous, ebullient nature asserted itself and he was holding her in his arms, rugs and cushions and all. She stiffened a little in his arms, and he was amazed how light her body was in spite of her condition. He had held her so gently that her resistance slackened and she abandoned herself to him.

'You must eat something this evening. I'll come and pay you a late call. I've something to talk to Reed about too. Tomorrow I'll carry you out on the balcony again.'

Ann Eliza seemed to have forgotten her cousin, who was impatiently looking out for her carriage. 'Tomorrow there'll be no more sun. just one more moment — oh please!' And softly she whispered into his ear: 'Go on holding me quite still like this, Glasberg. My only longing is to be cradled and cherished. Oh, I'd like to be a child, or even smaller, a doll for someone to play with, to be dressed and undressed — to have someone else to think and act for me.'

Yes, and that was just the way he had put her to bed, carefully straightening the bedclothes over her!

'. . . if I were a doll, my lover would drive me out into the park every night in a beautiful carriage, and the birds would be singing. I'd have a box at the opera with a trellis before it, and when we came home I'd sit alone opposite you at supper. But in the morning I'd be gently put back in my box, handled only with the fingertips.'

Her cousin seemed to be in a hurry to go now that her carriage had driven up to the door. Perhaps Reed was still at home drinking with her brothers. She did not dream of ever letting him go. She could put two and two together and work out for herself what these two here had to say to each other. She had seen how Ann Eliza's cheek had brushed the man's and how she had blushed fiery red. To Gwendolin's way of thinking such a familiarity could mean nothing but veiled adultery. As she waited for Glasberg, who was looking for a lantern, she could not resist the chance of seizing the certainty of it. Feeling the heat in Ann Eliza's face as she laid her hands round it, she said point-blank: 'Your heart is beating twice as fast as it should, and that gives you away. I believe you're on singularly intimate terms with Glasberg.'

Ann Eliza, who was wishing that Reed would come home early that evening, replied: 'There was only one time when I did not think of Reed, and that was when Glasberg first showed me the dead woman in the sycamore coffin.'

And when Reed had indeed soon come back, this time with his angler's basket empty, she had said to him: 'Reed, do you believe in a love beyond death? I should like to be in the mummy's place.'

Ann Eliza, Ann Eliza, I cannot bear such talk! Do you love me so little that your real thoughts stray elsewhere?'

'You say that out of pure egoism, Reed. The law only gives you the right to the living woman. Hold me fast lest you lose me. I am driven mad by the thought that you want to claim something of me beyond the limits of my life.'

At these words Glasberg also made a move to go, for that was surely not meant for his ears. Would Glasberg be so good as to look after Ann Eliza once more while he rode to the nearest market-town to get the midwife? Reed had flushed. 'Gwendolin is sure to be at home, and she'll show you the way to the woman.'

Ann smiled at that, yet she trembled a little as she watched Reed go.

So now the loving woman lay in the loved man's arms. There had been no more time for the night visit that it would have been his obligation, as a doctor, to pay. Yet was what was happening now any less an offense against the sacred laws of hospitality? Oh, anyone could see that this woman was too weak to bring the child into the world! It was late in the night — and where was Reed, who would not be looking for Ann Eliza at the cottage? Under this roof — the last place! Here and now I must decide whether to save the mother or the child. The beloved?

Weary to the very marrow of his bones, Glasberg, who had lain down in the adjacent room — which served at once as a sort of alchemist's kitchen and as a bedroom — picked up a stick of a beech-wood, which kept slipping from his grasp. He got up in order to take the bellows and blow the fire into life, but also to keep himself awake. That had been his intention. He thought and thought and could not tell if he was dreaming. Had he not meditated the catastrophe again and again, long enough foreseen the destruction of what had not even begun? On Reed's side there was the law, which brought its own solution with it. Oh yes, indeed, there was the law, binding on no one more than on a doctor. Even before dawn, when Reed did at last come to the cottage in search of his lost Ann Eliza, he had already decided, in the light of his knowledge and of his conscience as a doctor, to give up the mother and at least try to save the child.

'Deliberately, unaided, I undertook the desperately dangerous surgical intervention that Ann Eliza's insane action had made necessary. She ought never to have left her bed,' he said to himself.

His patient had written on a scrap of paper her last instructions for Reed. He had almost flung it into the fire — this piece of paper on which she told her husband that she was keeping her wedding ring on as a last covering of her nakedness, since her nightdress was to be removed. Then with ether he had anesthetized the naked woman, who must entrust her chastity to the doctor, and had set about the fearful deed. Reed, who would perhaps not see the patient alive again, was sobbing uncontrollably outside the door. After an eternity there was the cry of a newborn child, which the midwife took to Gwendolin, waiting outside with Reed until the operation was over, and laid it in her arms. And still Mrs. Reed did not stir! The anesthetic must surely have worn off long ago, yet in spite of massaging the heart and all attempts to bring her round there was no sign of a pulse! For a doctor such an end was, under the circumstances, not surprising.

'Why did I sidle along the wall of the library, creeping round the back, in order to avoid seeing Mrs. Reed bereft of life? I paused only to draw the sheet over Ann Eliza's head, waving my hand towards that motionless, veiled figure as a sign to the wan-faced father that the mistress of his house was dead. Whereupon Reed collapsed. For how still the beloved lies there now.'

The coffin containing Ann Eliza's corpse, which the people laid out this morning, is in the library. The bedroom is locked up and cloths have been thrown over the anatomical collection and the Egyptian chest, in order not to violate the dignity of death. The heavy old door shutting off the bedroom makes it impossible for anyone outside to know what is going on in there. There is still no alteration in the dead woman's color, no sign of decomposition setting in. Again it is night. Three nights long it is customary to watch by the dead, before the burial may take place. Reed and his child are being looked after up at the manor, and no one would have heard a sound if Glasberg had now fallen asleep in the next room. But he heard something. He rose in order to see whether a fox might have got entrapped in the library, as had happened once before. Flinging open the door, he saw Ann Eliza sitting up stark naked in the coffin, trying to cast off her shroud. It was the coffin lid that had fallen to the floor with a crash loud enough to be beard even through the oak door. The distressed woman was stiff holding a flaming stick in one hand. In the gleam from this torch he saw Ann Eliza groping for the wound at the same place in her side as the wound in the side of the painted woman on the sarcophagus lid. Blood began to flow, and although Glasberg was a man who did not know fear, now he had cause enough to fall back a pace as he saw how extremely malevolent was the expression on the face of this Ann Eliza who had awakened from seeming death. But a man must not forget that he is a doctor! The most urgent thing was to clean and bandage the gaping wound, which was stuffed with gauze. Ann Eliza accepted it all unprotestingly, for she believed herself to be already dead. Still in the grip of this delusion, she whispered to Glasberg, whose joy at seeing his beloved restored to life was outmatched by his despair at seeing a mad woman before him: 'Glasberg, you're man enough to do one last thing for me! Listen.' I don't want to be taken to the cemetery. I beg of you to let the mummy be put there in my place. And to make up for her having to go into the earth instead of me, she shall have the fine new coffin. I should also like you to take enough in the way of underclothing for her, take it from among my things, as much as she needs. Furthermore, I wish the service for the dead to be read there according to the Roman rite, lest Reed suspect anything. I have always hated the thought that he will bring up my child in that faith. However, that is a matter for the living. You must swear to me that you will fulfill my wishes to the letter. For it has turned out as I always wished. I should have to do penance down there if you were to suffer on my account. Because I could not be yours in life, now that according to the law I am of no more value to my husband I wish to be yours in death forever. The law is binding only upon the living. By giving my husband the child I have ransomed myself.'

She flung her arms round Glasberg's chest, pleading so earnestly that the mummy should be placed in the coffin in her stead that finally — and primarily to remove the object of her agitation from her sight, because she continually cast spiteful glances towards the place where the sarcophagus stood under its dust-covering — the doctor carried Ann Eliza into his room and put the mummy into the empty coffin. Doubtless Glasberg was himself acting in a state of temporary insanity. When he closed the coffin lid, he entirely forgot what he had done and why. Nor was there any time to think about that now, for the madwoman could not be left unattended and her wound required the greatest care. Was he himself now on the point of losing his reason?

And what of events meanwhile as they looked to those up at the manor? The parish priest had been to see Reed that morning and had insisted that he would dispense holy water and the blessing only at the cemetery, because he had heard tell of the sinful collection that Glasberg had in the cottage. What he particularly disapproved of, as did everyone on the farm and in the district round about, was that the doctor kept an unburied corpse there — and what if it *had* been only a heathen person! Baptized or unbaptized, she had once been a human being and thus should not be deprived of the last respects owed to the dead. After this Reed had himself gone with two men-servants and secretly carried the coffin away from Glasberg's library. They went about their work on tiptoe and were all out of the room again so quickly — how glad they were, too, to be out in the open air again! — that Glasberg had not put in an appearance, perhaps had not even heard them nailing the coffin lid down! He was fast asleep in his wizard's den behind the oak door, and he was not meant to come to the cemetery. For in the end it turned out that the whole ceremony was nothing more or less than Glasberg's trial and condemnation. The priest had carried the cross all around the cottage, after blessing the coffin outside, the incense rising towards the stars under which Ann Eliza was borne to her grave. The litanies were said softly, no more than a murmur. A curse upon the fellow Glasberg, in league with the Devil as he was, a curse upon him there in his wizard's den! After the mourners, both gentry and servants, had cast three handfuls of earth upon the coffin in the open grave, more than one of them kept a stone clutched in his fist, in his pocket. Might the earth lie lightly upon her! Let no evil spirit manifest itself in the vicinity! Then suddenly all plucked up their courage again and uttered the prescribed responses with a will. Each one took a deep draught from a new glass that would never be used again and drew into his lungs the smoke from a white clay pipe that was afterwards smashed. All the shards were thrown into a plain wooden box that was rotting away by the cemetery wall and which had been used for this purpose since the time when an emigrant had sent it over full of tins of corned beef. The morning was icy cold, the sun refused to come out, and the breath from the priest's mouth curled up like fumes as he spoke the last words: 'Peace be with you! A child has been left without a mother — may the earth rest lightly upon her — long live the laird!' The priest had pointed in the direction of the cottage and said, with a glance at Gwendolin: 'Let that visitor begone! It would have been well had he gone sooner. May the child be guided by true Christians, that it may live in the light of grace. Reed needs a woman to guide him into the way of righteousness. Cousin Gwendolin, take heed of the chance.'

For other reasons than those that the priest had — and he was no spoilsport so long as it was not a matter of freethinkers or the Scottish Kirk — all Reed's kinspeople were filled with resentment against Glasberg, whom they now regarded as their last enemy. They gathered round Reed. And now, as they marched off towards the cottage, with here one and there another joining the procession, he began to question the servants as to what was known about Glasberg. Reed was the first to enter the library, and he tore away the rags from the hated objects there. Gwendolin crossed herself as a safeguard against evil spirits. The sarcophagus was wrenched open and everyone peered into it. All could see that it was empty. Gwendolin's father called them to witness that they had obviously fallen a prey to a swindler who would use his hocus-pocus to get the farm for himself if measures were not swiftly taken to prevent it. In such a case there was no need to resort to the law-courts! Everyone got out his stone. When Reed saw all his kinspeople, men and women alike, storming in after him, it seemed to him it would be hard to defend his former friend, all the more since he himself was now as hostile to him as were the rest. It was not his friend that the doctor had been, but Ann Eliza's, and *she* was gone forever. And how could one defend someone against charges, anyway, if he stayed in hiding? Obviously the man had grounds to fear the verdict!

Since no amount of shouting and knocking and pounding on the oak door brought Glasberg forth, Reed assumed that his guilt was proven. Someone had an axe with him and managed to get the blade into the crack of the door. But when the neighbors saw the indignant Reed trying to get hold of the axe himself, with every sign of growing really violent, they did their best to prevent any extreme action — for that would too soon have put an end to this thrilling entertainment. People wanted some fun after the tragedy. For this reason Gwendolin advised luring the fox out of his lair by means of hunger and thirst. It was her sly notion to send a laborer to fetch food and a basket full of dusty bottles of brandy, whereupon all fell to and made short work of the refreshments. They were all big drinkers, and there is, after all, neither man nor woman who despises a fine old brandy. Reed, who did not forget his desire for vengeance even in his cups, had sworn not to break Glasberg's neck until as much had been done to all the bottles. Gradually they began to forget what had brought them there. There was still a great orgy going on in the room, with women screeching and the men growing bold, when suddenly they all held their breath. All at once, as at a single beat of a heart, the disturbers of the peace grew still. It was the sweetest sound they could have heard. Reed was still thanking Gwendolin, who could hardly keep on her feet either, when the key began to turn in the lock.

What have a riddle and a door in common? The fact that Something is where first there was Nothing. It is Glasberg who is turning the key. He has drunk the cup of bitterness to the dregs. In the end he is worn out, is unable to bear any more of it, simply cannot keep his eyes open. For this is the third day! Ann Eliza is raving. Chaste as she was while still in possession of her reason, now all this time she has beset him with a veritable rage of passion. Regardless of her wound she has entwined herself about Glasberg's body and legs and arms. What she wished was to make Him feel every bit of what was maddening her. However often he had laid her down in bed in these last hours, she had refused to stay there; tortured by her obsessions, she had knelt before him. Her explanation of his reluctance was this: 'You refuse to be happy because you're still alive. But I would jeopardize my eternal salvation if there were nothing I could do for you, now I am free.' When she was *in extremis*, her strength failed. In blank despair she kept on whimpering, over and over again: 'Glasberg is still alive, Glasberg's alive, and oh, I am dead!'

Glasberg had no choice but to agree with her. With tears in his eyes he begged her forgiveness for the wrong he had done her, blaming himself for not having been in more of a hurry to die. The time is coming, the hour is already striking, when it will be much better to be dead than alive. Now Ann Eliza has brought him to the point where he decides to put an end to it all. He hears Reed's voice. How should he look him in the eye? Besides, he now recalled his earlier action and the chest containing the contraband Egyptian priestess, which, to judge by the shouting on the other side of the door, was now being smuggled across the river of the nether world. The act could not be excused, and he himself could not quite explain why he had done it. Evidently in his exhaustion he had acted just as Ann Eliza prompted. It was perfectly clear to him now that each individual life, as a pheno- menon, lost all its meaning the moment one abandoned a personal attitude to it. When would all this be over? All at once the pendulum ceases to swing. . . .

Ann Eliza stirred again, saying: 'They have buried me alive.'

'Would I then be sitting beside you, Ann Eliza?' he murmured. He was no longer capable of thought. His imagination boggled. He was no longer even afraid.

'Is the table laid for the two of us? Then die, die, beloved! Die!' Realizing how Glasberg was deceiving her — for he had laid the table with his surgical instruments as though they were ordinary knives and forks — the delirious woman, in whose brain delusion mingled with a last remnant of rational perception, now formed her plan. In the very moment when he turned his back on her, opening the door in order to surrender to the enemies without — and to do so unconditionally — Mrs. Reed snatched up a scalpel from the table. In the instant when all those angry eyes were peering into the room, while Reed swung the axe high in both hands and Glasberg covered his face with his hands, knowing that he was about to meet his end, the wine-flushed faces were suddenly drained of color — for there was Ann Eliza in her nakedness, alive! Her white arm moved slowly forward, and then, as in a lightning flash, the blade slashed Glasberg's throat from ear to ear. All the faces as yet wore no expression other than amazement at seeing Ann Eliza risen from the dead; and in Gwendolin's face it lingered longest. Then all saw Glasberg's head slipping back and a thick jet of blood spurting forth, making a pool on the floor. Gwendolin's mouth opened wide — and then she heard no more. But it was the dying Glasberg who sighed — now no more than a gurgling head rolling in that pool of blood like a fragment of rock cracked by lightning. 'Here I am!'

Over the fallen man the naked woman stands, now lets the knife drop, now speaks commandingly, fiercely, to Reed. 'Reed, my husband — behold! Ann Eliza has herself executed the criminal who sought to alienate your wife's affections! Alas that it was I who had to do the deed, since you are not man enough!'

Reed had advanced timidly to where Glasberg lay in his blood, when the other Ann Eliza suddenly came to herself again. Hastily snatching the sheet off the table, she flung it over her.

She clutched her hair, which had turned quite white. In a low voice she asked what was happening. Then she inquired after her friend Glasberg, whom she vividly remembered. The clouds began to pass away from her brain. The atrocious things within her and around her bore witness to the fact that the Devil, or something of that kind, had been at work in that room. Ann Eliza was beginning to be a human being again. Reed's thoughts were nearer to the mystery of transsubstantiation than at any time since he had acknowledged the Church's authority. Just is the substance of the bread and wine is absolutely destroyed in the mystery of the alteration that takes place when the priest administers them, and yet the accidents of bread and wine by an inscrutable Will remain perceptible to the senses and the rational mind — so now for the first time did he apprehend that his marriage was a sacrament. 'Take this woman!' the priest had said at that time.

Ann Eliza drew the wedding ring from her finger, handed it to Reed, and said: 'Reed, if destiny grants that you may forget, then do you, in return, take me away from this place, tormented woman that I am, and do so forthwith and forever. Then give me the ring again.'

Not long after this Reed set out on a voyage together with his wife, now restored to health, and his child: he was going to San Domingo to inspect plantations that he had inherited there. Nor must I forget to mention that Gwendolin and the rest of the clan moved in and took over the estate, which Reed relinquished to them because Ann could never again live there. There it is the privilege of the lady of the house to hand each guest the salt for his daily bread, taking it out of the huge ram's head with the topaz eyes and the curling horns, an heirloom that reigns supreme over everything else on the table. Gwendolin is fundamentally not a bad person, even if she is mindful of what is due to her.

I come to my senses again after my swoon. The ground is firmer, I get a foothold, the sun breaks through the mist. Covered with peat, from head to foot, suddenly I stand on the shore of the sunken world, as one to whom life has been restored. My hand fumbles over an object that it has chanced to encounter, and I identify it as a sporran. As I open it, it disintegrates; it has been lying in the peat-bog for a long time, perhaps since the time when the Scots fought against the Hanoverians, under that Prince Charles whom even today they call their Bonny Charlie. Some crumbs of ocher pigment fall from the pouch, still quite unchanged. So then perhaps this sporran dates from as far back as heathen times, when bold warriors were so arrogant that each clan distinguished itself from all others not merely by means of the tartan kilt, with its own colors and pattern, but also by painting their faces in just the way that the Red Indians of North America do! For everyone far and wide should know which clan was meditating war and rapine. Like their rams, so too the heroes would at times be impelled by some obscure urge to break away from the flock and charge each other. We modern people cannot understand that sort of thing, because there are no longer the legions' glorious banners and eagles to proclaim our courage. We have ceased to employ those eloquent symbols since we took to creeping below ground, taking cover in trenches, and dressing in khaki in the attempt to escape from modern warfare's infernal engines. Our personal courage has become collective, taken over by the State, like everything else. But those were fearless heroes, those Peter Pans!

Now there's bright sunshine, and my clothes are drying off. What seemed like an eternity cannot really have been so very long. I realize I'm hungry. I feel as if newly born into this world, and I want to live in it. A ram comes towards me, quietly cropping. How good the wild herbs taste to him! Well, I'll try them too, mint and thyme and wild lavender, washed down by the delicious spray of the waterfall. What meal could taste better? The ram has strange eyes, like topaz, eyes like those of the ram rearing up on its hind legs before the Sumerian goddess in the British Museum. The maternal divinity sheared his fleece, span the woolen thread on her spindle, and then wove a garment of it. Her woolen dress was embroidered with colored flowers, butterflies, birds, animals, and all sorts of symbols to conjure

Nature with — fertility magic, the first garment ever to clothe a woman's shame. For never should any male eye behold the goddess's nakedness, when the maidens conducted her down to the sea for her ritual bath. The goddess of the Acropolis laid her curse on the Achaeans because they carried off her palladium. For that they perished together with Ilium.

No man shall gaze upon the naked body of another's wife. The heroes he encamped on the heights, their arms piled high about them, challenging each other, waiting always for the chance to avenge old crimes against domestic order in blood-soaked feuds that will be passed down from generation to generation.

What are three or four thousand years, or even more, in the lifetime of human society? How many populous cities are razed to the ground in such a span of time! Sometimes someone has the good fortune to excavate such a city in a district now barren and uninhabited, and wonderingly we always hear the archaeologists tell that its history was just the same as the history we know. An enemy takes a town by storm and burns it to the ground. So many contradictory reasons are invented to explain wars. One cannot help thinking that humanity devours its own children, like Ugolino, because it is a prey to madness. Even when Schliemann produced the treasures of Mycenae as evidence that Homer's storytelling was based on fact, his contemporaries were disinclined to believe him. That it was Helen's face that launched a thousand ships and burned the topless towers of Ilium may be assumed to have a fairly general application, so long as no better explanation has been found for all the other cases, and one, moreover, that would also do justice to human nature. An exclusively male society is not a natural thing.

There is a constriction round my heart. Suddenly I have remembered it all. It comes back to me now: the day and the hour when I was in the British Museum, contemplating the mummy of the Egyptian priestess, and suddenly felt the urge to escape from town. Here the sunlight sparkles in myriad colors in the waterfall that comes rushing in a narrow stream, plunging headlong, flashing into spray. The thunder of it makes the silence seem alive. The water is making all speed towards the sea, the mother of life itself. Glimmering, foam-drenched, on the cliff there is a marble slab engraved with the chalice of the memorial sacrifice and a date now grown illegible. Here the random traveler is reminded that 'the maiden . . . delighted to linger . . .' I can only just make out the letters of the name: ANN ELIZA.

All at once I see a little star glittering in the dear sky. It comes nearer, grows larger, and, silvery as an egret, with outspread wings glides down upon the water.

Afterword

How O. K. Told His Stories

In the late summer of 1934 Kokoschka came from Vienna to Prague, where he was to live and work for the next four years. I met him for the first time in my parents' house and immediately learned a new word which until then had not been in the vocabulary of my rather rudimentary Prague school German: *aufputschen* = 'to pep up.' It was Kokoschka's view that, when one was with other people, one ought to entertain them, give them something else to think about than the current wretched state of economic and political affairs. The political situation at the time is well known. Kokoschka had little cause to feel happy with the world and his place in it. His physical and moral strength were being tested to the utmost, and many of the people with whom he associated were in the same situation.

So he told 'stories.' Most of the stories in this book were actually told, each time a little differently, being added to and developed, depending on his audience. When he gave a talk in the *Urania* institute in Prague, he described being wounded in the war so vividly that one woman in the auditorium fainted.

In preparing the 1956 German edition of this book I came across five or six copies of the opening of the story that is called 'Easter in Cyprus' in this volume. The first sentences were always the same, but each then continued in a different fashion, and there was no end.

However, when he first came to our house I had great difficulty understanding his strong Viennese accent, until my school German gradually improved with practice. When, in late 1938, we fled to London, we took many manuscripts with us, despite the limited amount of luggage. Kokoschka used to enjoy working on them from time to time during the war. They are 'Poetry and Truth' in the truest sense of the word.

Olda Kokoschka

Ariadne Press
New Translations

The Secret of the Empire
By Heimito von Doderer
Translated by John S. Barrett

Ephemeral Aphorisms
By Phia Rilke
Translated by Wolfgang Mieder
and David Scrase

The Abbey
By Alois Brandstetter
Translated by Evelyn and
Peter Firchow

Donna Leopoldina
The Austrian Empress of Brazil
By Gloria Kaiser
Translated by Lowell A. Bangerter

The Stone Breakers
and Other Novellas
By Ferdinand von Saar
Translated by Kurt and Alice Bergel

Flight from Greatness
Six Variations on Perfection
in Imperfection
By Hans Weigel
Translated by Lowell A. Bangerter

Quotations of a Body
By Evelyn Schlag
Translated by Willy Riemer
Prefatory Note by
Claire Tomalin

Ornament and Crime
Selected Essays
By Adolf Loos
Selected by Adolf Opel
Translated by Michael Mitchell

The Tragic Demise of a
Faithful Court Official
By F. von Herzmanovsky-Orlando
Translated by David A. Veeder

The House of the Linsky Sisters
By Florian Kalbeck
Translated by Michael Mitchell

Springtime on the Via Condotti
By Gustav Ernst
Translated by Todd C. Hanlin

Woman's Face of Resistance
By Marie-Thérèse Kerschbaumer
Translated by Lowell A. Bangerter

Ice on the Bridge
By Erich Wolfgang Skwara
Translated by Michael Roloff

Constanze Mozart
An Unimportant Woman
By Renate Welsh
Translated by Beth Bjorklund

The Serf
By Josef Winkler
Translated by Michael Mitchell

Ariadne Press
Translations

Against the Grain
New Anthology of Contemporary
Austrian Prose
Selected by Adolf Opel

New Anthology of Contemporary
Austrian Folkplays
Edited by Richard H. Lawson

Walk About the Villages
A Dramatic Poem
By Peter Handke
Translated by Michael Roloff

Chasing after the Wind
Four Stories
By Barbara Frischmuth
Translated by Gerald Chapple
and James B. Lawson

The Convent School
By Barbara Frischmuth
Translated by Gerald Chapple
and James B. Lawson

In Foreign Cities
By Anna Mitgutsch
Translated by Michael Mitchell

The Register
By Norbert Gstrein
Translated by Lowell A. Bangerter

Shooting Rats,
Other Plays and Poems
By Peter Turrini
Translated by Richard Dixon

The Final Plaus
By Arthur Schnitzler
Translated by G.J. Weinberger

The Massive File on
Zwetschkenbaum
By Albert Drach
Translated by Harvey I. Dunkle

Hollywood Haven
Homes and Haunts of the European
Emigrés and Exiles in Los Angeles
By Cornelius Schnauber
Translated by Barbara Schoenberg

The Death of the Plover
and Trace of the Buckskin
By Marianne Gruber
Translated by Margaret T. Peischl

Dirt
By Robert Schneider
Translated by Paul F. Dvorak

Refractions
By Alois Vogel
Translated by Walter Kreeger

Ariadne Press
New Studies

Major Figures of
Nineteenth-Century Austrian
Literature
Edited by Donald G. Daviau

Felix Mitterer
A Critical Introduction
By Nicholas J. Meyerhofer
and Karl E. Webb

"I Am Too Many People"
Peter Turrini:
Poet, Playwright, Essayist
Edited by Jutta Landa

Phantom Empires
The Novels of Alexander
Lernet-Holenia and the Question of
Postimperial Austrian Identity
By Robert Dassanowsky

Out from the Shadows
Essays on Contemporary Austrian
Women Writers and Filmmakers
Edited by M. Lamb-Faffelberger

Thunder Rumbling at My Heels
Tracing Ingeborg Bachmann
Edited by Gudrun Brokoph-Mauch

Marie von Ebner-Eschenbach
The Victory of a Tenacious Will
By Doris M. Klostermaier

Barbara Frischmuth
in Contemporary Context
Edited by Renate S. Posthofen

Of Reason and Love
The Life and Works of Marie von
Ebner-Eschenbach
By Carl Steiner

Rilke's Duino Elegies
Cambridge Readings
Edited by Roger Paulin and
Peter Hutchinson

The Legacy of Kafka in Contemporary
Austrian Literature
By Frank Pilipp

Major Figures of Austrian Literature
The Interwar Years 1918-1938
Edited by Donald G. Daviau

Die Rezeption von
Arthur Schnitzlers Reigen:
Pressespiegel und andere
zeitgenössische Kommentare
Herausgegeben von Gerd K. Schneider

"Erst bricht man Fenster. Dann wir
man selbst eines." Zum 100.
Geburtstag von Heimito von Doder
Herausgegeben von Gerald Somme
und Wendelin Schmidt-Dengler